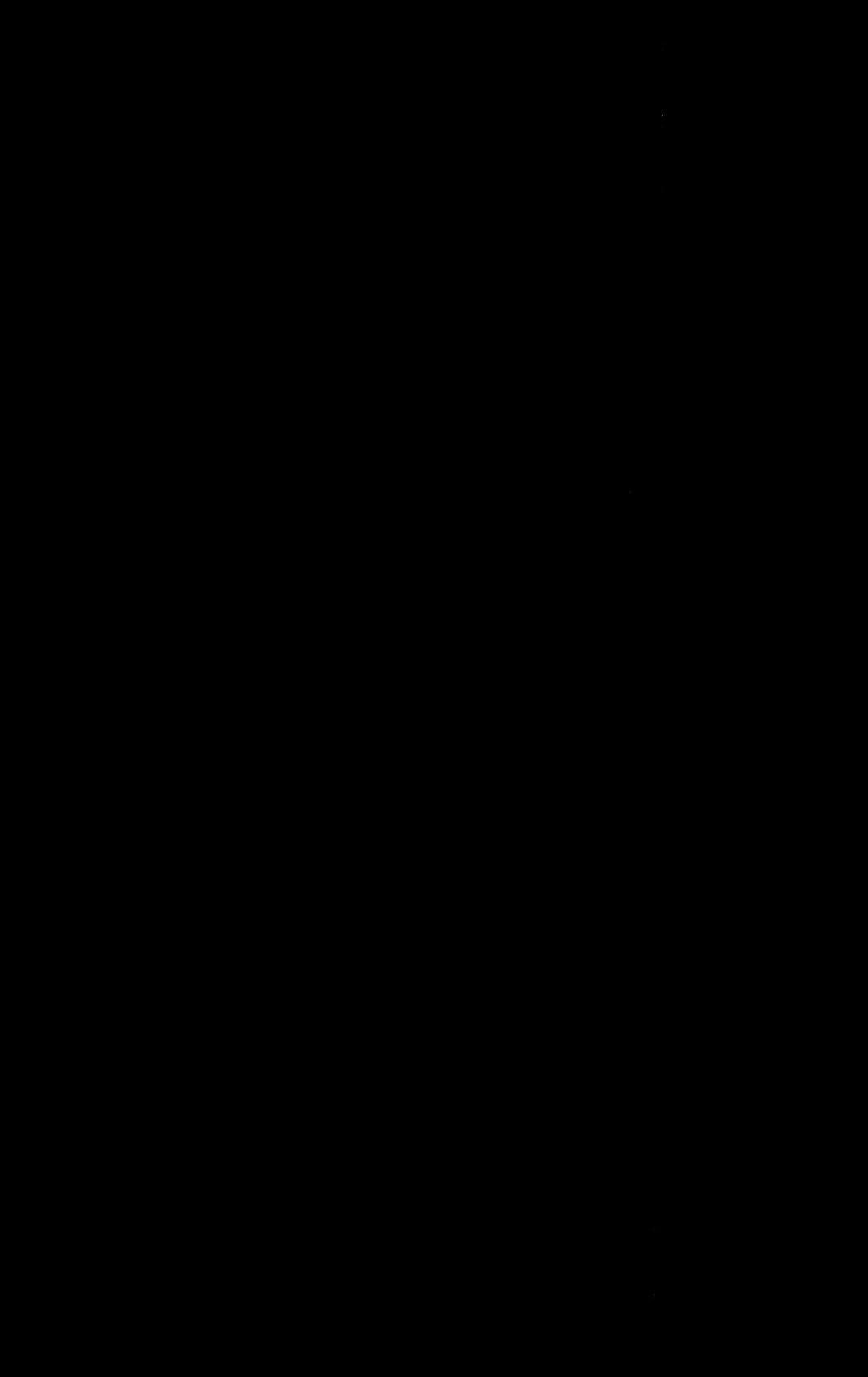

THE GUARDIAN OF THE BAHÁ'Í FAITH

This book is dedicated with tender affection to the youth, who deserve to know what Shoghi Effendi was like, and what he has given us for future generations.

'ABDU'L–BAHÁ'S ELDEST GRANDSON, SHOGHI EFFENDI
"Look at his eyes, they are like clear water" said 'Abdu'l-Bahá

THE GUARDIAN OF THE BAHÁ'Í FAITH

By

Rúḥíyyih Rabbani

BAHÁ'Í PUBLISHING TRUST
27 RUTLAND GATE, LONDON SW7

Published by the Bahá'í Publishing Trust,
27 Rutland Gate, London SW71PD

© RÚḤÍYYIH RABBANI 1988

All rights reserved including reproduction of any photographs herein not previously published under copyright. All rights foreign translations reserved by the author.

Cover design by Rúḥíyyih Rabbani and Audrey Marcus

Rabbani, Rúḥíyyih
 The Guardian of the Bahá'í Faith.
 1. Shoghi, *effendi*   2. Bahá'ís—Biography
 I. Title   297'.8961   BP395.S5
 ISBN 0-900125-59-4 cased
 ISBN 0-900125-97-7 paper

Printed in Great Britain by
Richard Clay Ltd, Bungay, Suffolk

CONTENTS

	Foreword	xiii
I	Childhood and Youth	1
II	'Abdu'l-Bahá's Ascension and its Consequences	13
III	Early Years of the Guardianship	29
IV	Martha Root and Queen Marie	39
V	A Many Splendoured Personality	53
VI	The Deepest Ties	65
VII	The War Years	71
VIII	The Writings of Shoghi Effendi	83
IX	Creation of a World Headquarters	99
X	The Heart and Nerve Centre	121
XI	The Rise of the Administrative Order	145
XII	Fundamental Truths and Guidelines	169
XIII	The Spiritual Conquest of the Globe	197
XIV	A Unique Ministry	229
	Index	241

LIST OF ILLUSTRATIONS

'Abdu'l-Bahá's eldest grandson, Shoghi Effendi	*Frontispiece*
Birthplace of the Guardian	Between pages 10-11
The Priceless Pearl	
Shoghi Effendi and his sister	
That child is born	
The young scholar at his ease	
The map maker's work	
Study years in Beirut	
'Abdu'l-Bahá on the steps of His home	
The Master's secretary	34-35
Shoghi Effendi in oriental robes	
Shoghi Effendi in his early twenties	
Shoghi Effendi before he became Guardian	
Shoghi Effendi with Harry Randall	
The samovar	
'Abdu'l-Bahá and Shoghi Effendi	50-51
Some distinguished Bahá'ís with 'Abdu'l-Bahá	
Shoghi Effendi in Alexandria, Egypt	
Shoghi Effendi, 1920-1921	
Balliol College, Oxford University	66-67
Balliol College, Junior Common Room	
A gathering in Manchester, England	
The first flight?	

ILLUSTRATIONS

Shoghi Effendi with Dr. J.E. Esslemont	82-83
The Guardian after his return to Haifa	
'Abdu'l-Bahá's home	
The Tomb of the Báb	
The Tomb of the Báb on Mt. Carmel	90-91
The Guardian and Bahíyyih <u>Kh</u>ánum	
The Guardian's handwriting	
Shoghi Effendi in the early 1920's	
The young Guardian in Switzerland	122-123
Interlaken, Switzerland	
Shoghi Effendi in the Alps	
Rivers, mountains and glaciers	
The Guardian became a mountaineer	
The indomitable enthusiast	
The top of the mountain	
Shoghi Effendi and his guide	
Mountain hazards	154-155
Shoghi Effendi walking in the Swiss Alps	
On top of the world	
Bicycling over snowy passes	
The mountaineer	162-163
A photograph by Shoghi Effendi	
Victoria Falls, Rhodesia, 1929	
A ferry on the Nile	
African views	178-179
A photograph by the Guardian	
Safari	

The Guardian studies his gardens
Two views of Mt. Carmel   194-195
The Shrine on Mt. Carmel
The Shrine of the Báb on Mt. Carmel
The development of Mt. Carmel by Shoghi Effendi
The transformation of Mt. Carmel   210-211
Buildings erected by Shoghi Effendi
That Sacred Spot
The Resting-place of the Greatest Holy Leaf
The handwriting of Shoghi Effendi
Aerial view of Bahjí
Bahá'u'lláh's Tomb in Bahjí   234-235
The Most Holy Tomb
Facsimile of Shoghi Effendi's handwriting
Facsimiles of Queen Marie's handwriting
The Guardian
The Funeral of Shoghi Effendi in London
The Grave of the Guardian

Foreword

Shoghi Effendi, Guardian of the Bahá'í Faith, and appointed Expounder of the Teachings of Bahá'u'lláh, its Founder, is the one human being in all history, past, present or future, to exercise the greatest influence on the ultimate shape and *modus operandi* of the social order of the world. He is the one who understood the vision of his great-grandfather Bahá'u'lláh and his grandfather 'Abdu'l-Bahá — respectively the Revealer and the Interpreter of teachings destined to reshape the divisive society of the present world and usher in an era of universal peace — and applied Their doctrines in practical terms to the organization of such a future state of society. There cannot be, on this planet, a greater social or political unit than World Order. It is Shoghi Effendi who, while not the architect of that consummation, is certainly its chief builder and engineer. He laid the foundations of the Administrative Order of a Faith which, as it develops, will come—as he stated—"to be regarded not only as the nucleus but the very pattern of the New World Order destined to embrace in the fullness of time the whole of mankind."

Only his widow, Rúḥíyyih Rabbani, could have written this book. For twenty years she was his wife, and for sixteen of those years his personal secretary; she was his close companion and his representative on many occasions. In a cable to the National Spiritual Assembly of Canada, her homeland, he designated her as "my helpmate, my shield in warding off the darts of Covenant-breakers and my tireless collaborator in the arduous tasks I shoulder." She shared in all the circumstances of his life and knew the pressures and restrictions both within and without the Bahá'í community which imposed themselves on his total dedication to his divinely-appointed task. She observed his deep love for his fellow Bahá'ís and his constant concern for their spiritual and material welfare.

It is apparent that countless eulogies, evaluations, acclamations, biographies and panegyrics of the God-given genius of Shoghi Effendi will be added in future to the already proliferating number. The prime depository of source material for such works will forever be *The Priceless Pearl*, Rúḥíyyih Rabbani's own version of her illustrious husband's life and mission, of which this sister volume constitutes a more compact presentation. We can offer the gratitude of posterity to Rúḥíyyih Rabbani for this clear and authentic account of his life and endeavours. But for the present generations, and particularly those of us who served under the beloved Guardian, no expressions of thanks can be adequate for the personal glimpses of our "true brother" — as he was wont to sign his letters — in action and in his daily life. This book, dealing so intimately with the life of a man who in 36 years of ministry left an indelible imprint on the fortunes of mankind, will outwear the ravages of time as it continues to bear authentic witness to the life and personality of Shoghi Effendi.

David Hofman

I

CHILDHOOD AND YOUTH

Salutation and praise, blessing and glory rest upon that primal branch of the Divine and Sacred Lote-Tree, grown out, blest, tender, verdant and flourishing from the Twin Holy Trees; the most wondrous, unique and priceless pearl that doth gleam from out the Twin Surging Seas.

Like a cloud-break in a stormy sky these words, even as a mighty shaft of sunlight, broke through the gloom and tempest of dangerous years and shone from on high upon a small boy, the grandson of a prisoner of the Sulṭán of Turkey, living in the prison-city of 'Akká in the Turkish province of Syria. The words were written by 'Abdu'l-Bahá in the first part of His *Will and Testament* and referred to His eldest grandchild, Shoghi Effendi.

Although already appointed the hereditary successor of his grandfather, neither the child, nor the ever-swelling host of followers of Bahá'u'lláh throughout the world, were made aware of this fact. In the Orient, where the principle of lineal descent is well understood and accepted as the normal course of events, there was hope, no doubt, that even as Bahá'u'lláh Himself had demonstrated the validity of this mysterious and great principle of primogeniture, so would 'Abdu'l-Bahá, His son and successor, do likewise. Many years before His passing, in answer to a question from some Persian believers as to whether there would be one person to whom all should turn after His death, 'Abdu'l-Bahá had written:

. . . Know verily that this is a well-guarded secret. It is even as a gem concealed within its shell. That it will be revealed is predestined. The time will come when its light will appear, when its evidences will be made manifest, and its secrets unravelled.

Until the Master passed away in November 1921, and His *Will and Testament* was found in His safe and opened and read, no one in the Bahá'í world knew that Shoghi Effendi was that "unique pearl", and just how unique and glorious a pearl it was that 'Abdu'l-Bahá left behind Him no one really understood until in November 1957 it was recalled to the Seas from which it had been born.

On the 27th day of Ramaḍán, 1314 of the Muslim calendar, Shoghi Effendi was born. This was Sunday, March 1, 1897 of the Gregorian calendar. These dates have been found in one of Shoghi Effendi's notebooks which he kept during his boyhood, written in his own hand. He was the eldest grandchild and first grandson of 'Abdu'l-Bahá, born of His oldest daughter, Ḍíyá'íyyih Khánum, and her husband, Mírzá Hádí Shírází, one of the Afnáns and a relative of the Báb. He was invariably addressed by his grandfather as "Shoghi Effendi"; indeed, He gave instructions that he should at all times have the "Effendi" added and even told Shoghi Effendi's own father he must address him thus and not merely as "Shoghi". The word "Effendi" signifies "sir" or "mister" and is added as a term of respect; for the same reason "Khánum", which means "lady" or "madame", is added to a woman's name.

At the time of Shoghi Effendi's birth 'Abdu'l-Bahá and His family were still prisoners of the Sulṭán of Turkey, 'Abdu'l Ḥamíd; it was not until the revolution of the Young Turks, in 1908, and the consequent release of political prisoners, that they were freed from an exile and bondage that, for Him and His sister at least, had lasted for over fifty years. In 1897 they were all living in a house known as that of 'Abdu'lláh Páshá, a stone's throw from the great Turkish military barracks where Bahá'u'lláh, 'Abdu'l-Bahá, and the company of believers who were with Them, had been incarcerated when they first landed in 'Akká in 1868. It was in this home that the first group of pilgrims from the Western World visited the Master in the winter of 1898–99, and many more of the early believers of the West; travelling along the beach in an omnibus drawn by three horses, they would proceed from Haifa to 'Akká, enter the fortified walls of the prison-city, and be welcomed as His guests for a few days in that house. It was from this home that 'Abdu'l-Bahá left to reside in freedom in Haifa, twelve miles away on the other side of the Bay of 'Akká. Entering through a passage across which the upper story of the building ran, one came upon a small enclosed garden where grew flowers, fruit trees, and a few tall palms, and in one corner of which a long stairway ran up to the upper floor and opened on an inner, unroofed court from which doors led to various rooms and to a long corridor giving access to other chambers.

To catch even a glimpse of what must have transpired in 'Abdu'l-Bahá's heart when this first grandson was born to Him at the age of fifty-three, one must remember that He had already lost more than one son, the dearest and most perfect of them, Ḥusayn, a beautiful and very dignified little boy, having passed away when only a few years old. Of the four surviving daughters of 'Abdu'l-Bahá three were to bear Him thirteen grandchildren, but it was this oldest one who bore witness to the saying "the child is the secret essence of its sire", not to be taken to mean in this case the heritage of his own father, but rather that he was sired by the Prophets of God and inherited the nobility of his grandfather 'Abdu'l-Bahá. The depths of 'Abdu'l-Bahá's feelings at this time are reflected in His own words in which He clearly states that the name Shoghi—literally "the one who longs" — was conferred by God upon this grandson:

> . . . O God! This is a branch sprung from the tree of Thy mercy. Through Thy grace and bounty enable him to grow and through the showers of Thy generosity cause him to become a verdant, flourishing, blossoming and fruitful branch. Gladden the eyes of his parents, Thou Who giveth to whomsoever Thou willest, and bestow upon him the name Shoghi so that he may yearn for Thy Kingdom and soar into the realms of the unseen!

By the signs Shoghi Effendi showed from earliest childhood and by his unique nature, he twined himself ever more deeply into the roots of the Master's heart. How great must have been the struggle of the grandfather to keep within bounds His love for this child lest the very blaze of that love endanger his life through the hatred and envy of His many enemies, ever seeking an Achilles heel to bring about His downfall. Many times when Shoghi Effendi spoke of the past and of 'Abdu'l-Bahá I felt not only how boundless and consuming had been his own love for the Master, but that he had been aware of the fact that 'Abdu'l-Bahá leashed and veiled the passion of His love for him in order to protect him and to safeguard the Cause of God from its enemies.

Shoghi Effendi was a small, sensitive, intensely active and mischievous child. He was not very strong in his early years and his mother often had cause to worry over his health. However, he grew up to have an iron constitution, which, coupled with the phenomenal force of his nature and will-power, enabled him in later years to overcome every obstacle in his path. The first photographs we have of him show a peaky little face, immense eyes and a firm, beautifully shaped chin which in his childhood gave a slightly elongated and heart-shaped appearance to his face. His eyes were of that deceptive hazel colour that sometimes led people who did not have the opportunity to look into them as often as I did to think they were brown or blue. The truth is they were a clear hazel which sometimes changed to a warm and luminous grey. I have never seen such an expressive face and eyes as those of the Guardian; every shade of feeling and thought was mirrored in his visage as light and shadow are reflected on water.

In the days of Shoghi Effendi's childhood it was the custom to rise about dawn and spend the first hour of the day in the Master's room, where prayers were said and the family all had breakfast with Him. The children sat on the floor, their legs folded under them, their arms folded across their breasts, in great respect; when asked, they would chant for 'Abdu'l-Bahá; there was no shouting or unseemly conduct. Breakfast consisted of tea, brewed on the bubbling Russian brass samovar and served in little crystal glasses, very hot and very sweet, pure wheat bread and goats' milk cheese. Dr. Zia Baghdádí, an intimate of the family, in his recollections of these days records that Shoghi Effendi was always the first to get up and be on time—after receiving one good chastisement from no other hand than that of his grandfather!

He also tells us the story of Shoghi Effendi's first Tablet from 'Abdu'l-Bahá. Dr. Baghdádí states that when Shoghi Effendi was only five years old he was pestering the Master to write something for him, whereupon 'Abdu'l-Bahá wrote this touching and revealing letter in His own hand:

> He is God!
> O My Shoghi, I have no time to talk, leave me alone! You said "write"—I have written. What else should be done? Now is not the time for you to read and write, it is the time for jumping about and chanting "O my God!", therefore memorize the prayers of the Blessed Beauty and chant them that I may hear them, because there is no time for anything else.

It seems that when this wonderful gift reached the child he set himself to memorize a number of Bahá'u'lláh's prayers and would chant them so loudly that the entire neighbourhood could hear his voice; when his parents and other members of the Master's family remonstrated with him, Shoghi Effendi replied, according to Dr. Baghdádí, "The Master wrote to me to chant that He may hear me! I am doing my best!" and he kept on chanting at the top of his voice for many hours every day. Finally his parents begged the Master to stop him, but He told them to let Shoghi Effendi alone. This was one aspect of the small boy's chanting. We are told there was another: he had memorized some touching passages written by 'Abdu'l-Bahá after the ascension of Bahá'u'lláh and when he chanted these the tears would roll down the earnest little face. From another source we are told that when the Master was requested by a western friend, at that time living in His home, to reveal a prayer for children He did so, and the first to memorize it and chant it was Shoghi Effendi who would also chant it in the meetings of the friends.

In his recollections of those early years one of the Bahá'ís has written that one day Shoghi Effendi entered the Master's room, took up His pen and tried to write. 'Abdu'l-Bahá drew him to His side, tapped him gently on the shoulder and said, "Now is not the time to write, now is the time to play, you will write a lot in the future." Nevertheless the desire of the child to learn led to the formation of classes in the Master's household for the children, taught by an old Persian believer. I know that at one time in his childhood, most likely while he was still living in 'Akká, Shoghi Effendi and other grandchildren were taught by an Italian, who acted as governess or teacher; a grey-haired elderly lady, she came to call shortly after I was married.

Although these early years of Shoghi Effendi's life were spent in the prison-city of 'Akká, enclosed within its moats and walls, its two gates guarded by sentries, this does not mean he had no occasion to move about. He must have often gone to the homes of the Bahá'ís living inside the city, to the Khán where the pilgrims stayed, to the Garden of Riḍván and to Bahjí. Many times he was the delighted companion of his grandfather on these excursions. We are told that sometimes he spent the night in Bahjí in the house now used as a pilgrim house; 'Abdu'l-Bahá would Himself come and tuck him in bed, remarking, "I need him."

When 'Abdu'l-Bahá first moved into the new home in Haifa (which was in use by members of His family in February 1907, if not earlier) the rooms were occupied by all the members of His family;

eventually the families of two of His daughters moved to homes of their own near His, but the house was always crowded with relatives, children, servants, pilgrims and guests.

Shoghi Effendi entered the best school in Haifa, the *Collège des Frères*, conducted by the Jesuits. He told me he had been very unhappy there. Indeed, I gathered from him that he never was really happy in either school or university. In spite of his innately joyous nature, his sensitivity and his background—so different from that of others in every way—could not but set him apart and give rise to many a heart-ache; indeed, he was one of those people whose open and innocent hearts, keen minds and affectionate natures seem to combine to bring upon them more shocks and suffering in life than is the lot of most men. Because of his unhappiness in this school 'Abdu'l-Bahá decided to send him to Beirut where he attended another Catholic school as a boarder, and where he was equally unhappy. Learning of this in Haifa the family sent a trusted Bahá'í woman to rent a home for Shoghi Effendi in Beirut and take care of and wait on him. It was not long before she wrote to his father that he was very unhappy at school, would refuse to go to it sometimes for days, and was getting thin and run down. His father showed this letter to 'Abdu'l-Bahá Who then had arrangements made for Shoghi Effendi to enter the Syrian Protestant College, which had a school as well as a university, later known as the American College in Beirut, and which the Guardian entered when he finished what was then equivalent to the high school. Shoghi Effendi spent his vacations at home in Haifa, in the presence as often as possible of the grandfather he idolized and Whom it was the object of his life to serve. The entire course of Shoghi Effendi's studies was aimed by him at fitting himself to serve the Master, interpret for Him, and translate His letters into English.

It is very difficult to trace the exact course of events in these years. All eyes were fixed on the grandfather and much as people loved and respected the eldest grandson, when the sun shines the lamp is ignored! Some pilgrims' accounts, like that of Thornton Chase, the first American believer, who visited the Master in 1907, mentioned meeting "Shogi Afnan". Indeed Chase published a photograph showing Shoghi Effendi in what must have been his usual costume in those days, short pants, long dark stockings, a fez on his head, a jacket and a huge sailor's collar covering his shoulders. But there is not enough material available at present to fill in all the gaps. Even those who accompanied 'Abdu'l-Bahá on His journeys to the West, and kept careful diaries, did not think to record very much about the comings and goings of a child who was only thirteen when 'Abdu'l-Bahá set forth on His historic visits to Europe and America.

No sooner had 'Abdu'l-Bahá been freed from His long imprisonment and taken up His permanent residence in Haifa, than He began to contemplate this journey. A report published in America in "Bahá'í News", 1910, states: "You have asked for an account of 'Abdu'l-Bahá's departure for the land of Egypt. 'Abdu'l-Bahá did not inform anyone that He was going to leave Haifa . . . within two days He summoned to His presence M.N., Shoghi Effendi and K. and this servant." One of the Bahá'ís recalls that a little before sunset, on that September afternoon when 'Abdu'l-Bahá's ship set sail for Port Said in Egypt, Shoghi Effendi was seated on the steps of the Master's house, disconsolate and forlorn, and remarked: "The Master is now on board the ship. He has left me behind, but surely there is a wisdom in this!" or words to this effect. Well knowing what was passing in the heart of His grandson the loving Master no doubt sent for the child to soften the blow of this first, serious separation from Him; but more reference than this to that event has not been found. We know the Master stayed about a month in Port Said, later proceeding to Alexandria rather than to Europe, which was His original intention, and that Shoghi Effendi was with Him. As school opened in early October one presumes he returned to Syria. In April 1911, Shoghi Effendi was again with the Master, in Ramleh, a suburb of Alexandria, for a visiting Bahá'í from America, Louis Gregory, the first negro Hand of the Cause, mentions meeting, on April 16th, "Shogi", a beautiful boy, a grandson of 'Abdu'l-Bahá, and says he showed great affection for the pilgrims.

'Abdu'l-Bahá's thoughts, in spite of the arduous nature of His daily preoccupations during those exhausting months in America and later in Europe, must have often gone to His beloved grandson. We find mention of Shoghi Effendi in three of the letters the Master wrote to His sister, the Greatest Holy Leaf, Bahíyyih Khánum, during His travels, showing His anxiety over Shoghi Effendi and revealing His great love for him: "Write to me at once about Shoghi Effendi's condition, informing me fully and hiding nothing; this is the best way."; "Kiss the light of the eyes of the company of spiritual souls, Shoghi Effendi"; "Kiss the fresh flower of the garden of sweetness, Shoghi Effendi". Such references clearly indicate

His anxiety over a child who had not always been well and who, He well knew, missed Him terribly and suffered. We also have a Tablet of 'Abdu'l-Bahá addressed to Shoghi Effendi, expressing His concern about his health, but at what period it was written I do not know:

> *He is God!*
> *Shoghi Effendi, upon him be the glory of the All-Glorious! Oh thou who art young in years and radiant of countenance, I understand you have been ill and obliged to rest; never mind, from time to time rest is essential, otherwise, like unto 'Abdu'l-Bahá from excessive toil you will become weak and powerless and unable to work. Therefore rest a few days, it does not matter. I hope that you will be under the care and protection of the Blessed Beauty.*

Shoghi Effendi was always active in corresponding with Bahá'í friends through personal letters. We learn from one of these, addressed to "Syed Mustafa Roumie" in Burma, and dated "Caiffa, Syria, July 28, 1914", in which he says he is much pleased with the "glad tidings of the rapid progress of the Cause in the Far East", that he shared this letter with the Master and "a Holy tender smile ran over his radiant Face and his heart overflowed with joy. I then came to know that the Master is in good health for I recollected his sayings which I quote now. 'Whenever and wherever I hear the glad tidings of the Cause my physical health is bettered and ameliorated.' I therefore tell you that the Master is feeling very well and is happy. Convey this happy news to the Indian believers. I do hope that this will double their courage, their firmness, and their zeal in spreading the Cause."

Shoghi Effendi also played a dominant role in the activities of the Bahá'í students studying in Beirut, through which passed so many of the pilgrims from Persia and the Far East on their way to and from Haifa. He writes, in a letter from Beirut dated May 3, 1914: "Going back to our college activities our Bahá'í meetings, which I have spoken to you about, are reorganized and only today we are sending letters, enclosing glad tidings of the Holy Land, to the Bahá'í Assemblies in various countries."

The war years, during most of which Shoghi Effendi was studying to obtain his Bachelor of Arts degree at the American University, must have often cast a deep shadow of anxiety on him, in spite of his naturally buoyant and joyous nature. They were years of ever-increasing danger for his beloved grandfather, years of dire starvation for much of the population, of privations shared by all, including his own family.

It was in 1918 that Shoghi Effendi received his Bachelor of Arts degree. In a letter to a friend in England dated November 19th of that year, he wrote: "I am so glad and privileged to be able to attend to my Beloved's services after completing my course of Arts and Sciences in the American University at Beirut. I am so anxious and expectant to hear from you and of your services to the Cause for by transmitting them to the Beloved I shall make him happy, glad and strong. The past four years have been years of untold calamity, of unprecedented oppression, of indescribable misery, of severe famine and distress, of unparalleled bloodshed and strife, but now that the dove of peace has returned to its nest and abode a golden opportunity has arisen for the promulgation of the Word of God. This will be now promoted and the Message delivered in this liberated region without the least amount of restriction. This is indeed the Era of Service." Nothing could be more revealing of the character of the future Guardian than these lines, in which his devotion to the work of the Master, his consuming longing to make Him happy and well, his concise summary of where his own life now stands in relation to this service, his analysis of what the war's end signifies for the immediate future of Bahá'í work are all clearly shown. His nascent rhetorical style, still hampered by an imperfect command of the English language, but already showing the bare bones of its future greatness is reflected in passages such as this: "the friends . . . are all . . . large and small, old and young, healthy and sick, at home and abroad, glad of the events that have recently transpired; they are all one soul in different bodies, united, agreed, serving and aiming to serve the oneness of humanity."

Shoghi Effendi was now twenty-one years old. His personal relationship to 'Abdu'l-Bahá was made clear in some of these early letters, for the most part written in 1919, in which he refers to "my grandfather, 'Abdu'l-Bahá" and signs himself "Shoghi Rabbani (grandson of 'Abdu'l-Bahá)". One must remember that in the immediate months after the war ended, when contact was being re-established between the Master and the believers in so many countries which had been cut off from Him during the long years of hostilities, it was highly desirable that Bahá'ís and non-Bahá'ís alike should know who this "Shoghi Rabbani" was who was now acting as the Master's secretary and right-hand man. The *Star of the*

West, in its issue of September 27, 1919, published a full length photograph of Shoghi Effendi, entitled, "Shoghi Rabbani, Grandson of 'Abdu'l-Bahá" and states he is the translator of recent Tablets and his Diary Letters begin in this issue. Personally I believe, knowing from experience how completely Shoghi Effendi directed even minutiae at the World Centre, that it is probable the Master Himself directed him to make clear their family relationship.

The work of 'Abdu'l-Bahá increased from day to day as floods of letters, reports, and eventually pilgrims poured into Haifa. This is reflected in Shoghi Effendi's personal letters to various Bahá'í friends: ". . . this interruption of correspondence with you on my part has been solely due to a great pressure of work in connection with the dictation and translation of Tablets . . . The whole afternoon has been spent in translating for him only the contents of a part of the supplications from London." He ends up by saying, "I enclose, out of my Bahá'í and particular affection for you, two photographs . . ."; "My head is in a whirl, so busy and so eventful was the day. No less than a score of callers from prince and pasha to a simple private soldier have sought interview with 'Abdu'l-Bahá."; "The Beloved from morn till eve, even at midnight is engaged in revealing Tablets, in sending forth his constructive, dynamic thoughts of love and principles to a sad and disillusioned world."; "As I am writing these lines, I am again moved to present myself in his presence and take down his words in response to the recently arrived supplications." Every word reflects the boundless energy, devotion and enthusiasm of this princeling standing at the side of the old king, serving and supporting Him with all the vitality of his youth and the singular eagerness of his nature.

Shoghi Effendi frequently accompanied the Master to the steadily increasing number of official functions to which He was invited. This included visits to the British Military Governor of Haifa and interviews with the Commander-in-Chief, Sir Edmund Allenby, the General who had led the Allied forces in Palestine and who later became Lord Allenby and was largely responsible for 'Abdu'l-Bahá's receiving a knighthood from the British Government. Shoghi Effendi wrote: "This was the second time 'Abdu'l-Bahá had called on the General and this time the conversation centred around the Cause and its progress . . . He is a very gentle, modest and striking figure, warm in affection, yet imposing in his manner." In these circles the grandson of 'Abdu'l-Bahá was now becoming known. An official letter, from the Military Governor to 'Abdu'l-

BIRTHPLACE OF THE GUARDIAN
In this house Shoghi Effendi was born in 1897, in the prison-city of 'Akká

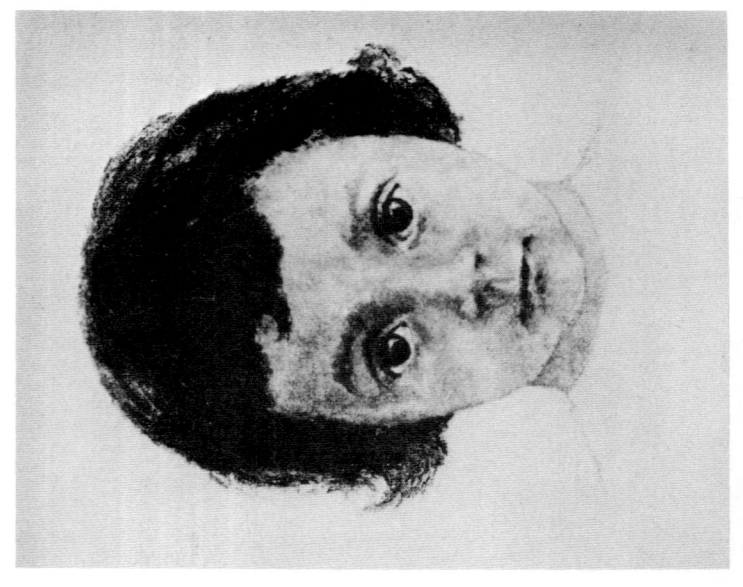
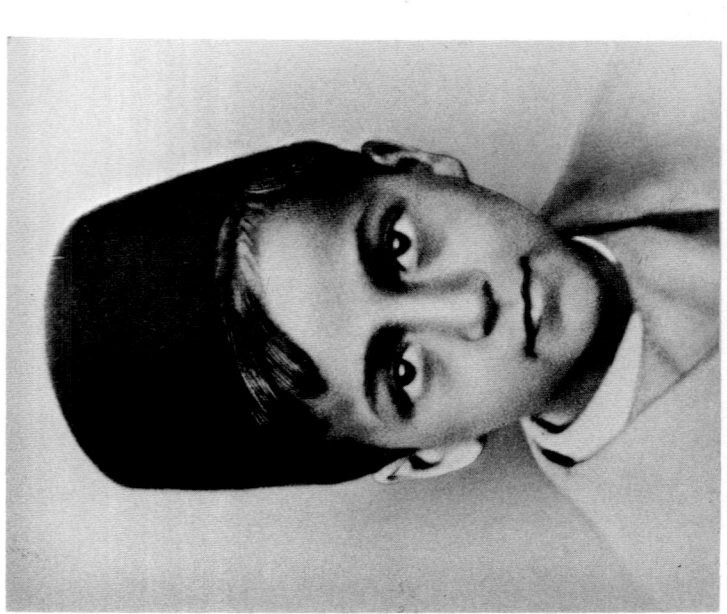

THE PRICELESS PEARL

Shoghi Effendi, 'Abdu'l-Bahá's eldest grandson

"*O God! This is a branch sprung from the tree of Thy mercy... bestow upon him the name Shoghi so that he may yearn for Thy Kingdom....*"

'Abdu'l-Bahá

SHOGHI EFFENDI AND HIS SISTER
Taken in the prison-city of 'Akká circa 1902

THAT CHILD IS BORN

"Verily, that child is born and is alive and from him will appear wondrous things… in the future."

'Abdu'l-Bahá

THE YOUNG SCHOLAR AT HIS EASE

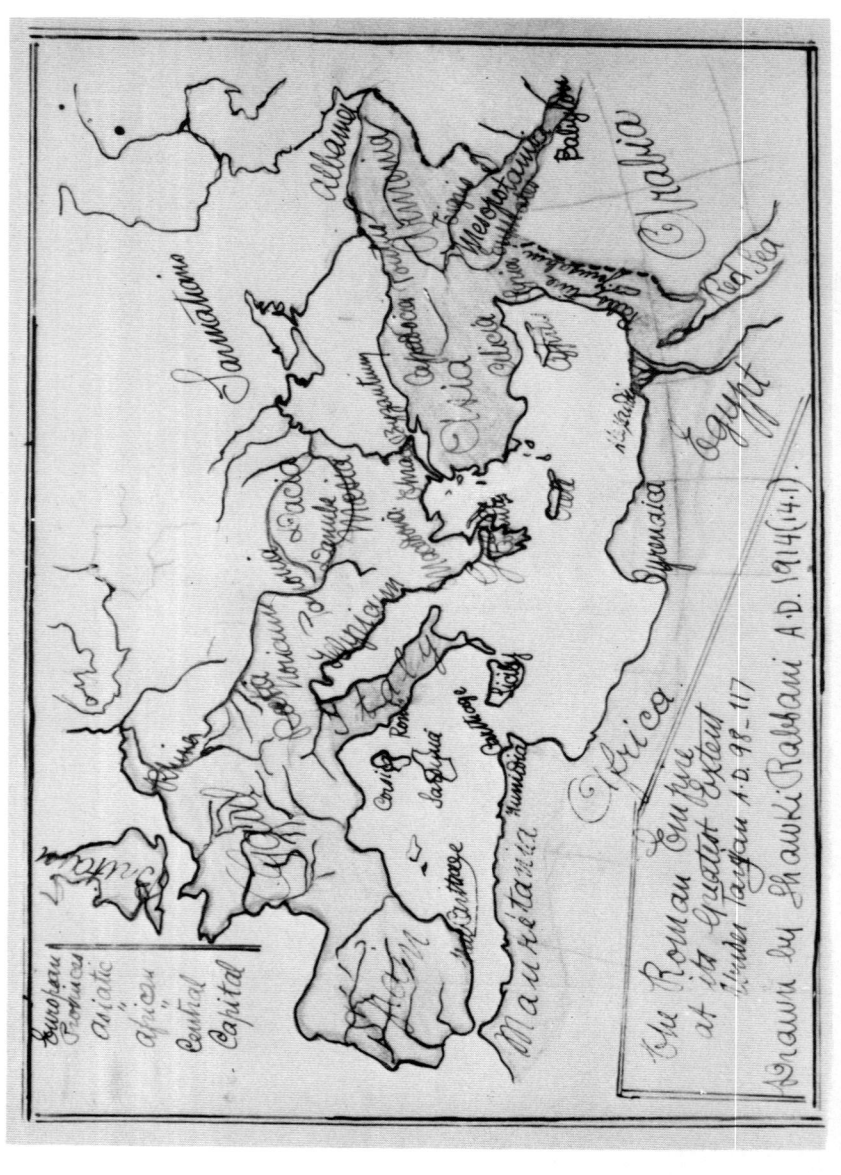

THE MAP-MAKER'S WORK

One of the earliest of Shoghi Effendi's maps, drawn in 1914, showing the Roman Empire

STUDY YEARS IN BEIRUT

Standing, in the first row (third from the left), is Shoghi Effendi with his class at the Syrian Protestant College; circa 1914

'ABDU'L-BAHÁ ON THE STEPS OF HIS HOME

The future Guardian is standing in the first row, third from the right; circa 1914

Bahá says: "Your Eminence: I have today received from your grandson the sum of . . ." This was in response to Shoghi Effendi's having called upon him with a further contribution from the Master to the "Haifa Relief Fund". Shoghi Effendi also spent much time with the pilgrims, not only in the presence of 'Abdu'l-Bahá, during which he eagerly obtained detailed information from them about the progress of Bahá'í activities in various countries.

Wherever 'Abdu'l-Bahá went, as often as possible the beloved grandson went with Him. This constant companionship, which lasted for about two years, must have been a deep satisfaction to them both and have exerted a profound and decisive influence on Shoghi Effendi. During these years, when the star of 'Abdu'l-Bahá's fame was rising locally, as well as internationally, Shoghi Effendi had the opportunity of observing how the Master dealt with high officials and the numerous men of distinction drawn to one Whom many regarded as little less than an oriental prophet and the greatest religious figure in Asia, as well as how the Master conducted Himself in the face of the ever-present envy and intrigue of His enemies and ill-wishers. The lessons learned were to be reflected in the thirty-six years of Shoghi Effendi's own ministry to the Faith of Bahá'u'lláh.

The decision of Shoghi Effendi to leave 'Abdu'l-Bahá, after less than two years spent constantly in His service, and at a time when the Master's vast post-war correspondence was steadily increasing, was based on a number of factors: if he intended to pursue his studies the sooner he did so the better; 'Abdu'l-Bahá now had a number of people acting as His secretaries; Shoghi Effendi's eldest cousin had finished his studies in Beirut and was now at home; the Master's own condition and plans were propitious.

Very few of us, least of all when we are twenty-three years old, imagine our loved ones dying. So it is not surprising that Shoghi Effendi should have left 'Abdu'l-Bahá, some time in the spring of 1920, with a tranquil conscience, fully believing he would return to His side better equipped to serve Him.

Oxford and Cambridge are still words to conjure with; in 1920 they shone in even more splendid academic isolation than they do in these days when universities and university education have become more prevalent. Balliol, to which Shoghi Effendi was admitted, had a very high standing, being one of Oxford's oldest colleges. I was conducted, years later, by the Guardian, to see the streets he had passed through, the Bodleian Library, the placid river in its greensward surroundings beyond the wrought iron gates, to thousand-year-old Christ Church with its vast kitchen and fairy web of Gothic arches, to Magdalen and its beauties and to the peaceful quad inside the walls of Balliol, which Shoghi Effendi crossed to his studies, to the dining hall where he ate, and to gaze on the narrow entrance that led to the room he had once lived in as a student.

The Guardian's own idea of why he was at Oxford was quite clear; fortunately we have an expression of this in a letter he wrote to an oriental believer on October 18, 1920: "My dear spiritual friend . . . God be praised, I am in good health and full of hope and trying to the best of my ability to equip myself for those things I shall require in my future service to the Cause. My hope is that I may speedily acquire the best that this country and this society have to offer and then return to my home and recast the truths of the Faith in a new form, and thus serve the Holy Threshold." There is no doubt he was referring to his future translation of the teachings into the perfect English for which he laid the foundation during his sojourn in England.

From his Beirut days until practically the end of his life Shoghi Effendi had the habit of writing vocabularies and typical English phrases in notebooks. Hundreds of words and sentences have been recorded and these clearly indicate the years of careful study he put into mastering a language he loved and revelled in. For him there was no second to English. He was a great reader of the King James version of the Bible, and of the historians Carlyle and Gibbon, whose styles he greatly admired, particularly that of Gibbon whose *Decline and Fall of the Roman Empire* Shoghi Effendi was so fond of that I never remember his not having a volume of it near him in his room and usually with him when he travelled.

II

'ABDU'L-BAHÁ'S ASCENSION AND ITS CONSEQUENCES

The address of Major Tudor Pole, in London, was often used as the distributing point for cables and letters to the Bahá'ís. Shoghi Effendi himself, whenever he went up to London, usually called there. On November 29, 1921, at 9:30 in the morning the following cable reached that office:

> Cyclometry London
>   His Holiness 'Abdu'l-Bahá ascended Abhá Kingdom. Inform friends.
>   Greatest Holy Leaf

In notes he made of this terrible event and its immediate repercussions Tudor Pole records that he immediately notified the friends by wire, telephone and letter. I believe he must have telephoned Shoghi Effendi, asking him to come at once to his office, but not conveying to him at that distance a piece of news which he well knew might prove too much of a shock. However this may be, at about noon Shoghi Effendi reached London, went to 61 St. James' Street (off Piccadilly and not far from Buckingham Palace) and was shown into the private office. Tudor Pole was not in the room at the moment but as Shoghi Effendi stood there his eye was caught by the name of 'Abdu'l-Bahá on the open cablegram lying on the desk and he read it. When Tudor Pole entered the room a moment later he found Shoghi Effendi in a state of collapse, dazed and bewildered by this catastrophic news. He was taken to the home of Miss Grand, one of the London believers, and put to bed there for a few days.

Owing to passport difficulties Shoghi Effendi cabled Haifa he could not arrive until the end of the month. He sailed from England on December 16th, accompanied by Lady Blomfield and

Rouhangeze, and arrived in Haifa by train at 5:20 p.m. on December 29th, from Egypt where his boat from England had docked. Many friends went to the station to bring him home; it is reported he was so overcome on his arrival that he had to be assisted up the steps. Awaiting him in the house was the only person who could in any measure assuage his suffering—his beloved great-aunt, the sister of 'Abdu'l-Bahá. She had already—so frail, so quiet, so modest at all times—shown herself in these past weeks to be a strong rock to which the believers clung in the midst of the tempest that had so suddenly burst upon them. The calibre of her soul, her breeding, her station, fitted her for the role she played in the Cause and in Shoghi Effendi's life during this extremely difficult and dangerous period.

When 'Abdu'l-Bahá so unexpectedly and quietly passed away, after no serious illness, the distracted members of His family searched His papers to see if by chance He had left any instructions as to where He should be buried. Finding none they entombed Him in the centre of the three rooms adjacent to the inner Shrine of the Báb. They discovered His Will—which consists of three Wills written at different times and forming one document—addressed to Shoghi Effendi. It now became the painful duty of Shoghi Effendi to hear what was in it; a few days after his arrival they read it to him.

There is no doubt that the Greatest Holy Leaf, and probably a selected few of the Master's family knew, before Shoghi Effendi reached Haifa, the gist at least of what was in the Will because it had been examined to see if He had made any provisions for His own burial. That this is so is borne out by cables sent to the Persian and to the American believers, by the Greatest Holy Leaf, on December 21, 1921. The one to America read as follows: "Memorial meeting world over January seven. Procure prayers for unity and steadfastness. Master left full instructions in His Will and Testament. Translation will be sent. Inform friends." But the provisions of the Will were not made known until it was first read to Shoghi Effendi and, indeed, until it was officially read on January 3, 1922.

It was befitting that the Greatest Holy Leaf, and not Shoghi Effendi himself, should announce to the Bahá'í world the provisions of the Master's Will. On January 7th she sent two cables to Persia as follows: "Memorial meetings all over the world have been held. The Lord of all the worlds in His Will and Testament has revealed His instructions. Copy will be sent. Inform believers." and "Will and Testament forwarded Shoghi Effendi Centre Cause." On

January 16th she cabled: "In Will Shoghi Effendi appointed Guardian of Cause and Head of House of Justice. Inform American friends." In spite of the fact that from the very beginning Shoghi Effendi exhibited both a tactful and masterful hand in dealing with the problems that continually faced him, he leaned very heavily on the Greatest Holy Leaf, whose character, station and love for him made her at once his support and his refuge.

Immediately after these events Shoghi Effendi selected eight passages from the Will and circulated them among the Bahá'ís; only one of these referred to himself, was very brief and was quoted as follows: "O ye the faithful loved ones of 'Abdu'l-Bahá! It is incumbent upon you to take the greatest care of Shoghi Effendi . . . For he is, after 'Abdu'l-Bahá, the guardian of the Cause of God, the Afnán, the Hands (pillars) of the Cause and the beloved of the Lord must obey him and turn unto him." Of all the thundering and tremendous passages in the Will referring to himself, Shoghi Effendi chose the least astounding and provocative to first circulate among the Bahá'ís. Guided and guiding he was from the very beginning.

These early years of his Guardianship must be seen as a continual process of being floored and rising to his feet again, often staggering from the terrible blows he had received, but game to the core. It was his love for 'Abdu'l-Bahá that always carried him through: "yet I believe," he cries out, "and firmly believe in His power, His guidance, His ever-living presence . . ." In a letter written in February 1922, to Nayyir Afnán, a nephew of 'Abdu'l-Bahá, the agony of his soul is clearly reflected: "Your . . . letter reached me in the very midst of my sorrows, my cares and afflictions . . . the pain, nay the anguish of His bereavement is so overwhelming, the burden of responsibility He has placed on my feeble and my youthful shoulders is so overwhelming . . ." He goes on to say: "I am enclosing for you personally the copy of the dear Master's Testament, you will read it and see what He had undergone at the hands of His kindred . . . you will also see what a great responsibility He has placed on me which nothing short of the creative power of His word can help me to face . . ." This letter is not only indicative of his feelings but in view of the fact that the one he wrote it to belonged to those who had been the enemies of the Master in the days after Bahá'u'lláh's ascension and were of that breed of kindred He had so strongly denounced in His Will, shows how courageously Shoghi Effendi holds up the mirror of the past and at the same time appeals for his support and loyalty in the new situation which exists.

His earliest letters reveal Shoghi Effendi's characteristic strength, wisdom and dignity. To one of the professors of the American University in Beirut he wrote, on March 19, 1922, clearly and unequivocally stating his own position: "Replying to your question as to whether I have been officially designated to represent the Bahá'í Community: 'Abdu'l-Bahá in his testament has appointed me to be the head of the universal council which is to be duly elected by national councils representative of the followers of Bahá'u'lláh in different countries . . ."

It must not be thought, however, that the act of promulgating the Master's Will solved all problems and ushered in a new era in the Cause with the greatest of ease. Far from it. Before Shoghi Effendi reached Haifa the Greatest Holy Leaf had been obliged to cable America on December 14th: "Now is period of great tests. The friends should be firm and united in defending the Cause. Nakeseens [Covenant-breakers] starting activities through press other channels all over world. Select committee of wise cool heads to handle press propaganda in America."

One of the oldest and most staunch of the American believers wrote to Shoghi Effendi on January 18, 1922, less than two weeks after the public announcement of the provisions of 'Abdu'l-Bahá's Will: "As you know we are having great troubles and sorrows with violators in the Cause in America. This poison has penetrated deeply among the friends . . ." In many reports, in great detail, accusations and facts poured in upon the newly-made Guardian. There was, of course, another aspect. With touching pure-heartedness and trust the Bahá'ís of East and West rallied round their young leader and poured out avowals of their love and loyalty: "We long to assist the Guardian in every way and our hearts are responsive to the burdens upon his young shoulders . . ."; "Word has reached us here in Washington that our beloved Master has placed the guidance and protection of the Holy Cause in your hands and that He named you as the head of the House of Justice. I write you these few lines responding with all my heart to the sacred instructions of our Beloved Lord and assuring all the support and fidelity of which I am capable . . ."; "Beloved of our beloved," he was addressed by two pillars of the Faith in America, "how our hearts sang with joy at the news that the Master had not left us comfortless but had made you, His beloved, the centre of the unity of His Cause, so that the hearts of all the friends may find peace and certainty.";

"Our lives have been in utter darkness until the blessed cablegram of the Greatest Holy Leaf arrived with the first ray of light, and that is your appointment by the Merciful Lord as our Guardian and our Head as well as the Guardian of the Cause of God and the Head of the House of Justice."; "Whatever the Guardian of the Cause wishes or advises these servants to do, that is likewise our desire and intention."

On January 16th the Guardian wrote his first letter to the Persian Bahá'ís, encouraging them to remain steadfast and protect the Faith and sharing with them in moving terms his grief at the passing of the beloved Master. On January 22nd Shoghi Effendi cabled the American Bahá'ís: "Holy Leaves comforted by Americans' unswerving loyalty and noble resolve. Day of steadfastness. Accept my loving cooperation." The day before he had written his first letter to them, beginning: "At this early hour when the morning light is just breaking upon the Holy Land, whilst the gloom of the dear Master's bereavement is still hanging thick upon the hearts, I feel as if my soul turns in yearning love and full of hope to that great company of His loved ones across the seas . . ." Already he has placed his hand on the tiller and sees the channels he must navigate clearly before him: "the broad and straight path of teaching", as he phrased it, unity, selflessness, detachment, prudence, caution, earnest endeavour to carry out the Master's wishes, awareness of His presence, shunning of the enemies of the Cause—these must be the goal and animation of the believers. Four days later he is writing his first letter to the Japanese Bahá'ís: "Despondent and sorrowful though I be in these darksome days, yet whenever I call to mind the hopes our departed Master so confidently reposed in the friends in that Far-Eastern land, hope revives within me and drives away the gloom of His bereavement. As His attendant and secretary for well nigh two years after the termination of the Great War, I recall so vividly the radiant joy that transfigured His face whenever I opened before Him your supplications . . ."

While Shoghi Effendi was thus occupied and was gathering his powers and beginning to write letters such as these to the Bahá'ís in different countries, he received the following letter from the High Commissioner for Palestine, Sir Herbert Samuel, dated January 24, 1922:

Dear Mr. Rabbani,
I have to acknowledge receipt of your letter of Jan. 16, and to

thank you for the kind expression it contains.

It would be unfortunate if the ever to be lamented death of Sir 'Abdu'l-Bahá were to interfere with the completion of your Oxford career, and I hope that may not be the case.

I am much interested to learn of the measures that have been taken to provide for the stable organization of the Bahá'í Movement.

Should you be at any time in Jerusalem it would be a pleasure to me to see you here.

Yours sincerely,
Herbert Samuel

However friendly its tone, it demanded on the part of His Majesty's Government to be informed of what was going on. And this is not the least surprising in view of the activities of Muḥammad 'Alí. Shortly after 'Abdu'l-Bahá's ascension, this disgruntled and perfidious half-brother had filed a claim, based on Islamic law (he who pretended he had still a right to be the successor of Bahá'u'lláh!) for a portion of the estate of 'Abdu'l-Bahá which he now claimed a right to as His brother. He had sent for his son, who had been living in America and agitating his father's claims there, to join him in this new and direct attack on the Master and His family. Not content with this exhibition of his true nature he applied to the civil authorities to turn over the custodianship of Bahá'u'lláh's Shrine to him on the grounds that he was 'Abdu'l-Bahá's lawful successor. The British authorities refused on the grounds that it appeared to be a religious issue; he then appealed to the Muslim religious head and asked the Muftí of 'Akká to take formal charge of Bahá'u'lláh's Shrine; this dignitary, however, said he did not see how he could do this as the Bahá'í teachings were not in conformity with Sharí'ah law. All other avenues having failed he sent his younger brother, Badí'u'lláh, with some of their supporters, to visit the Shrine of Bahá'u'lláh where, on Tuesday, January 30th, they forcibly seized the keys of the Holy Tomb from the Bahá'í caretaker, thus asserting Muḥammad 'Alí's right to be the lawful custodian of his father's resting-place. This unprincipled act created such a commotion in the Bahá'í Community that the Governor of 'Akká ordered the keys to be handed over to the authorities, posted guards at the Shrine, but went no further, refusing to return the keys to either party.

It does not require much imagination to conceive this was another terrible shock to Shoghi Effendi, the news arriving after dark, by a panting and excited messenger, all the believers aroused and distressed beyond words at the thought that for the first time in decades the Most Sacred Remains had fallen into the hands of the inveterate enemy of the Centre of His Covenant.

The situation in which Shoghi Effendi now found himself was truly crushing. Although the body of the believers was loyal, the Cause was being attacked from all sides by enemies emboldened by and rejoicing over the death of 'Abdu'l-Bahá.

The strain of this was more than he could bear. He appointed a body of nine people to act tentatively as an Assembly and we find that on April 7, 1922, this body enters in its records that a letter has been received from the Greatest Holy Leaf in which she states that "the Guardian of the Cause of God, the Chosen Branch, the Leader of the people of Bahá, Shoghi Effendi, under the weight of sorrows and boundless grief, has been forced to leave here for a while in order to rest and recuperate, and then return to the Holy Land to render his services and discharge his responsibilities." She goes on to say that in accordance with his letter, which she encloses, he has appointed her to administer, in consultation with the family of 'Abdu'l-Bahá, and a chosen Assembly, all Bahá'í affairs during his absence. Shoghi Effendi had already left Haifa for Europe, on April 5th, accompanied by his eldest cousin.

On April 8th the Greatest Holy Leaf wrote a general letter to the friends. She first acknowledges the letters of allegiance they have sent and says Shoghi Effendi is counting upon their co-operation in spreading the Message; the Bahá'í world must from now on be linked through the Spiritual Assemblies and local questions must be referred to them. She then goes on to say: "Since the ascension of our Beloved 'Abdu'l-Bahá, Shoghi Effendi has been moved so deeply . . . that he has sought the necessary quiet in which to meditate upon the vast task ahead of him, and it is to accomplish this that he has temporarily left these regions. During his absence he has appointed me as his representative, and while he is occupied in this great endeavour, the family of 'Abdu'l-Bahá is assured that you will all strive to advance triumphantly the Cause of Bahá'u'lláh . . ." The typewritten letter in English is signed in Persian "Bahá'íyyih" and sealed with her seal.

It all looked very calm on paper but behind it was a raging storm in the heart and mind of Shoghi Effendi. "He has gone", the

Greatest Holy Leaf wrote, "on a trip to various countries". He left with his cousin and went to Germany to consult doctors. I remember he told me they found he had almost no reflexes, which they considered very serious. In the wilderness, however, he found for himself a partial healing, as so many others had found before him. Some years later, in 1926, to Hippolyte Dreyfus, who had known him from childhood and whom he evidently felt he could be open with as an intimate friend, he wrote that his letter had reached him "on my way to the Bernese Oberland which has become my second home. In the fastnesses and recesses of its alluring mountains I shall try to forget the atrocious vexations which have afflicted me for so long . . . It is a matter which I greatly deplore, that in my present state of health, I feel the least inclined to, and even incapable of, any serious discussion on these vital problems with which I am confronted and with which you are already familiar. The atmosphere in Haifa is intolerable and a radical change is impracticable. The transference of my work to any other centre is unthinkable, undesirable and in the opinion of many justly scandalous . . . I cannot express myself more adequately than I have for my memory has greatly suffered."

In the early years after 'Abdu'l-Bahá's passing, although Shoghi Effendi often travelled about Europe with the restless interest of not only a young man but a man haunted by the ever-present, towering giants of his work and his responsibility, he returned again and again to those wild, high mountains and their lofty solitude.

In spite of his withdrawal—for that is really what this first absence from the Holy Land amounted to—the forces Shoghi Effendi had set in motion were bearing fruit. One of the returning pilgrims informed the American Bahá'í Convention, held in April 1922, that: "our visit was at the summons of Shoghi Effendi. At Haifa we met Bahá'ís from Persia, India, Burma, Egypt, Italy, England and France . . . On arrival the impression that came strongly over me was that God is in His Heaven and all is well with the world . . . We met Shoghi Effendi, dressed entirely in black, a touching figure. Think of what he stands for today! All the complex problems of the great statesmen of the world are as child's play in comparison with the great problems of this youth, before whom are the problems of the entire world . . . No one can form any conception of his difficulties, which are overwhelming . . . the Master is not gone. His Spirit is present with greater intensity and power . . . In the center of this radiation stands this youth, Shoghi Effendi.

The Spirit streams forth from this young man. He is indeed young in face, form and manner, yet his heart is the center of the world today. The character and spirit divine scintillate from him today. He alone can . . . save the world and make true civilization. So humble, meek, selfless is he that it is touching to see him. His letters are a marvel. It is the great wisdom of God in granting us the countenance of this great central point of guidance to meet difficult problems. These problems, much like ours, come to him from all parts of the world. They are met and solved by him in the most informal way . . . The great principles laid down by Bahá'u'lláh and 'Abdu'l-Bahá now have their foundation in the external world of God's Kingdom on earth. This foundation is being laid, sure and certain, by Shoghi Effendi in Haifa today."

Being by nature very methodical Shoghi Effendi in these early years kept fairly complete records and copies of letters sent; he lists 67 centres that he wrote to, East and West, during the months he was in the Holy Land in 1922. From December 16, 1922, to February 23, 1923 he records 132 places he wrote to, some more than once. In a letter dated December 16, 1922 he wrote: ". . . I shall now eagerly await the joyful tidings of the progress of the Cause and the extension of your activities and will spare no effort in sharing with the faithful, here and in other lands, the welcome news of the progressive march of the Cause." The correspondence of this period covers 21 countries and 67 cities, but he does not seem to have written to more than a score of individuals, many of whom were not Bahá'ís. The countries he corresponded with at the very outset of his ministry included Persia, Britain, France, Germany, Italy, Sweden, Switzerland, United States, Canada, Australia, Pacific Islands, Japan, India, Burma, Caucasus, Turkistán, Turkey, Syria, Mesopotamia, Palestine and Egypt.

In his first letter to the newly-elected National Assembly of America he writes, on December 23rd, that: "To have been unable, owing to unforeseen and unavoidable circumstances, to correspond with you ever since you entered upon your manifold and arduous duties is to me a cause of deep regret and sad surprise." These are the words of a man coming up from the depths of nightmare and reflect how deep had been the abyss of affliction into which he had fallen during the past year of his life. "I am however", he goes on to say, "assured and sustained by the conviction, never dimmed in my mind, that whatever comes to pass in the Cause of God, however disquieting in its immediate effects, is fraught with infinite Wisdom and tends ultimately to promote its interests in the world."

In these early letters he invites the Assemblies to write to him, and he asks them to inform him of their "needs, wants and desires, their plans and their activities", so that he may "through my prayers and brotherly assistance contribute, however meagrely, to the success of their glorious mission in this world." He is deeply grateful for the manner in which "my humble suggestions" have been carried out, and assures the friends of his "never-failing brotherly assistance."

"I am now", Shoghi Effendi wrote to Tudor Pole in 1923, "fully restored to health and am intensely occupied with my work at present." Correspondence, however, was far from being his only activity; he was also "engaged in the service of the various pilgrims that visit in these days this sacred Spot." It was customary for him, in these early days of his ministry, to hold regular meetings in the home of 'Abdu'l-Bahá. In December 1922, five days after his return, he writes: "I have shared fully your news with those loving pilgrims and resident friends in the Holy Land whom I meet regularly in what was the audience chamber of the Master."

These might be described as the more pleasant phases of his work in the discharge of his high office, though they exacted from him a great deal of time and energy. But what really burdened him beyond all endurance were the activities of the Covenant-breakers. It was, in Shoghi Effendi's own words, "amidst the heat and dust which the attacks launched by a sleepless enemy precipitated" that he had to carry on his work.

The position of the Faith necessitated the cultivation of careful relations with the Mandatory authorities. 'Abdu'l-Bahá had been well known and highly esteemed, though it is unlikely that anyone in Palestine had the faintest inkling of the vast implications of the "Movement", as it was so often referred to in the early days, of which they accepted Him as Head. On December 19, 1922 Shoghi Effendi had wired to the High Commissioner for Palestine in Jerusalem: "Pray accept my best wishes and kind regards on my return to Holy Land and resumption of my official duties." As there must have been a considerable buzz of gossip, ardently fed no doubt by the Covenant-breakers, about his eight months' withdrawal, this was a carefully calculated move on Shoghi Effendi's part as well as an act of courtesy.

The matter which concerned Shoghi Effendi most, however, was the Shrine of Bahá'u'lláh at Bahjí. The keys of the inner Tomb were still held by the authorities; the right of access to other parts of the Shrine was accorded Bahá'ís and Covenant-breakers alike; the Bahá'í custodian looked after it as before, and any decision seemed in a state of abeyance. Shoghi Effendi never rested until, through representations he made to the authorities, backed by insistent pressure from Bahá'ís all over the world, he succeeded in getting the custody of the Holy Tomb back into his own hands. On February 7, 1923, he wrote to Tudor Pole: "I have had a long talk with Col. Symes and have fully explained to him the exact state of affairs, the unmistakable and overwhelming voice of all the Bahá'í Community and their unshakeable determination to stand by the Will and Testament of 'Abdu'l-Bahá. Recently he sent a message to Muḥammad 'Alí requiring from him the sum of £108 for the expenses of the policeman, contending that he being the aggressor is liable to this expense. So far he has not complied with this request and I await future developments with great anxiety."

The following day Shoghi Effendi received this telegram from his cousin, who was in Jerusalem:

> His Eminence Shoghi Effendi Rabbani, Haifa.
> Letter received immediate steps taken the final decision by the High Commissioner is in our favour the key is yours.

The letter referred to was one written by Sir Gilbert Clayton, Chief Secretary of the Palestine Administration, to the High Commissioner. Shoghi Effendi, in another letter to Tudor Pole, informed him that he was on very warm terms with the Governor of Haifa, Col. G. Stewart Symes and had met Sir Gilbert; it was no doubt due to these contacts that the authorities decided in favour of the Guardian and the key was officially returned to the legitimate Bahá'í keeper of the Shrine, from whom it had been wrested by force over a year before.

Though the safety of the Qiblih of the Bahá'í world was now assured once and for all time, the house Bahá'u'lláh had occupied in Baghdád was still in the hands of the Shí'ah enemies of the Faith, and continues to be so until the present day; the battle to get it back into Bahá'í custody was to worry and to exercise Shoghi Effendi for many years.

Every time one goes into the details of any particular period in the Guardian's life one is tempted to say, "this was the worst period", so fraught with strain, problems, unbearable pressures was his entire ministry. But there is a pattern, there are themes, higher and lower points were reached. The pattern of 1922, 1923 and 1924 reveals itself, insofar as his personal life is concerned, as an heroic attempt to come to grips with this leviathan—the Cause of God—he had been commanded to bestride.

With the passing of 1923 one could almost say that the winged Guardian emerged from the chrysalis of youth, a new being; the wings may not yet be fully stretched, but their beat gains steadily in sweep and assurance as the years go by until, in the end, they truly cast a shadow over all mankind. In his early writings one sees this mastery unfolding, in style, in thought, in power. Let us pick certain facts and quotations at random and see how clearly they substantiate this evolution that was taking place. From the very beginning he turned to the believers, with that inimitable trusting and confiding touch that won all hearts, and asked them to pray for him, that he might, in collaboration with them, achieve the "speedy triumph of the Cause of God" in every land. His questions are challenging, his thoughts incisive: "Are we to be carried away by the flood of hollow and conflicting ideas, or are we to stand, unsubdued and unblemished, upon the everlasting rock of God's Divine Instructions?"; ". . . are we to believe that whatever befalls us is divinely ordained, and in no wise the result of our faint-heartedness and negligence?" Already in 1923 he sees the world and the Cause as two distinct things, not to be mixed up in our minds into one sentimental and haphazard lump. The Will of God he asserts is "at variance with the shadowy views, the impotent doctrines, the crude theories, the idle imaginings, the fashionable conceptions of a transient and troublous age."

Shoghi Effendi's interest in the Pacific and his awareness of the future development of the Cause in that area is manifested in the first years of his Guardianship. He wrote to the Pacific Islands, in delightfully romantic terms, in January 1923, that "their very names evoke within us so high a sense of hope and admiration that the passing of time and the vicissitudes of life can never weaken or remove", and addressed a letter in January 1924 "To the dearly-beloved ones of 'Abdu'l-Bahá throughout Australia, New Zealand, Tasmania, and the adjoining islands of the Pacific. Friends and heralds of the Kingdom of Bahá'u'lláh! A fresh breeze laden with the perfume of your love and devotion to our beloved Cause was wafted again from your distant Southern shores to the Holy

Land and has served to remind us one and all of that unquenchable spirit of service and self-sacrifice which the passing of our Beloved has in these days kindled in almost every corner of the world."

The words he wrote to one of the American Assemblies in December 1923 sound almost like a soliloquy: "The inscrutable wisdom of God has so decreed that we, who are the chosen bearers of the world's greatest Message to suffering humanity, should toil and promote our work under the most trying conditions of life, amidst unhelpful surroundings, and in the face of unprecedented trials, and without means, influence or support, achieve, steadily and surely, the conquest and regeneration of human hearts." Many of these early letters to various Spiritual Assemblies have this quality, not of disquisition, but of voicing his own innermost considerations. That same month he wrote: ". . . True, the progress of our work, when compared to the sensational rise and development of an earthly cause, has been painful and slow, yet we firmly believe and shall never doubt that the great spiritual Revolution which the Almighty is causing to be accomplished, through us, in the hearts of men is destined to achieve, steadily and surely, the complete regeneration of all mankind."; "However great our tribulation may be, however unexpected the miseries of life, let us bear in mind the life He [the Master] has led before us, and, inspired and grateful, let us bear our burden with steadfastness and fortitude, that in the world to come, in the divine Presence of our loving Comforter, we may receive His true consolation and reward of our labours."; "Whatever may befall us, and however dark the prospect of the future may appear, if we but play our part we may rest confident that the Hand of the Unseen is at work, shaping and moulding the events and circumstances of the world and paving the way for the ultimate realization of our aims and hopes for mankind."; "Our primary duty is to create by our words and deeds, our conduct and example, the atmosphere in which the seeds of the words of Bahá'u'lláh and 'Abdu'l-Bahá cast so profusely during well-nigh eighty years, may germinate and give forth those fruits that alone can assure peace and prosperity to this distracted world."; ". . . let us arise to teach His Cause with righteousness, conviction, understanding and vigour . . . let us make it the dominating passion of our life. Let us scatter to the uttermost corners of the earth, sacrifice our personal interests, comforts, tastes and pleasures, mingle with the divers kindreds and peoples of the world; familiarize ourselves with their manners, traditions, thoughts and customs". The tone of some of these sounds like his great messages during the prosecution of the Divine Plan, but they were written in the winter of 1923–1924. He had set himself the task of seeing that the Faith emerged into "the broad daylight of universal recognition", a term he used that same year.

Steeped in the Teachings from his infancy, privileged to hear, read and write so many of the Master's words during his youth, Shoghi Effendi firmly guided the friends in East and West along their destined course. Already in March 1922, in one of his first letters to the American believers, he had stated: "the friends of God the world over are strictly forbidden to meddle with political affairs". He is using the term "pioneer", in his earliest letters, and in 1925 is keeping a list of Bahá'í centres throughout the world!

In spite of what he described as the "thorny path of my arduous duties", in spite of the "oppressive burden of responsibility and care which it is my lot and privilege to shoulder", he was clear in expressing and brilliant in understanding the needs of the Cause and the tasks facing the believers. He was equally clear in defining what relationship he wished the Bahá'ís to have with him and in what manner they should regard him. On February 6, 1922 he wrote to one of the Persian Bahá'ís: "I wish to be known, to realize myself however far I may proceed in future, as one and only one of the many workers in His Vineyards . . . whatever may betide I trust in His ['Abdu'l-Bahá's] wondrous love for me. May I in no wise by my deeds, thoughts or words, impede the stream of His sustaining Spirit which I sorely need in facing the responsibilities He has placed on my youthful shoulders . . ." and on March 5th he added the following postscript to a letter to the American friends: "May I also express my heartfelt desire that the friends of God in every land regard me in no other light but that of a true brother, united with them in our common servitude to the Master's Sacred Threshold, and refer to me in their letters and verbal addresses always as Shoghi Effendi, for I desire to be known by no other name save the one our Beloved Master was wont to utter, a name which of all other designations is the most conducive to my spiritual growth and advancement." In 1924 he cabled India clearly and succinctly: "My birthday should not be commemorated". In 1930 his secretary wrote on his behalf: "Concerning Shoghi Effendi's station: he surely has none except what the Master confers upon him in His Will and that Will also states what Shoghi Effendi's station is. If anyone misinterprets one part of the Will he misinterprets all the

Will." When Shoghi Effendi wrote the general letter known as *The Dispensation of Bahá'u'lláh* he made clear, once-for-all, his own position, disassociating himself categorically from the prerogatives and station Bahá'u'lláh had conferred upon 'Abdu'l-Bahá: "In the light of this truth to pray to the Guardian of the Faith, to address him as lord and master, to designate him as his holiness, to seek his benediction, to celebrate his birthday, or to commemorate any event associated with his life would be tantamount to a departure from those established truths that are enshrined within our beloved Faith." In 1945 his secretary wrote on his behalf: ". . . he has never gone so far as to forbid the friends to have pictures of himself in their possession; he merely would rather they placed the emphasis on the beloved Master."

III

EARLY YEARS OF THE GUARDIANSHIP

It is time to ask ourselves what manner of man this was who wrote such things about himself, what impression did he create, how did he appear to others?

From the diary of one of the American believers whom Shoghi Effendi called to Haifa, in March 1922, we have the following description: ". . . Shoghi Effendi appeared and greeted me most kindly and affectionately. I had not seen him for eight years, and of course I was surprised at the change and development in him, for instead of the boy I had known there was now a man very young in years but premature in poise and depth of spirit and thought . . ." He goes on to describe his impressions of Shoghi Effendi: "As I used to sit at table looking at Shoghi Effendi, I was struck by his resemblance to the Master. In the shape and poise of his head, his shoulders, his walk and his general bearing. Then I felt the terrible weight and responsibility which had been placed upon that young boy. It seemed overwhelming that he, whose life was just starting, so to speak from the human worldly standpoint, should have had this great responsibility thrust upon him, a weight which would so consume him and place him aside by himself as to eliminate from his life the freedom and joy of the human side of life, which though not eternal, has a certain call for each of us human beings."

In 1929 an Indian Bahá'í pilgrim wrote of Shoghi Effendi: "We must understand Shoghi Effendi in order to be able to help him accomplish the stupendous task he has entrusted to us. He is so calm and yet so vibrant, so static and yet so dynamic." This is little short of a brilliant characterization of one aspect of the Guardian. The impression he created on the first American Bahá'í to be called to Haifa after the second World War, in 1947, reveals other aspects of his nature: "My first impression is of his warm, loving smile and handclasp, making me feel instantly at ease . . . In the course of these interviews, I was to become increasingly conscious of his many great qualities—his nobility, dignity, fire and enthusiasm—his ability to run the scale from sparkling humour to deep outrage, but always, always, putting the Bahá'í Faith ahead of everything . . . In his practical, logical manner, Shoghi Effendi made me feel both a welcome guest and a needed helper, he outlined some of my duties which started the very next day! His advice, given me on that initial visit, was to overshadow all my efforts on his behalf; he said he wanted me to follow his instructions explicitly, if I was unsuccessful, or ran into difficulties, to report to him precisely and he would give me a new plan of action . . . For the Bahá'ís working at the International Center, during this period at least, there was no special day of rest. It was then that one learned that each moment belonged to the Faith . . ." She then tells of those evenings when Shoghi Effendi shared with us at the dinner table special plans, cables and messages he was sending out and occasionally precious documents in his possession: ". . . Sparkling with excitement and new plans, he would produce messages and letters from his pockets, oftentimes pushing his dinner plate away untouched, calling for paper and pencil and thrill us all with his new ideas and hopes for the Bahá'ís to carry out . . . The beloved Guardian disliked very much to have his picture taken, therefore any photographs extant do not reflect his true 'image'. In the first place, the emotions flowed so rapidly over his features that one would need a series to catch his many moods. It was a delight to see and hear him laugh . . . he seemed to twinkle like a star when some plan had been successfully brought to a conclusion. His sense of humour was a joy! He was like a high mountain, strong, always there, but never conquered, filled with unexpected heights and depths . . . he was extremely thorough and taught us all a new sense of perfection and attention to detail . . . he was in close touch with the expenditure of all funds . . . He was enthusiastically concerned with Bahá'í statistics . . . We could never appreciate his grasp of all affairs connected with activities at the 'grass roots' right up to the World Center . . ."

Professor Alaine Locke of Howard University in Washington, who was one of the Bahá'í pilgrims to visit Haifa during the first years of Shoghi Effendi's Guardianship, describes the impressions he received as he walked with Shoghi Effendi in the gardens of the Báb's Shrine: "Shoghi Effendi is a master of detail as well as of principle, of executive foresight as well as of projective vision. But I have never heard details so redeemed of their natural triviality as when talking to him of the plans for the beautifying and laying out of the terraces and gardens. They were important because they all were meant to dramatize the emotion of the place and quicken the soul even through the senses."

Shoghi Effendi continually added to these gardens and their fame increased steadily. By the end of his life as many as 90,000 people a year were visiting them and the Shrine of the Báb. What one visitor wrote to him in 1935 expressed in the simplest terms the impression such a visit creates on many people; she had been "deeply impressed by the reticent beauty of the Shrines and by the happiness of the gardens."

It was his practice each year to enlarge the cultivated area around the Shrines of the Báb and 'Abdu'l-Bahá. No doubt the very first impulse in this direction came from his ever-conscious desire to follow in every field the wishes of his departed Master. He knew 'Abdu'l-Bahá had planned a series of terraces from the old German Colony up to the Báb's Sepulchre; indeed the Master had begun developing the first terrace. Shoghi Effendi set himself, over the years, to finish these and in the course of studying this plan he no doubt evolved a concept of his gardens around the Shrine—for gardens they are, not one garden. To understand and appreciate the extraordinarily beautiful effect Shoghi Effendi has created on Mt. Carmel and in Bahjí one must know his method.

Shoghi Effendi studied the surrounding barren mountain side and began to develop, piece by piece, year after year, separate sections. With the exception of the terraces it must be borne in mind that he never had an over-all plan. This is what gives the gardens on Mt. Carmel their unique character. As he walked about Shoghi Effendi would get an idea for a piece of garden that fitted the topography of the land. With no fuss, no advice and no help except the unskilled farmers who did duty as gardeners, he would make his plan for this "piece". If necessary he would have the spot surveyed and curves or long lines laid out, but very often he dispensed with this and did it all himself.

It is hard to understand why most people do things so slowly when Shoghi Effendi did them so fast. Just to twitter faithfully that he was "guided by God" does not seem to me a sufficient explanation. I believe great people see things in great dimensions, little people get tripped up by little details. Shoghi Effendi, being truly great, having clearly in mind what he wanted to do, saw no reason why a lot of puny details—such as that one usually gave instructions to subordinates and let them go their own pace in carrying them out—should prevent him from getting the whole thing done, under his own eyes, in one operation. He organized it perfectly and it was accomplished immediately and perfectly; anything he could do himself was always done this way. The delays and frustrations usually occurred when he had to refer his work to others.

Shoghi Effendi had a faultless sense of proportion. It is the combination of this sense of proportion, and an originality unhampered by tradition or too much information that made his gardens so unique, so fascinating and beautiful. If he (so he claimed) lacked the power of visualizing a thing completed, he possessed to a strong degree the other creative faculty of the true artist, the capacity to let a thing shape up under his hands, to receive an inspiration in the middle of a plan and pursue the soaring course of that inspiration rather than be tied to the preconceived idea.

Shoghi Effendi—like the Master before him—was a great lover of light. He hated gloomy interiors. This love of bright light was so pronounced that I used to remonstrate with him for working with a powerful desk lamp practically shining in his eyes as I was afraid it was too much for them. His own room was always brilliantly lit, the Shrines were all full of lights, large and small, and one of his first acts as Guardian was to have placed over the door of the Báb's Shrine that faces the terraces and the straight avenue at the foot of the mountain that leads to the sea, a bright light.

Gradually the gardens in both Haifa and Bahjí were all illumined with beautiful four-branched wrought iron lamp posts, ninety-nine of them being erected in Bahjí alone. When the night came that these were lighted for the first time, on the occasion of the Riḍván Feast in 1953, and we approached Bahjí by car the sky glowed as if we were approaching a small city! The Guardian told the Persian pilgrims that it had always been light, but now it was "light upon light". (In the original there is a beautiful play of words alluding to Bahá'u'lláh as light.) In addition to this the Shrine in Haifa was illuminated at night by flood-lights, as were the resting-places of the Greatest Holy Leaf, and those of the mother and brother of 'Abdu'l-Bahá, and high-powered reflectors were ordered to illumine the International Archives Building.

Shoghi Effendi came to grips with the harsh fact that he was to all intents and purposes alone and he placed increased reliance on himself. He set himself to do all the work and did it, using as secretaries various members of the Master's family, facing an ever-

EARLY YEARS OF THE GUARDIANSHIP 33

increasing spirit of disaffection on their part, resigning himself to the unending drudgery of petty tasks as well as major ones, accepting his fate with resignation, often with despair, always with loyalty and fortitude. It can truly be said of him that single-handed he effected the world-wide establishment of the Faith of his Divine Forefathers and proved that he belonged to that same sovereign caste.

It was during these years, when Shoghi Effendi was trying so hard to gather about him a group of competent co-workers, that a crisis of unprecedented dimensions burst upon him. The sea of the Cause of God, whipped by the winds of both destiny and chance which blow upon it from the outside world, was now lashed into a storm whose waves beat remorselessly upon Shoghi Effendi's mind, his strength, his nerves and his resources. The blessed House occupied by Bahá'u'lláh in Baghdád, and ordained by Him, in Shoghi Effendi's words, as a "sacred, sanctified and cherished object of Bahá'í pilgrimage and veneration" had already in the days of 'Abdu'l-Bahá been seized by the Shí'ahs, after a series of nefarious manoeuvres, but had been returned by the British authorities to its legitimate custodians. When news of 'Abdu'l-Bahá's passing reached the inveterate enemies of the Faith, they once again renewed their attack and laid claim to the House; in 1922 the government had taken over the keys of the House in spite of the assurance of King Feisal that he would respect the claims of the Bahá'ís to a building that had been occupied by their representatives ever since Bahá'u'lláh's departure from Baghdád and who now, for political reasons, went back on his word; and in 1923, the keys had been most unjustly delivered again to the Shí'ahs. From shortly after the passing of 'Abdu'l-Bahá until November 1925 there had been a continuous struggle on the part of the Bahá'ís to protect the Most Holy House. The Shí'ahs had first taken the case to their own religious court from which it was speedily lifted out to the Peace court and then brought before the local Court of First Instance, which decided in favour of the rights of the Bahá'ís. This decision was then taken to the Court of Appeals, the Supreme Court of 'Iráq, which gave its verdict in favour of the Shí'ahs.

When the Guardian was informed of this flagrant miscarriage of justice he immediately mustered the Bahá'í world to take action: he sent nineteen cables to various individuals and national bodies comprising the believers in Persia, the Caucasus, Turkistán, 'Iráq, Japan, Burma, China, Turkey, Moscow, India, Australia, New

Zealand, Canada, the United States, Germany, Austria, France, Great Britain and the Pacific Islands. His instructions were that the Bahá'ís should cable and write their protest at this decision to the British High Commissioner in 'Iráq. Persia and North America—where the Bahá'í communities were numerically strong—were informed that in addition to every local Assembly voicing its protest directly, the National Assembly should not only contact the High Commissioner, but protest directly to both King Feisal of 'Iráq and the British authorities in London. The Assembly of India and Burma was likewise to protest to the King himself, but not to London. In places where the Bahá'ís were few in number, such as France and China, Shoghi Effendi advised that the protest should go over the signature of individuals. All these instructions markedly display the strategist in Shoghi Effendi. In his cables to the Bahá'í world he stated the situation was "perilous" and the "consequences of the utmost gravity"; all must request "prompt action to safeguard spiritual claims of Bahá'ís to this dearly-beloved Spot", "this sanctified abode", "Bahá'u'lláh's Sacred House". He put the proper phrases into the mouths of those he advised, the eastern friends being told to "fervently and courteously", "in firm considerate language", earnestly appeal "for consideration of their spiritual claims to its possession" and to the "British sense of justice", while the western believers were informed that "effective prompt action urgently required . . . protesting vigorously against Court's glaring injustice, appealing for redress to British sense of fairness, asserting spiritual claims of Bahá'ís . . . declaring their unfailing resolve to do their utmost to vindicate their legitimate and sacred rights." With his usual thoroughness Shoghi Effendi advised America that the messages sent by the local Assemblies "should not be identical in wording."

The exchange, during a six-month period, of well-nigh a hundred cables, in addition to a continual correspondence with various agents working to safeguard the Most Holy House, testify in bulk and substance to Shoghi Effendi's preoccupation with this problem. One of his first acts, on receiving the news of the decision of the Supreme Court, was to cable the High Commissioner in Baghdád that: "The Bahá'ís the world over view with surprise and consternation the Court's unexpected verdict regarding the ownership of Bahá'u'lláh's Sacred House. Mindful of their long-standing and continuous occupation of this property they refuse to believe that Your Excellency will ever countenance such manifest injus-

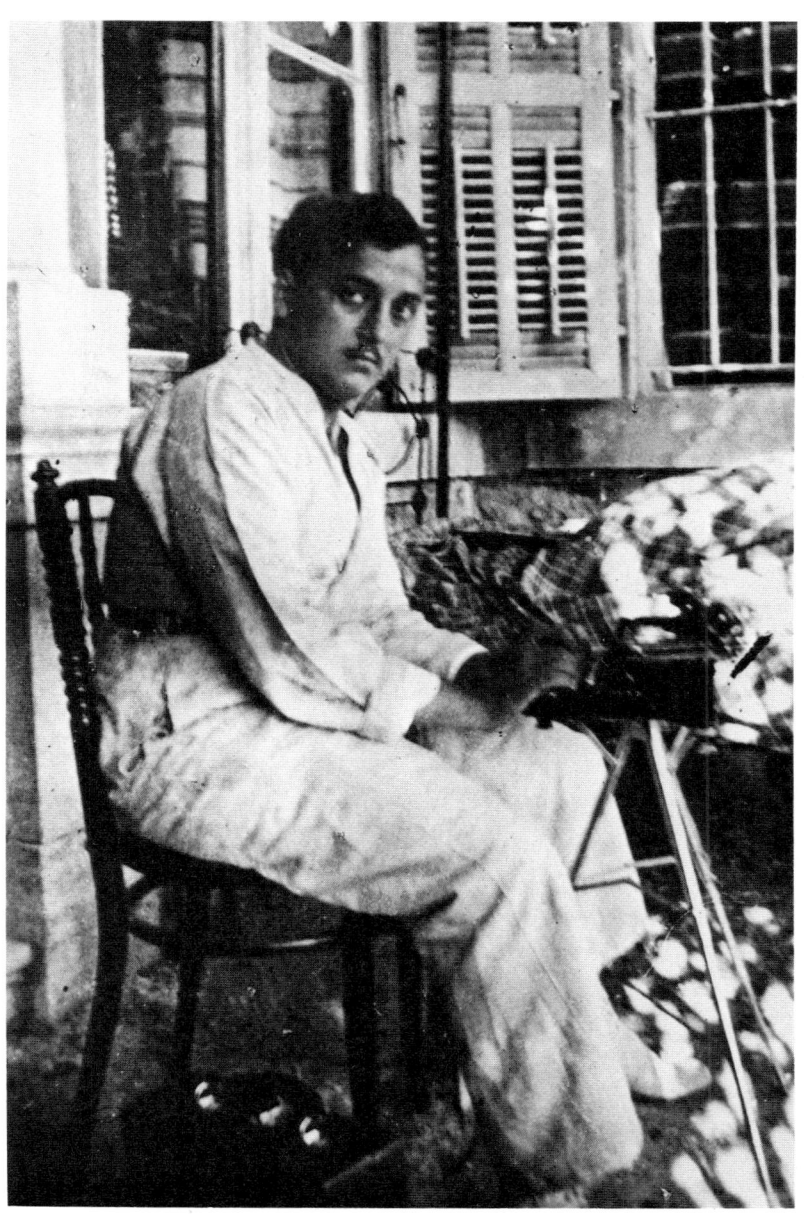

THE MASTER'S SECRETARY

Shoghi Effendi at his small typewriter, on the balcony of the room he occupied next to 'Abdu'l-Bahá's, probably working on the translation of his grandfather's Tablets; circa 1919

SHOGHI EFFENDI IN ORIENTAL ROBES
Before he went to study in England the Guardian used to dress in this manner

SHOGHI EFFENDI IN HIS EARLY TWENTIES

SHOGHI EFFENDI BEFORE HE BECAME GUARDIAN

SHOGHI EFFENDI WITH HARRY RANDALL
Taken in the Garden of the Riḍván, near 'Akká, 1919

THE SAMOVAR

Shoghi Effendi (centre) on the roof of the barn at 'Abdu'l-Bahá's home in Haifa

tice. They solemnly pledge themselves to stand resolutely for the protection of their rights. They appeal to the high sense of honour and justice which they firmly believe animates your Administration. In the name of the family of Sir 'Abdu'l-Bahá 'Abbás and the whole Bahá'í Community, Shoghi Rabbani". On the same day he cabled the heart-broken Keeper of Bahá'u'lláh's House: "Grieve not. Case in God's hand. Rest assured."

During the ensuing months many cables from Shoghi Effendi included such phrases as "House case should be strenuously pursued." He cabled a number of prominent non-Bahá'ís, and constantly co-ordinated the efforts of his lieutenants in different parts of the world. When over a month had passed Shoghi Effendi cabled various National Assemblies, instructing them to enquire in "courteous terms" from the High Commissioner "results of investigation" which the British authorities had promised to undertake. It was a losing battle, for the political and religious elements in 'Iráq had common cause and refused to bow to the pressure brought upon them, including that of the British Government.

Shoghi Effendi, however, did not accept defeat so lightly and never rested until the case of the Holy House was brought before the League of Nations Permanent Mandates Commission, in November 1928; the Mandatory Power had upheld the right of the Bahá'ís to the possession of the House, and the Mandates Commission recommended to the Council of the League of Nations that it request the British Government to make representations to the 'Iráqí Government to redress the denial of justice to the Bahá'ís in this case. The Bahá'ís continued to press the matter, from 1928 until 1933, but to no avail because the instruments for enforcing the decision were lacking and the power of the Shí'ahs inside 'Iráq was such as to cause the entire question to be dropped by the 'Iráqí Government, whenever that decision was pressed upon it.

A brief résumé of events such as these conveys none of the day-to-day suspense that attends them, the fluctuations between hope and despair, the good news and bad news that alternate with each other and wear away the heart and strength. The first impact of the Supreme Court's decision had scarcely been received when Dr. Esslemont suddenly died. Coming at such a time of crisis the loss of his friend was a doubly grievous blow to the Guardian.

So heavy was this burden that in February 1926 he wrote to one of the believers: "I am submerged in a sea of activities, anxieties and preoccupations. My mind is extremely tired and I feel I am becoming inefficient and slow due to this mental fatigue." This condition became so acute that he was forced to go away for a brief rest. "The overwhelming burden of pressing cares and responsibilities", he wrote towards the end of March, "necessitated my departure at a time when . . . I was most anxious to receive my friends and co-workers from various parts of the world". He must have been ill, indeed, to have absented himself from Haifa and his guests, but whatever his condition in February and March it was mild compared to that into which he was plunged by a wire from Persia, sent on April 11th, from Shíráz, which baldly stated: "Twelve friends in Jahrom martyred agitation may extend elsewhere," to which he replied the same day, "Horrified sudden calamity. Suspend activities. Appeal central authorities. Convey relatives tenderest sympathy". He also wired that same day to Ṭihrán a message so significant of the spirit of the Faith that its conjunction with the events in Jahrum cannot be ignored: "I earnestly request all believers Persia Turkistan Caucasus participate whole-heartedly in renewal Spiritual Assemblies election. No true Bahá'í can stand aside. Results should be promptly forwarded Holy Land through central Assemblies communicate immediately with every centre. Proceed cautiously. Imploring Divine assistance." The following day, having received a more detailed wire from Shíráz advising that the chief instigator of the agitation there had been arrested and giving certain suggestions, Shoghi Effendi telegraphed Ṭihrán: "Grief-stricken Jahrom martyrdom. Convey His Majesty on behalf all Bahá'ís and myself our profound appreciation his prompt intervention and our earnest entreaty to inflict immediate punishment on perpetrators of such atrocious crime. Urge all Persian Assemblies send similar message." It is a slight, but significant indication of his mental state, that in the first cables he spells "Jahrom" phonetically, but later switches to the transliterated "Jahrum".

What all this meant to Shoghi Effendi is expressed by him in a letter to one of his co-workers, written on the 24th of April. After acknowledging receipt of his many letters, he explains that his delay in answering them has been due to "my unfortunate illness, amounting almost to a break-down, combined with the receipt of the most distressing news from Persia reporting the martyrdom of twelve of our friends in the town of Jahrum, south of Shíráz. I have wired for full particulars and will communicate them to the various Bahá'í centres immediately I receive detailed information. Political considerations and personal rivalries appear to have played no small part . . . I have transmitted a message to the Sháh through the Persian National Spiritual Assembly . . . I have also requested foreign Assemblies to give in an unoffensive language full publicity to these reports in their respective newspapers, but have thought it premature for them to get into direct relation with the Sháh . . ."

Yet in this state Shoghi Effendi managed to do what he thought could be done: "I feel that with patience, tact, courage and resource we can utilize this development to further the interests and extend the influence of the Cause." He had mustered the forces of the Bahá'í world in defence of the oppressed Persian Community, ensured that wide publicity in the foreign press be given to these martyrdoms, and constantly directed various National Assemblies in the action they should take in this respect as well as in the case of the Most Holy House.

Such is the tale of one period of the Guardian's life; how many blows rained on him in a little over six months, at a time when he was still struggling to get the load that had been placed on his shoulders at the time of the Master's passing properly balanced so that he could carry it!

IV

MARTHA ROOT AND QUEEN MARIE

Shoghi Effendi used to remark that out of his sufferings something always seemed to be born. He would go through these ordeals by fire—for indeed he seemed to fairly burn with suffering—and then some rain from heaven, in the form of good news, would shower upon him and help to revive him. I am afraid the mystery of sacrifice still remains a mystery to me, but certainly the Holy Ones of this world buy their victories dearly.

It was at this time, when affliction was literally engulfing the Guardian, that, on May 4th, the "Toronto Daily Star" published a highly appreciative statement made by Queen Marie of Rumania on the Bahá'í Faith, a statement, followed by others during the course of her visit to the United States and Canada, which was printed in about two hundred newspapers and constituted some of the widest and most spectacular publicity the Faith has ever received. In a confidential letter written on May 29th the Guardian refers to this as "this most astonishing and highly significant event in the progress of the Cause".

The acceptance of Bahá'u'lláh's station by the Rumanian Queen—the first crowned head to embrace the Faith—is a chapter in itself in the life of Shoghi Effendi and is inextricably bound up with the services of Martha Root, that "star-servant of the Faith of Bahá'u'lláh", as Shoghi Effendi called her, and the part she played in his life—indeed no account of his life could ever be complete without mention of the relationship of this noble soul to him. Miss Martha Root was a journalist by profession and came of a distinguished American family. She met the Master during His visit to the United States and, fired by His *Tablets of the Divine Plan*, arose in 1919 and commenced her historic travels in the service of the Cause, not only travelling longer and farther than any single Bahá'í has ever done since its inception, but often, as the Guardian said, "in extremely perilous circumstances". It was her great teaching journeys—four of which took her entirely round the world—combined with her truly outstanding qualities, that so endeared her to Shoghi Effendi and led him to call her the "archetype of Bahá'í itinerant teachers". The services of no other believer ever afforded him the satisfaction that her singular victories brought him. Of her Shoghi Effendi wrote in October 1926: "In her case we have verily witnessed in an unmistakable manner what the power of dauntless faith, when coupled with sublimity of character, can achieve, what forces it can release, to what heights it can rise."

From the inception of Shoghi Effendi's ministry she not only turned her great loving heart to him but constantly sought his advice as to her plans. It would not be exaggerating to say they had a partnership in all her undertakings, marked by a mutual love and confidence all too rare in the harassed life of the Guardian. They kept in close touch, a flow of letters and cables apprising him of her plans, her needs, her victories, her requests for guidance and his unfailing answers giving encouragement and advice. We find in his letters to her, whom he characterized, in 1923, as that "indomitable and zealous disciple of 'Abdu'l-Bahá", over and over again phrases such as these, in which he expresses the warmth of his feelings, that he has read her letters with "pride and gratitude", that they "have as usual gladdened my heart", that "It is always a joy to hear from you, beloved Martha." He wrote to her in July 1926, when she was making so many contacts with the royalty of Europe: ". . . write me fully and frequently for I yearn to hear of your activities and of every detail of your achievements. Assuring you of my boundless love for you . . .", and in August he says, "I hunger for every minute detail of your triumphal advance in the field of service . . . I am enclosing a copy of my letter to the Queen. Do not share its contents with anyone." But he had hastened to share it himself with her who had taught that Queen. In September he wrote, "I am glad to share with you the contents of the Queen of Rumania's answer to my letter. I think it is a remarkable letter, beyond our highest expectations. The change that has been effected in her, her outspoken manner, her penetrating testimony and courageous stand are indeed eloquent and convincing proof of the all-conquering Spirit of God's living Faith and the magnificent services you are rendering to His Cause."

She turned to him at all times, unhesitatingly making requests of him which she felt were in the interests of the Faith. The Guardian was well aware of both the purity of her motives and her good judgement and almost invariably acceded to these requests, which ranged from letters of encouragement to individuals to cabled messages to figures of great prominence.

On one occasion she cabled the Guardian: ". . . perhaps you will think wise send me immediately greetings President Hoover", to which Shoghi Effendi replied by cable the following day: "Kindly convey President Hoover on behalf followers Bahá'u'lláh world over expression their fervent prayers for success his unsparing efforts in promoting cause of international brotherhood and peace—a cause for which they have steadfastly laboured well nigh a century". Exactly one year before, during a visit to Japan in November 1930, we find a similar exchange of cables taking place; Martha's said: "Love beautiful you cable me greetings Emperor", to which Shoghi Effendi replied, the same day: "Kindly transmit His Imperial Majesty Emperor Japan on behalf myself and Bahá'ís world over expression of our deepest love as well as assurance our heartfelt prayers for his well-being and prosperity his ancient realm." Love begets love. Martha's great love for Shoghi Effendi called forth his love and his responses the way the capacity of a diamond to reflect light captures its rays and casts them back brilliantly.

In March of 1927, Shoghi Effendi wrote to Martha: ". . . I assure you, dearest Martha that wherever you be, in Scandinavia, Central Europe, Russia, Turkey or Persia, my fervent and continued prayers will accompany you and I trust that you may be protected, strengthened and guided to fulfil your unique and unprecedented mission as the exemplary advocate of the Bahá'í Faith."

The years rolled by and Martha Root continued, white haired, frail and indomitable, her ceaseless journeys, until she was stricken by "a deadly and painful disease", as Shoghi Effendi wrote, and in Honolulu on September 28, 1939 she passed away. She had been on fire with pain during the last weeks of a tour of the Antipodes and, on her way back to America, to assist in the prosecution of the first Seven Year Plan, she literally dropped in her tracks, yielding up a life the Guardian said might well be regarded as the fairest fruit the Formative Age of the Dispensation of Bahá'u'lláh had yet produced.

I well remember the day the cable conveying the news of her death reached Shoghi Effendi. He himself was very ill with sand fly fever, had a high temperature (104 degrees Fahrenheit) and, alas, should never have had to receive such news in such a condition! But there was no way we could withhold it from him. He was the Guardian, it was Martha Root who had died. Against the strong remonstrances of his mother, his brother and myself, he pulled himself up to a sitting position in his bed, white, terribly weak, and very shaken by this sudden news, and dictated a cable to America announcing her death. He said what else could he do—the whole Bahá'í world was waiting to hear what he would say. In that long message he said, amongst other things: "Martha's unnumbered admirers throughout Bahá'í world lament with me earthly extinction her heroic life . . . Posterity will establish her as foremost Hand . . . first Bahá'í Century . . . first finest fruit Formative Age Faith . . ." He said he was impelled to share the expenses of building her grave with the American National Assembly, the grave of one whose "acts shed imperishable lustre American Bahá'í Community."

Martha Root was firmly convinced that in her possession was the most priceless gem the world had ever seen—the Message of Bahá'u'lláh. She believed that in showing this gem and offering it to anyone, king or peasant, she was conferring the greatest bounty upon him he could ever receive. It was this proud conviction that enabled her, a woman of no wealth or social prestige, plain, dowdily dressed and neither a great scholar nor an outstanding intellectual, to meet more kings, queens, princes and princesses, presidents and men of distinction, fame and prominence and tell them about the Bahá'í Faith than any other Bahá'í in the history of this Cause has ever done.

Martha Root reported to Shoghi Effendi the account of the first of her eight interviews with Queen Marie of Rumania, which took place on January 30, 1926, in Controceni Palace in Bucharest, at the request of the Queen herself, after she had received Dr. Esslemont's book, *Bahá'u'lláh and the New Era*, sent to her by Martha. The Queen had evidently been attracted to the Teachings and when it was bruited about that she might visit North America, Shoghi Effendi wrote to the American National Spiritual Assembly the following instructions, conveyed in the writing of his secretary, on August 21, 1926: "We read in *The Times* that Queen Marie of Rumania is coming to America. She seems to have obtained a great interest in the Cause. So we must be on our guard lest we do an act which may prejudice her and set her back. Shoghi Effendi desires, that in case she takes this trip, the friends will behave with great reserve and wisdom, and that no initiative be taken on the part of the friends except after consulting the National Assembly."

It was during this visit that Her Majesty, her heart deeply stirred by the teachings of the Faith which she had been studying, testified, "in a language of exquisite beauty", as Shoghi Effendi put it, "to the power and sublimity of the Message of Bahá'u'lláh, in open letters widely circulated in newspapers of both the United States and Canada". As a result of the first of these letters Shoghi Effendi was "moved by an irresistible impulse" to write to the Queen of the "joyous admiration and gratitude" of himself and the Bahá'ís of both the East and the West for her noble tribute to the Faith. On August 27, 1926 the Queen responded to this first communication from the Guardian and wrote to him, what he described as a "deeply touching letter":

Bran, August 27th, 1926
Dear Sir,
 I was deeply moved on reception of your letter.
 Indeed a great light came to me with the message of Bahá'u'lláh and 'Abdu'l-Bahá. It came as all great messages come at an hour of dire grief and inner conflict and distress, so the seed sank deeply.
 My youngest daughter finds also great strength and comfort in the teachings of the beloved masters.
 We pass on the message from mouth to mouth and all those we give it to see a light suddenly lighting before them and much that was obscure and perplexing becomes simple, luminous and full of hope as never before.
 That my open letter was balm to those suffering for the cause, is indeed a great happiness to me, and I take it as a sign that God accepted my humble tribute.
 The occasion given me to be able to express myself publically, was also His Work, for indeed it was a chain of circumstances of which each link led me unwittingly one step further, till suddenly all was clear before my eyes and I understood why it had been.
 Thus does He lead us finally to our ultimate destiny.
 Some of those of my caste wonder at and disapprove my courage to step forward pronouncing words not habitual for Crowned Heads to pronounce, but I advance by an inner urge I cannot resist.
 With bowed head I recognize that I too am but an instrument in greater Hands and rejoice in the knowledge.

Little by little the veil is lifting, grief tore it in two. And grief was also a step leading me ever nearer truth, therefore do I not cry out against grief!

May you and those beneath your guidance be blessed and upheld by the sacred strength of those gone before you.

Marie

Among the things Queen Marie, who was not only a famous beauty, but an authoress and a woman of character and independence, wrote in her "open letters" published during 1926, on May 4th and September 28th, in the *Toronto Daily Star* and September 27th in the Philadelphia *Evening Bulletin*, were words such as these: "A woman brought me the other day a Book. I spell it with a capital letter because it is a glorious Book of love and goodness, strength and beauty . . . I commend it to you all. If ever the name of Bahá'u'lláh or 'Abdu'l-Bahá comes to your attention, do not put their writings from you. Search out their Books, and let their glorious, peace-bringing, love-creating words and lessons sink into your hearts as they have into mine. One's busy day may seem too full for religion. Or one may have a religion that satisfies. But the teachings of these gentle, wise and kindly men are compatible with all religion, and with no religion. Seek them, and be the happier." "At first we all conceive of God as something or somebody apart from ourselves . . . This is not so. We cannot, with our earthly faculties entirely grasp His meaning—no more than we can really understand the meaning of Eternity . . . God is all, Everything. He is the power behind all beginnings. He is the inexhaustible source of supply, of love, of good, of progress, of achievement. God is therefore Happiness. His is the voice within us that shows us good and evil. But mostly we ignore or misunderstand this voice. Therefore did He choose His Elect to come down amongst us upon earth to make clear His Word, His real meaning. Therefore the Prophets; therefore Christ, Muhammad, Bahá'u'lláh, for man needs from time to time a voice upon earth to bring God to him, to sharpen the realization of the existence of the true God. Those voices sent to us had to become flesh, so that with our earthly ears we should be able to hear and understand."

Shoghi Effendi wrote to Martha Root on May 29th, after he had just received from Canada a copy of the first of the Queen's "open letters", that this was "a well deserved and memorable testimony of your remarkable and exemplary endeavours for the spread of our beloved Cause. It has thrilled me and greatly reinforced my spirit and strength, yours is a memorable triumph, hardly surpassed in its significance in the annals of the Cause." In that same letter he asks her to ponder the advisability of approaching Her Majesty with the news of the Jahrum martyrdoms and possibly enlisting her sympathy in the cause of the Persian persecutions. That this consideration influenced the Queen in making her further courageous statements on the Faith there can be no doubt, as her letter to Shoghi Effendi indicates that this was the case. The news of this victory had reached Shoghi Effendi on the eve of the commemoration of the passing of Bahá'u'lláh in Bahjí, at a time when, as he described it in one of his general letters, ". . . His sorrowing servants, had gathered round His beloved Shrine supplicating relief and deliverance for the down-trodden in Persia" and Shoghi Effendi goes on to say: "With bowed heads and grateful hearts we recognize in this glowing tribute which Royalty has thus paid to the Cause of Bahá'u'lláh an epoch-making pronouncement destined to herald those stirring events which, as 'Abdu'l-Bahá has prophesied, shall in the fullness of time signalize the triumph of God's Holy Faith."

This marked the inception of a relationship not only with the Queen, but with other crowned heads and royalty in Europe on the part of Martha Root, and in a few instances of Shoghi Effendi himself. He not only greatly encouraged and guided her in these relationships but, always staying within the bounds of dignity and good breeding, always sincere in the human relationship, he nevertheless used these contacts to serve the interests of the Cause through heightening its prestige in the eyes of the public and through seeing that they were pointedly brought to the attention of the enemies of the Faith.

Until the time of the Queen's death, in 1938, Martha Root kept in close touch with her, keeping her informed of Bahá'í activities and receiving from her letters, written in her own hand, that were both friendly and reflected her attachment to the Teachings of Bahá'u'lláh. There was also an exchange of letters and cables between Shoghi Effendi and the Queen; but often he sent her messages through Martha, which was a more intimate way of contacting her and less demanding of the high positions both he and the Queen occupied in their respective spheres. There was another factor that could not be lightly put aside and this was the constant pressure on the Queen, who occupied such an exalted rank in her nation—a nation so storm-tossed politically during her own reign and during her period as Dowager Queen, from both ecclesiastical and political factions—to keep silent about a religion which was not then widely known as it is today, which was viewed by the ignorant as Islamic in nature, and her open sponsorship of which they not only heartily disapproved but considered impolitic in the highest degree.

The Queen herself mentions, in her very first letter to the Guardian, that "Some of those of my caste wonder at and disapprove my courage to step forward pronouncing words not habitual to Crowned Heads to pronounce . . ." It required outstanding courage and deep sincerity for her to repeatedly write testimonials of her personal feelings on the subject of the Bahá'í Faith and grant permission for these to be made public—indeed Her Majesty wrote some of these deliberately for publication in *The Bahá'í World*. On January 1, 1934 she wrote to Martha, enclosing one of her precious tributes and giving personal news of herself and her family: "Will this do for Vol. V? The difficulty is to not repeat myself . . ."

In 1927, on October 25th, Shoghi Effendi wrote to Martha: "I am in receipt of your most welcome letters . . . and I am thrilled by the news they contained, particularly your remarkable and historic interview with the Queen and Princess. I am sending you a number of Bahá'í stones . . . to be presented by you on my behalf to the Queen, the Princess and any other member of the Royal Family whom you think would appreciate and prize them . . . Please assure the Queen and Princess of our great love for them, of our prayers for their happiness and success and of our warm and cordial invitation to visit the Holy Land and be received in the Beloved's home."

Behind this interview with the Queen, which Shoghi Effendi refers to in the above letter, undoubtedly lay his own influence and the confirmations which flowed from his instruction to Martha in a letter written on June 29th of that same year in which he said: "I hope you will succeed in meeting not only the Rumanian Queen but her daughter the Queen of Serbia and King Boris of Bulgaria as well and I trust you will not hesitate to send me all particulars and details regarding your work in such an important field."

There was a constant vigilance on the part of the Guardian regarding all contact with the Royal families of Europe as witnessed by the cable he sent following the death on July 20, 1927, of His Majesty King Ferdinand of Rumania:

Her Majesty Queen Marie Bucarest
Abdulbahas family and Bahais world over tender Your Majesty heartfelt condolences.

                                                                           Shoghi

The Queen replied by cable, on July 27, as follows:

Shoghi Effendi, Haifa
Grateful thanks you and all yours with whom I feel spiritually so closely in touch.

                                                                           Marie

Martha Root succeeded also in following the other instruction of Shoghi Effendi, for in May 1928 he writes to her: ". . . Your marvellous and historic interviews with members of the Rumanian and Serbian Royal Families have inspired and thrilled us all . . ."

Earlier in April, Queen Marie and her daughter Ileana were on a visit to Cyprus and the Guardian says, in his letter to Martha Root, that the papers have published the news that the Queen intended to visit Haifa and he wonders "whether they had in mind such a visit and whether these premature disclosures deterred them from accomplishing their intended pilgrimage . . ." During the Queen's visit to Cyprus the Guardian cabled Sir Ronald Storrs, the Governor of Cyprus, with whom the royal party was staying, the following message: "Kindly convey to Her Majesty Queen of Rumania and Her Royal Highness Princess Ileana on behalf 'Abdu'l-Bahá's family and friends our heartfelt appreciation of the noble tribute paid by them both to the ideals that animate the Bahá'í Faith. Pray assure them of our best wishes and profound gratitude." Sir Ronald transmitted the appreciative reply of the Queen and Princess to Shoghi Effendi.

The following draft, in the Guardian's own hand, of a long letter he wrote to the Queen is of historic interest:

                                                 Haifa, Palestine,
                                                 December 3, 1929

Her Majesty
The Dowager Queen Marie of Rumania
Bucarest
Your Majesty

I have received through the intermediary of my dear Bahá'í sister Miss Martha Root, the autograph portrait of Your

Majesty, bearing in simple and moving terms, the message which Your Majesty has graciously been pleased to write in person. I shall treasure this most excellent portrait, and I assure you, that the Greatest Holy Leaf and the Family of 'Abdu'l-Bahá share to the full my feelings of lively satisfaction at receiving so strikingly beautiful a photograph of a Queen whom we have learned to love and admire.

I have followed during the past few years with profound sympathy the disturbed course of various happenings in your beloved country, which I feel must have caused you much pain and concern. But whatever the vicissitudes and perplexities which beset Your Majesty's earthly path, I am certain that even in your saddest hours, you have derived abundant sustenance and joy from the thought of having, through your glowing and historic utterances on the Bahá'í Faith as well as by your subsequent evidences of gracious solicitude for its welfare, brought abiding solace and strength to the multitude of its faithful and long suffering adherents throughout the East. Yours surely, dearly beloved Queen, is the station ordained by Bahá'u'lláh in the realms beyond to which the strivings of no earthly power can ever hope to attain.

I have immediately upon the publication of the second volume of the Bahá'í World, by the American Bahá'í Publishing Committee, forwarded directly to Bucarest, to the address of Your Majesty and that of Her Royal Highness Princess Ileana, copies of this most recent and comprehensive of Bahá'í publications. I will take the liberty of presenting in the course of the coming year the III Volume of this same publication which I trust will prove of interest to Your Majesty.

May I, in closing, reiterate the expression of profound appreciation and joy which the Family of 'Abdu'l-Bahá and Bahá'ís in every land universally feel for the powerful impetus which Your Majesty's outspoken and noble words have lent to the onward march of their beloved Faith.

The Family also join me in extending to Your Majesty, as well as to Her Royal Highness Princess Ileana, a most cordial welcome should Your Majesty ever purpose to visit the Holy Land to 'Abdu'l-Bahá's home in Haifa as well as to those scenes rendered so hallowed and memorable by the heroic lives and deeds of Bahá'u'lláh and 'Abdu'l-Bahá.

Shoghi

In 1930 Her Majesty visited Egypt with her daughter Ileana. Shoghi Effendi, having had the unfortunate experience of indiscreet publicity during her visit to Cyprus, wired Alexandria on February 19th: "Advise Assembly in case Queen visits Egypt convey only written expression of welcome and appreciation on behalf Bahá'ís. Letter should be briefly carefully worded. No objection sending flowers. Individual communications should be strictly avoided. Inform Cairo."

In the hope that at last the Queen would be able to visit the Bahá'í Holy Places in Palestine the Guardian had had Bahá'u'lláh's Tablet to her grandmother, Queen Victoria, copied in fine Persian calligraphy, and illuminated in Ṭihrán. On the 21st of February he cabled Ṭihrán: "Illuminated Tablet Queen Victoria should reach Haifa not later than March tenth on one or several pages." This was to be his gift to Her Majesty. Hearing no news of the Queen's plans once she had reached Egypt he wired to her direct on March 8th: "Her Majesty, the Dowager Queen Marie of Rumania, aboard Mayflower, Aswan. Family of 'Abdu'l-Bahá join me in renewing the expression of our loving and heartfelt invitation to your gracious Majesty and Her Royal Highness Princess Ileana to visit His home in Haifa. Your Majesty's acceptance to visit Bahá'u'lláh's Shrine and prison-city of 'Akká will apart from its historic significance be a source of immeasurable strength joy and hope to the silent sufferers of the Faith throughout the East. Our fondest love, prayers and best wishes for Your Majesty's happiness and welfare."

Receiving no reply to this communication Shoghi Effendi sent another wire on March 26th to the Queen at the Hotel Semiramis in Cairo: "Fearing my former letter and telegram in which Family of 'Abdu'l-Bahá joined me in extending invitation to Your Majesty and Her Royal Highness Princess Ileana may have miscarried, we are pleased to express anew the pleasure it would give us all should Your Majesty find it feasible to visit Bahá'u'lláh's and 'Abdu'l-Bahá's Shrines and the prison-city of 'Akká. Deeply regret unauthorized publicity given by the Press." Two days later the Rumanian Minister in Cairo wired Shoghi Effendi: "Her Majesty regrets she will not be able to visit you."

The cancellation of the visit of the Queen and her daughter to the Bahá'í Holy Places, which she had definitely set her heart upon, was a source of deep disappointment not only to the Guardian but also to the Queen herself. Behind the scenes there must have taken place a real struggle between the courageous and independent

Queen and her advisers for, after a long silence, she wrote to Martha Root, in her own hand, describing at least a little of what had taken place. In a letter dated June 28, 1931, she stated: "Both Ileana and I were cruelly disappointed at having been prevented going to the holy shrines and of meeting Shoghi Effendi, but at that time were going through a cruel crisis and every movement I made was being turned against me and being politically exploited in an unkind way. It caused me a good deal of suffering and curtailed my liberty most unkindly. There are periods however when one must submit to persecution, nevertheless, however high-hearted one may be, it ever again fills one with pained astonishment when people are mean and spiteful. I had my child to defend at that time; she was going through a bitter experience and so I could not stand up and defy the world. But the beauty of truth remains and I cling to it through all the vicissitudes of a life become rather sad . . . I am glad to hear that your traveling has been so fruitful and I wish you continual success knowing what a beautiful message you are carrying from land to land." This letter ends with a sentence, after Her Majesty's signature, that was perhaps more significant of her attitude and character than anything else: "I enclose a few words which may be used in your Year Book."

The loyalty of this "royal convert", as Shoghi Effendi styled her, in the face of her increasing isolation, advancing age and the political trends in Europe which were gradually to engulf so many of her royal kin, deeply touched Shoghi Effendi. In 1934, on January 23rd, he wrote to her again:

> Your Majesty,
>
> I am deeply touched by the splendid appreciation Your Majesty has graciously penned for the Bahá'í World, and wish to offer my heartfelt and abiding gratitude for this striking evidence of Your Majesty's sustained interest in the Cause of Bahá'u'lláh.
>
> I was moved to undertake its translation in person, and feel certain that the unnumbered followers of the Faith in both the East and the West will feel greatly stimulated in their unceasing labours for the eventual establishment of the Most Great Peace foretold by Bahá'u'lláh.
>
> I am presenting to Your Majesty, through the care of Miss Martha Root, a precious manuscript in the handwriting of Bahá'u'lláh, illumined by a devoted follower of His Faith in Ṭihrán.

'ABDU'L-BAHÁ AND SHOGHI EFFENDI

The Centre of the Covenant and the future Guardian taken in Haifa on the steps of the Master's house during the last years they were together

SOME DISTINGUISHED BAHÁ'ÍS WITH 'ABDU'L-BAHÁ

Shoghi Effendi, His successor (second from left), Agnes Parsons (behind 'Abdu'l-Bahá), J.E. Esslemont and Lotfullah Hakim (top row, right to left). Taken before

SHOGHI EFFENDI IN ALEXANDRIA, EGYPT

This was taken on March 21, 1920, shortly before he sailed for Europe; Shoghi Effendi is shown seated (third from the right); behind him is standing Lotfullah Hakim

SHOGHI EFFENDI, 1920-1921
During the period of his studies in England

May it serve as a token of my admiration for the spirit that has prompted Your Majesty to voice such noble sentiments for a struggling and persecuted Faith.

With the assurance of my prayers at the threshold of Bahá'u'lláh for Your Majesty's welfare and happiness,

I am yours very sincerely,

Shoghi

After sending the Queen a copy of his recently translated *Gleanings from the Writings of Bahá'u'lláh*, and receiving from her a letter conveying her "most grateful thanks", which she ends by saying "May the Great Father, be with us in spirit, helping us to live and act as we should", Shoghi Effendi wrote to her as follows:

Haifa, Feb. 18, 1936

Your Majesty,

Miss Root has transmitted to me the original copy of the appreciation penned by Your Majesty for the forthcoming issue of Bahá'í World. I am deeply touched, and feel truly grateful for this further evidence of Your Majesty's sustained interest in and admiration for the Bahá'í Teachings.

Bahá'í Communities the world over will ever recall, with feelings of pride and gratitude, these beautiful, impressive and historic testimonies from the pen of Your Majesty—testimonies that will no doubt greatly inspire and hearten them in their continued labours for the spread of the Cause of Bahá'u'lláh.

I am so pleased and encouraged to learn that Your Majesty has derived much benefit from the reading of the Gleanings and I feel that my efforts in translating these extracts are fully rewarded.

I am presenting to Your Majesty through the kindness of Mrs. McNeill the latest photograph recently received from America showing the progress in the construction of the Bahá'í House of Worship in Wilmette. May the Spirit of Bahá'u'lláh ever bless and sustain Your Majesty in the noble support you are extending to His Cause.

With deepest affection and gratitude,

Shoghi

The Mrs. McNeill mentioned in this letter lived near 'Akká in the Mansion at Mazra'ih once occupied by Bahá'u'lláh. She had known the Queen as a child in Malta and when she learned through the Guardian of the Queen's interest in the Faith she informed her of her own interest and the associations of the house she lived in. The Queen had written to her: "It was indeed nice to hear from you, and to think that you are of all things living near Haifa and are, as I am, a follower of the Bahá'í teachings . . . the house you live in . . . made precious by its associations with the Man we all venerate . . ."

Her Majesty's last published tribute to the Faith, in 1936, two years before she died, seemed to aptly describe what Bahá'u'lláh's Message had meant to her: "To those searching for light the Bahá'í Teachings offer a star which will lead them to deeper understanding, to assurance, peace and good will with all men." She had won for herself, Shoghi Effendi wrote, "imperishable renown . . . in the Kingdom of Bahá'u'lláh" through her "bold and epochal confession of faith in the Fatherhood of Bahá'u'lláh"; "this illustrious Queen may well deserve to rank as the first of those royal supporters of the Cause of God who are to arise in future, and each of whom, in the words of Bahá'u'lláh Himself, is to be acclaimed as *'the very eye of mankind, the luminous ornament on the brow of creation, the fountain-head of blessings unto the whole world.'* "

One sees from all this, which began early in 1926, that the severe crises which followed upon the inception of Shoghi Effendi's Guardianship, released, as ever, the spiritual forces inherent in the Faith and brought about such victories as the conversion of the first Bahá'í Queen.

V

A MANY SPLENDOURED PERSONALITY

That Shoghi Effendi was stern in all matters affecting the protection of the Faith does not mean he could not be gentle and kind also. He was fundamentally a very tender-hearted person and when left sufficiently at peace within himself expressed this innate kindness and tenderness not only to those who surrounded him but to the believers personally in many ways. There are numerous examples of this in his cable files. Over and over, when disaster struck in some country where there were Bahá'ís, he would send an enquiry such as this one to Persia: "Wire safety friends. Anxious earthquake reports Persia Turkistan". Very often this would be followed by financial help for those who were in desperate need. When an American Bahá'í, stricken in Persia by infantile paralysis, was returning with his wife to the United States, Shoghi Effendi cabled the friends in Beirut, Alexandria and New York, requesting that they meet his boat and assist in every way they could. The Guardian sent seven wires, in a short space of time, in connection with a single Bahá'í who had various difficulties in getting to Haifa and leaving after her pilgrimage was over. His thoroughness in such matters, as well as his consideration, are delightfully reflected in this telegram to Egypt: "Dewing New Zealand Bahá'í arriving tonight Cairo for one day. Urge meet him station. He wears helmet. If missed meet him next morning Cooks office nine o'clock. Extend utmost kindness." On another occasion we find Shoghi Effendi cabling, in connection with a Bahá'í who for some reason had not been able to land in Haifa, to "comfort him my behalf".

Sometimes the spirit animating a Bahá'í was such as to persuade Shoghi Effendi to change his own instructions. An instance of this is the case of Marion Jack, whom 'Abdu'l-Bahá called "General Jack" and the Guardian called an "immortal heroine", saying she was a shining example to pioneers of present and future generations in both the East and the West, and that no one had surpassed her in "constancy, dedication, self-abnegation, fearlessness" except the "incomparable Martha Root". Jackie—as she was usually called—lived in Sofia, Bulgaria and when war broke out Shoghi Effendi, concerned over her dangerous position, wired her: "Advise return Canada wire whether financially able". She replied, ". . . how about Switzerland" but assured him of her implicit obedience. Shoghi Effendi then wired, "Approve Switzerland" but she still did not want to leave her pioneer post and begged to be allowed to remain in Bulgaria, to which the Guardian replied: "Advise remain Sofia love."

There is a great mystery involving the levels of service. Shoghi Effendi always advised the friends to pursue a moderate and wise course, but if they did not, and chose to rise to heights of heroism and self-sacrifice, he was immensely proud of them. After all, there is nothing either wise or moderate in being martyred—yet our crowning glory as a religion is that our first Prophet was martyred and twenty thousand people followed in His footsteps. I have tried to understand this mystery, moderation on one side and Bahá'u'lláh's words on the other: ". . . *then write with that crimson ink that hath been shed in My path. Sweeter indeed is this than all else . . .*" and it seems to me that the best example is an aeroplane: when it trundles along on the ground on its wheels it is in the dimension of the ground, going along steadily on an earthly plane, but when it soars in the air and folds its wheels away and leaps forward at dazzling speeds, it is in a celestial realm and the values are different. When we are on the ground we get good sound earthly advice, but if we choose to spurn the soil and leap into the realms of higher service and sacrifice we do not get that kind of advice any more, we win immortal fame and become heroes and heroines of God's Cause.

Shoghi Effendi worked through everything; everything that he encountered, individual, object or piece of land, that could be turned to an advantageous use for the Faith he seized upon and used. Although in general he worked through Assemblies and Committees, he also worked directly through individuals. An example of this is Victoria Bedekian, known as "Auntie Victoria". For years she wrote letters, widely circulated in the West and the East, and the Guardian encouraged her in this activity and even told her what she should emphasize in her communications.

He was not fussy about sources of information; by this I mean he did not always wait until official channels corroborated the arrival of a pioneer at his post or some piece of good news which had been conveyed to him through a personal letter or by a pilgrim, but would incorporate his encouraging information in his messages. This latitude which Shoghi Effendi allowed himself meant that the whole work of the Faith was bowled forward at a far faster pace than if he had done otherwise. Like all great leaders he possessed something of the quality of a good press man who realizes that the time factor in conveying news is of great importance and that speed itself has an impact and stimulates the imagination. This practice of his should not, however, mislead us into thinking that he was not extraordinarily thorough. The exactitude with which he compiled statistics, sought out historic facts, worked on every minute detail of his maps and plans was astonishing.

The whole of Shoghi Effendi's life activity as the Guardian, his mind and his feelings, his reactions and instructions, can be found reflected in miniature in his cables and telegrams; often they were more intimate, more powerful and revealing than the thousands of letters he wrote to individuals because in his letters his secretary usually dealt with details and thus the words are not the Guardian's own words, except for the postscripts which he wrote himself and which most of the time conveyed the assurance of his prayers, his encouragement and his statement of general principles.

Shoghi Effendi, like his grandfather and great-grandfather before him, had a delightful sense of humour which was ready to manifest itself if he were given any chance to be happy or enjoy a little peace of mind. His eyes would fairly dance with amusement, he would chuckle delightedly and sometimes break out into open laughter. Inside his family, with those he was familiar with, he liked to tease.

On one side so majestic, on the other so engagingly confiding, innocent-hearted and youthful, such was our Guardian! One of my tasks, once Shoghi Effendi knew I could paint a little, was to colour various things for him and one of these was a map showing the plots owned by the Bahá'í Community on Mt. Carmel. One day when I was adding colour to some newly-acquired areas Shoghi Effendi told me to paint them lighter. I asked why. Why, he said, to show they are a "recent acquisition". It was such a clear reflection of the joy these newly-purchased plots afforded him.

This recalls another aspect of Shoghi Effendi's richly endowed personality. He was very tenacious of his purposes, very determined, but never unreasonable. Although he never changed his objectives he sometimes changed the course he had planned to take to reach them.

All through the Guardian's ministry we see the light of Divine Guidance shining on his path, confirming his decisions, inspiring his choice. But there are always unforeseeable factors in every plan. Acts of God, and the sum of human endeavour, constantly change plans, little or big. This has always happened to the greatest as well as the smallest human beings, and the words of the Prophets themselves attest it. Shoghi Effendi was subject to such forces, but he also frequently modified his own plans. Examples of this are many and interesting: at one time he conceived the idea of placing the Mausoleum of Bahá'u'lláh on Mt. Carmel, but later gave this up entirely and fixed its permanent place in Bahjí; what became known as the World Crusade or Ten Year Plan was at first announced as a Seven Year Plan; one Temple to be built during this Plan became three Temples; the original eight European goal countries became ten; and so on. If outside forces over which the Guardian had no control frustrated some plan of his—as opposed to his modifying or expanding some plan of his own in the light of circumstances—he immediately compensated, so that the Cause, if a temporary defeat or humiliation was inflicted upon it, came out in the end with an augmented victory, a richer endowment.

Shoghi Effendi might be deflected from his course but he was never defeated in his purpose and his ingenuity was remarkable. A good example of this is the way he arranged for two of the three great new Continental Bahá'í Temples of the Ten Year Plan to be built. He extracted from the architect he had at hand the designs he felt were suitable for the Sydney and Kampala Houses of Worship. These were dignified, pleasing in proportion, conservative in style and relatively modest in cost. Since the architect was not in a position to carry out the detailed drawings or supervise the actual construction, Shoghi Effendi, not making a great circumstance of what to a fussy and small-minded man would have imposed an insuperable obstacle, proceeded to instruct the two National Assemblies involved to get local architectural firms to carry out the details and erect the buildings. Shoghi Effendi himself modified the expensive suggestions these firms at first made and got both Temples built within what he considered a reasonable price for the Cause to pay. Over and over his shrewdness and sound judgement saved the money of the Faith so that it could be spent on the many all-important tasks and not create temporary bankruptcy through the unwise prosecution of a single project.

Economy was a very rigid principle with Shoghi Effendi and he had very stern ideas on money matters. He more than once refused to permit an individual to make the pilgrimage who he knew was in debt, saying he must first pay his debts. I never saw the Guardian settle a bill he had not first carefully added up, whether it was for a meal or a payment of thousands of dollars! If there was an overcharge he pointed it out—and also if there was an undercharge. Many times I went to astonished people and called to their attention that their addition was wrong and they should do it again or they would be the losers. He also was a determined bargainer, never paying what he felt was too much for a thing. More than once, when a beautiful ornament for the Shrines, Archives, or gardens was too expensive, and the seller could not or would not meet the Guardian's price, he would not buy it even though he wanted it and had the money. He just considered it wrong and would not do it. Although Shoghi Effendi for many years had had a private automobile and chauffeur (like 'Abdu'l-Bahá before him), because spare parts were not procurable for it during the worst years of the war he had it sold and used taxis. I have no doubt that as with sufficient money one can usually buy anything he could have procured another car, but it never entered his mind. He was against extravagance, ostentation and luxury as such, denying himself and others many things because he felt they were either not justified or not appropriate.

Another of the strongly marked characteristics of the Guardian was his openness. The believers were his confidants. Freely, majestically, aloof but with a most endearing and heart-captivating confidence, he would share with the pilgrims who were his guests not only his ideas and his interpretations of the Teachings, but his projects and plans. There were no privileged communicants who received his thought as of right. In spite of the fact that the National Assemblies were his channels through which he passed on his great Plans and the bodies by which they were prosecuted, he was wont to share these Plans in almost full detail with those he met, to such an extent that many a returning pilgrim was in possession of nearly all the details that were soon to be communicated to the Bahá'í world officially. The same was true of his work at the World Centre. So complete was this frankness that he sometimes drew little sketches at the table to illustrate what he was now doing in the gardens on

Mt. Carmel, how the "arc" would be, what buildings might be erected on it, and so on.

Each new thing he was setting in motion, nationally or internationally, one might almost say followed the same pattern as the dawn of a day: the first light, feelers of vision, would be discerned in his words to visiting pilgrims, or lie half-hidden in his communications to the Bahá'í world; then would come the glimmering of goals beginning to take shape as the sun of his concept rose higher and he focussed the brilliant energy of his mind upon it; finally, in a clear burst of illumination, would come the whole idea in all its splendour—a Seven Year Plan, a Ten Year Plan, the warnings and promises in some new and wonderful general letter, the complete instructions regarding such major projects as the completion of the Shrine of the Báb, the International Archives, one of the great new Houses of Worship, or the exposition of certain fundamental themes contained in such books as *The Advent of Divine Justice* and *The Promised Day Is Come*.

The relationship of Shoghi Effendi to the pilgrims, his courtesy as a host, his kindness shown to them in so many little ways, the things he so openly discussed with them, had a tremendous effect on the work the Bahá'ís were accomplishing in so many countries, for when these fortunate believers returned to their own communities they acted as a leaven, stimulating their fellow Bahá'ís to greater efforts, making the Guardian a more real person to those who had not been privileged to meet him face to face, creating a sense of nearness both to him and to the World Centre that by any other method would have been hard to achieve.

But in spite of all he showered upon the pilgrims—from providing for their physical comfort as his guests to tearing the veils from their eyes and educating them in their Faith—whenever one of them would seek to express his or her deep gratitude for the honour of meeting him, he would instantly turn this aside, saying the purpose of the pilgrimage was to visit the Holy Shrines.

The last year of the Guardian's life two Swiss pilgrims came to Haifa. Their presence stirred up all his memories of Switzerland and his love for their country poured out in a manner wholly unlike his usual reserve about his personal life and feelings. I had been ill in bed and not present at dinner in the Pilgrim House but when Shoghi Effendi came home he told me he had said everything, about the mountains he had climbed, the walks he had taken, the scenes he loved so much. It was very atypical of him, very rare and a clear index of something deep in his own heart.

He was moved to inform them that he wished Switzerland to have its own Temple site, which was to be situated near the capital city of Bern and have a clear view of the Bernese Alps, where he had spent so many months of his life walking and climbing. On August 12, 1957 he communicated to what was then the National Spiritual Assembly of the Bahá'ís of Italy and Switzerland his wishes in this matter. His secretary wrote: "As he explained to ——, he is very anxious for Switzerland to purchase a plot, however small in size, and modest a beginning it might be, for the future Mashriqu'l-Adhkár of that country. He feels this should be in the outskirts of Bern, overlooking the Bernese Oberland; and he is very happy to be able to present this land himself to the Swiss Community. No publicity whatsoever should be given to this matter lest an opposition resembling that which has arisen in Germany should be provoked amongst the orthodox element in Bern. Whenever the committee responsible for finding this land has located a suitable plot, he would like your Assembly to inform him of the details." This was a gift of a unique nature, no other community in the Bahá'í world having been thus honoured. The plot of land, almost 2,000 square metres in area, on the outskirts of Bern, overlooks the Gürberthal and from it can be seen the famous Finsteraarhorn, Mönch, Eiger and Jungfrau mountains, the scene of many of the Guardian's mountaineering exploits, the scene also of many of the most agonizing hours he passed after the ascension of his grandfather.

On one occasion a pilgrim from Canada had informed the Guardian that in teaching the Faith to the Eskimo people it was very difficult for them to understand the meaning in such similes as the nightingale and the rose because these things were entirely unknown to them. The reaction of Shoghi Effendi to this was typical. When he said good-bye to this friend he gave her a small vial of the Persian attar of rose, the quintessence of what a rose is, and told her to anoint the Eskimos with it, saying that perhaps in this way they would get an inkling of what Bahá'u'lláh meant when He wrote of the rose.

Another incident comes to my mind. Among the last pilgrims to leave Haifa before Shoghi Effendi himself left in June 1957, never to return, were two American negro believers. As long as I live I will never forget the look on the face of one of them as she sat opposite the Guardian at the Pilgrim House table. One could see that in meeting him—who met all men as the creation of God, with no other feeling than pleasure that they were as God had made them—the hurts and sorrows of a lifetime were melted away. She looked at him with a combination of the great loving heart of a mother and the reverence due him in his glorious station that I think must be the look on the faces of the angels in Paradise as they gaze upon their Lord.

Those who had the privilege of being near the Guardian, no matter how much experience they had had or how long they had been Bahá'ís—some, like myself from birth—were constantly having their concept of the greatness of this Cause expanded by Shoghi Effendi's words, his reactions and his example. I remember my surprise when, in his long Riḍván Message to the Bahá'í world in 1957, he mentioned (obviously with pride or he would not have included it) the "recently converted Bahá'í inmates" in Kitalya Prison in Uganda. It had never occurred to me that one would mention a Bahá'í being in a prison without shame! But here he was proclaiming that we had a group of the followers of Bahá'u'lláh in a prison. He often referred to this in his talks to the pilgrims and as I pondered over this and the things he said about it I realized that as this Faith is for all men, the saints and the sinners, there were two principles involved. One was the fact that society must be governed by laws, protected by laws and men punished through laws; and the other was that belief in the Manifestation of God should be universal and include everyone, because the act of faith is the spark that sets the soul alight and gives it eternal awareness of its God, and this was something each soul had a right to, no matter what his sins might be. In more than one letter, at different times to different people, Shoghi Effendi encouraged the Bahá'ís to teach in prisons.

The sympathy which all the Prophets of God have shown towards the down-trodden, the meek, the poor and the outcast, singling them out for particular succour, protection and loving encouragement, was always manifested in the Guardian's acts and words. But we must not confuse this attitude with the fundamental truth that many groups of people who at present fall into these categories not only deserve to receive special attention but have within themselves reserves of power and spiritual greatness needed by the entire world. Take, for example, the Indians of the Western Hemisphere. 'Abdu'l-Bahá had written: "You must attach great importance to the Indians, the original inhabitants of America. For these souls may be likened unto the ancient inhabitants of the Arabian Peninsula, who, prior to the Revelation of Muḥammad, were like savages. When the Muḥammadan Light shone forth in their midst, they became so enkindled that they shed illumination upon the world. Likewise, should these Indians be educated and properly guided, there can be no doubt that through the Divine teachings they will become so enlightened that the whole earth will be illumined." Throughout his ministry Shoghi Effendi never forgot these words and repeatedly urged the believers throughout Canada and the Americas to enlist these souls under the banner of Bahá'u'lláh. Some of the last letters he wrote, in July 1957, to various National Assemblies in the Western Hemisphere, again forcibly stressed this subject and referred to the "long overdue conversion of the American Indians". I quote an excerpt from his instructions written by his secretary on his behalf:

"He was particularly happy to see that some of the Indian believers were present at the Convention. He attaches the greatest importance to teaching the original inhabitants of the Americas the Faith. 'Abdu'l-Bahá Himself has stated how great are their potentialities, and it is their right, and the duty of the non-Indian Bahá'ís, to see that they receive the Message of God for this day. One of the most worthy objectives of your Assembly must be the establishment of all-Indian Spiritual Assemblies. Other minorities should likewise be especially sought out and taught. The friends should bear in mind that in our Faith, unlike every other society, the minority, to compensate for what might be treated as an inferior status, receives special attention, love and consideration . . ."

To a pilgrim belonging to the Mongolian race the Guardian stated that as the majority of the people in the world were not white there was no reason why the majority of Bahá'ís inside the Faith should be white; on the contrary, the Cause should reflect the situation existing in the world. To Shoghi Effendi differences were not something to be eliminated but rather the legitimate, necessary, indeed fascinating, ingredients that made the whole so much more beautiful and perfect.

Not only did Shoghi Effendi constantly inculcate in the Bahá'ís the respect due to people of different ethnic backgrounds, he also taught them what respect, and above all what reverence, as qualities needed to round out a noble human character, really are. Reverence for holy things is sadly lacking in the Western World today. In an age when the mistaken idea of equality seems to imply that every blade of grass must be exactly the same height, the Guardian's own profound respect for those above himself in rank was the best example one could find. The extreme reverence he showed to the Twin Manifestations of God and to 'Abdu'l-Bahá, whether in his writings, his speech or the manner in which he approached Their resting-places provides a permanent pattern for all Bahá'ís to follow. Whenever Shoghi Effendi was near one of the Shrines one could sense his awareness of this in his whole being. The way he walked as he neared it, the way he quietly and with great dignity and reverence approached the threshold, knelt and placed his forehead upon it, the way he never turned his back when inside the Shrine on that spot where one of these infinitely holy and precious beings was interred, the tone of his voice, his dignified lack of any levity on such occasions, all bore witness to the manner in which man should approach a holy of holies, going softly on sacred ground. It is really with the soul that man has to do in this life, for it is all he will take with him when he leaves it. It is this fundamental concept—so obscured and forgotten in present-day philosophies—that endows even the dust of noble beings with a mystic potency. So strong is the perfume of some roses that even years after they have withered and dried out one can still smell the rose in them. This is a feeble example of the power which remains in the very dust that has been associated with the towering spirits of divine souls when they were in this world.

This wonderful emotion of reverence—which seems when it sweeps over us to blow away so much of the dross in our immature natures—was a deep characteristic of the Guardian, who learned it in his childhood as he sat on his heels, arms crossed on breast, before his exalted grandfather. It is not a ritualistic thing that is at stake here. There are no rituals in the Bahá'í Faith. It is an attitude. Although the Guardian was wont to prostrate himself before the thresholds of the Holy Tombs, He was at pains to explain to the pilgrims that they were free to do so or not. He did it because it was a custom in the part of the East from which his ancestors came. But the reverence was another matter; one thing was a form of expression the individual could choose for himself, the other was the proper spirit that should dwell in the heart of a devotee as he approaches those things that are most sacred in this world.

No picture of Shoghi Effendi's personality would ever be complete that did not depict the truly extraordinary artistic sense he possessed. This does not mean he could have been a painter; he was a writer *par excellence*. But he certainly had a painter's and an architect's eye. This was coupled with that fundamental quality without which I cannot see how anyone can achieve greatness in any of the arts or the sciences—a perfect sense of proportion, a sense of proportion measured in millimetres rather than centimetres. It was he who fixed the style of the Shrine of the Báb through his instructions—mostly not in detail but in principle—to my father. It was he who set the design for the International Archives Building, to such an extent that its architect would invariably state it was Shoghi Effendi's design, not his. The Guardian, with no help and no advice, laid out his superb gardens in Bahjí and Haifa, every measurement being his own. But what people do not perhaps realize is that the appearance of the Shrine interiors, the Mansion of Bahá'u'lláh, the House of 'Abbúd, the Mansion at Mazra'ih, was not created by anyone, however slight the detail, except the Guardian himself. He not only steadily added to the ornaments, photographs, lamps and furnishings that make these places so beautiful, but everything was placed where it was under his supervision. Not a picture hung on the walls that was not placed exactly where it was, to within a centimetre, by him. He not only created the effect of beauty that meets the eye as one enters those places, but he produced it all at a minimum cost, buying things not so much because of their style and period but because they were inexpensive and could achieve an effect regardless of their intrinsic worth. His visits to the Shrines and gardens were my only opportunities to have his room cleaned. How often I remember how, in spite of my efforts and the maid's to get the many objects on his desk back into their exact positions, he would enter his bedroom, in which he did all his work, go to his desk, cast an eye over it automatically, reach out his hand and give an almost infinitesimal twist to the different objects which he detected were slightly out of the position he liked them to be in, though I am sure the difference was practically invisible to any eye but his. Needless to add that all this went with a neatness and tidiness that was phenomenal.

Unhampered by tradition in matters of taste Shoghi Effendi was extremely original and ingenious in the way he achieved his effects. He did things no over-instructed authority on a series of do's and don't's would ever have attempted. Take for instance the interior decoration of the Greek style Archives Building. In order to acquire more space as a single giant hall in which to exhibit the many objects, sacred or otherwise, with which he intended to furnish it, Shoghi Effendi had two narrow balconies built, running its full length on either side, which were protected by a purely renaissance, excellent in style, wooden balustrade. Most of the cabinets he chose to line the walls of the hall downstairs were Japanese lacquer or Chinese carved teak wood. The six great chandeliers suspended from the ceiling were of cut crystal and purely European in design. When I asked the Guardian what furniture he would place on the balconies he said he would use some of the cabinets from the previous Archives, which were really of no style at all but just modern veneer furniture such as people have in their homes these days. Yet this strange assortment of things representing different periods and different countries, including innumerable *objets d'art*, have combined to create an impression of beauty, of dignity, of richness and splendour it would be hard to equal anywhere.

VI

THE DEEPEST TIES

The supreme influence on Shoghi Effendi's life was his beloved grandfather, 'Abdu'l-Bahá, and next to this came his lifelong relationship with the Master's sister, known as the Greatest Holy Leaf, who watched over him from babyhood with more than a mother's love and care. When she passed away in 1932 the news reached him in Interlaken, Switzerland. Although he was well aware of her condition, which he described in 1929 when he wrote that the Greatest Holy Leaf was "now in the evening of her life, with deepening shadows caused by failing eyesight and declining strength swiftly gathering about her"; although he had had a premonition of her swiftly approaching death, when he wrote in March 1932 to the American believers urging them to press on with the completion of the dome of "our beloved Temple" and said that "my voice is once more reinforced by the passionate, and perhaps, the last, entreaty, of the Greatest Holy Leaf, whose spirit, now hovering on the edge of the Great Beyond, longs to carry on its flight to the Abhá Kingdom . . . an assurance of the joyous consummation of an enterprise, the progress of which has so greatly brightened the closing days of her earthly life"; although she was now eighty-six years old—none of this softened the blow or mellowed the grief that overwhelmed the Guardian. On July 15th he cabled America announcing that her spirit had taken its flight to that Great Beyond, bewailing the "sudden removal of my sole earthly sustainer, the joy and solace of my life", and informing the friends that "So grievous a bereavement necessitates suspension for nine months throughout Bahá'í world every manner religious festivity"; memorial meetings were to be held everywhere, locally and nationally, for her, the "last remnant of Bahá'u'lláh".

But it was on July 17th that he wrote to the American and Canadian believers a letter that provides a glimpse of what was passing in the surging sea of his heart and in which he eulogizes the life, station and deeds of 'Abdu'l-Bahá's sister, pouring forth his love in an unforgettable torrent of words.

Dearly-beloved Greatest Holy Leaf! Through the mist of tears that fill my eyes I can clearly see, as I pen these lines, thy noble figure before me, and can recognize the serenity of thy kindly face. I can still gaze, though the shadow of the grave separate us, into thy blue, love-deep eyes, and can feel, in its calm intensity, the immense love thou didst bear for the Cause of thine Almighty Father, the attachment that bound thee to the most lowly and insignificant among its followers, the warm affection thou didst cherish for me in thine heart. The memory of the ineffable beauty of thy smile shall ever continue to cheer and hearten me in the thorny path I am destined to pursue. The remembrance of the touch of thine hand shall spur me on to follow steadfastly in thy way. The sweet magic of thy voice shall remind me, when the hour of adversity is at its darkest, to hold fast to the rope thou didst seize so firmly all the days of thy life.

Bear thou this my message to 'Abdu'l-Bahá, thine exalted and divinely-appointed Brother: If the Cause for which Bahá'u'lláh toiled and laboured, for which Thou didst suffer years of agonizing sorrow, for the sake of which streams of sacred blood have flowed, should, in the days to come, encounter storms more severe than those it has already weathered, do Thou continue to overshadow, with Thine all-encompassing care and wisdom, Thy frail, Thy unworthy appointed child.

What the Greatest Holy Leaf had done for Shoghi Effendi at the time of the Master's passing and in the years that followed is beyond calculation. She had played, as he said, a unique part throughout the tumultuous stages of Bahá'í history, not the least of which had been the establishment of Shoghi Effendi's own ministry after the death of 'Abdu'l-Bahá. "Which of the blessings am I to recount," wrote Shoghi Effendi, "which in her unfailing solicitude she showered upon me, in the most critical and agitated hours of my life?" He says that to him she had been an incarnation of 'Abdu'l-Bahá's all-encompassing tenderness and love. As her life had waned his had waxed. With what deep satisfaction she must have seen, as the tide of her own life receded from the shores of this world, that Shoghi Effendi was become strong in his Guardianship, able to face

BALLIOL COLLEGE, OXFORD UNIVERSITY
Showing buildings much frequented by Shoghi Effendi as a student

BALLIOL COLLEGE JUNIOR COMMON ROOM

Shoghi Effendi is standing behind the man wearing a striped tie in the third row, fourth from the left, 1920

A GATHERING IN MANCHESTER, ENGLAND
Shoghi Effendi (second row, third from left) often visited the
Manchester Baháʼís while studying at Oxford

THE FIRST FLIGHT?

Shoghi Effendi was a great believer in travel by air, even as

the incessant blows he received with the fortitude of a man now fully grown into his stupendous task.

So close was the communion between Shoghi Effendi and his great-aunt that over and over, in cables and other communications, particularly during the early years of his Guardianship, he included her with himself in such phrases as "assure us", "the Greatest Holy Leaf and I", "we", and so on. In a cable sent in 1931 he even signs it "Bahíyyih Shoghi". Nothing could be more revealing of this intense love he had for her than the fact that on the day we were married it was to her room, where everything is preserved as it was in her days, standing beside her bed, that the Guardian went to have the simple Bahá'í marriage ceremony of hand in hand performed and we each repeated the words in Arabic: "We will all, verily, abide by the Will of God."

This love the Guardian had for the Greatest Holy Leaf, who had watched over him for thirty-five years as far more than a mother, continued to be demonstrated for the remainder of his life. When the news of her death reached him in Switzerland his first act was to plan for her grave a suitable memorial which he hastened to Italy to order. No one could possibly call this exquisitely proportioned monument, built of shining white Carrara marble, anything but what it appears—a love temple, the embodiment of Shoghi Effendi's love. He had undoubtedly conceived its design from buildings of a similar style and, under his supervision, an artist now incorporated his concept in the monument he planned to erect on her resting-place. Shoghi Effendi used to compare the stages in the Administrative Order of the Faith to this monument, saying the platform of three steps was like the local Assemblies, the pillars like the National Assemblies, and the dome that crowned them and held them together like the Universal House of Justice, which could not be placed in position until the foundations and pillars were first firmly erected. After the Greatest Holy Leaf's monument had been completed in all its beauty he had a photograph of it sent to many different Assemblies, as well as to a special list of individuals to whom he wished to present so tender a memento.

In every act of his life he associated the Greatest Holy Leaf with his services to the Faith. When he entombed the remains of the mother and brother of Bahíyyih <u>Kh</u>ánum on Mt. Carmel he cabled: ". . . cherished wish Greatest Holy Leaf fulfilled", referring to her often expressed desire to be buried near them. On that momentous occasion he said he rejoiced at the privilege of pledging one thousand pounds as his contribution to the Bahíyyih Khánum Fund designed to inaugurate the final drive connected with the completion of the American Temple. He wrote that this transfer and reburial were events of "capital institutional significance". He said "the conjunction of the resting-place of the Greatest Holy Leaf with those of her brother and mother incalculably reinforces the spiritual potencies of that consecrated Spot", which was "destined to evolve into the focal centre of those world-shaking, world-embracing, world-directing Administrative institutions, ordained by Bahá'u'lláh . . ."

When 'Abdu'l-Bahá's mantle, as Head of the Faith, fell on Shoghi Effendi's shoulders a great change came over him. What the nature of that change was spiritually it is not for us—so infinitely remote in both station and stature—to either grasp or seek to define. Shoghi Effendi was never really intimate with anyone except the closest members of his family and, in the early days, those who acted as his help-mates and secretaries. As years went by and his burdens increased, even this intimacy grew less.

Surely the simplicity of the marriage of Shoghi Effendi—reminiscent of the simplicity of 'Abdu'l-Bahá's own marriage in the prison-city of 'Akká—should provide a thought-provoking example to the Bahá'ís everywhere. No one, with the exception of his parents, my parents and a brother and two sisters of his living in Haifa, knew it was to take place. He felt strongly urged to keep it a secret, knowing from past experience how much trouble any major event in the Cause invariably stirred up. It was therefore a stunning surprise to both the servants and the local Bahá'ís when his chauffeur drove him off, with me beside him, to visit the Holy Tomb of Bahá'u'lláh on the afternoon of March 24, 1937. His heart drew him to that Most Sacred Spot on earth at such a moment in his life. I remember I was dressed entirely in black for this unique occasion. I wore a white lace blouse, but otherwise I was a typical example of the way oriental women dressed to go out into the streets in those days, the custom being to wear black. Although I was from the West Shoghi Effendi desired me to fit into the pattern of the life in his house—which was a very oriental one—as naturally and inconspicuously as possible and I was only too happy to comply with his wishes in every way. When we arrived at Bahjí and entered the Shrine he requested me to give him his ring, which I was wearing concealed about my neck, and this he placed on the ring-finger of my right hand, the same finger that corresponded to the one of his own on which he himself had always worn it. This was the only gesture he made. He entered the inner Shrine, beneath the floor of which Bahá'u'lláh is interred, and gathered up in a handkerchief all the dried petals and flowers that the keeper of the Shrine used to take from the threshold and place in a silver receptacle at the feet of Bahá'u'lláh. After he had chanted the Tablet of Visitation we came back to Haifa. There was no celebration, no flowers, no elaborate ceremony, no wedding dress, no reception. His mother and father, in compliance with the laws of Bahá'u'lláh, signified their consent by signing our marriage certificates and then I went back to the Western Pilgrim House across the street and joined my parents (who had not been present at any of these events), and Shoghi Effendi went to attend to his own affairs. At dinner-time, quite as usual, the Guardian appeared, showering his love and congratulations on my mother and father. He took the handkerchief, full of such precious flowers, and with his inimitable smile gave them to my mother, saying he had brought them for her from the inner Shrine of Bahá'u'lláh. My parents also signed the marriage certificate and after dinner and these events were over I walked home with Shoghi Effendi, my suitcases having been taken across the street by Fujita while we were at dinner. We visited for awhile with the Guardian's family and then went up to his two rooms which the Greatest Holy Leaf had had built for him so long ago.

The quietness, the simplicity, the reserve and dignity with which this marriage took place did not signify that the Guardian considered it an unimportant event—on the contrary. Over his mother's signature, but drafted by the Guardian, the following cable was sent to America: "Announce Assemblies celebration marriage beloved Guardian. Inestimable honour conferred upon handmaid of Bahá'u'lláh Rúḥíyyih <u>Kh</u>ánum Miss Mary Maxwell. Union of East and West proclaimed by Bahá'í Faith cemented. Ziaiyyih mother of the Guardian." A telegram similar to this was sent to Persia. This news, so long awaited, naturally produced great rejoicing amongst the Bahá'ís and messages flooded in to Shoghi Effendi from all parts of the world. To that received from the National Assembly of the Bahá'ís of the United States and Canada Shoghi Effendi replied: "Deeply moved your message. Institution Guardianship, head cornerstone Administrative Order Cause Bahá'u'lláh, already ennobled through its organic connection with Persons of Twin Founders Bahá'í Faith, is now further reinforced through direct association with West and particularly with American believers, whose spiritual destiny is to usher in World Order Bahá'u'lláh. For my part desire congratulate community American believers on acquisition tie vitally binding them to so weighty an organ of their Faith." To innumerable other messages his practically universal answer was merely an expression of loving appreciation for their felicitations.

The most significant point, however, associated with the Guardian's marriage is the stress he laid on the fact that it had drawn the Occident and the Orient closer to each other. It had not only done this but other ties had also been reinforced and established. In reply to an inquiry from the American Assembly: "Request advice policy concerning announcement marriage" Shoghi Effendi stated: "Approve public announcement. Emphasize significance institution Guardianship union East West and linking destinies Persia America. Allude honour conferred British peoples"—a direct allusion to my Scotch Canadian father.

All this had such an effect on the American Community that its national body informed the Guardian it was sending $19.00 from each one of its seventy-one American Assemblies "for immediate strengthening new tie binding American Bahá'ís to institution Guardianship"—truly a most unusual, pure-hearted wedding gift to the Cause itself.

VII

THE WAR YEARS

Shoghi Effendi was the keenest observer of political events and kept abreast of all happenings. His intelligence and analytical faculties did not permit him to lull himself into any false complacency, induced by the rather childish idea people sometimes have of what "faith" means. He well knew that to have faith in God does not mean one should not use one's mind, appraise dangers, anticipate moves, make the right decisions during a crisis.

Steeped in the Teachings from his childhood, the alert and observant companion of his grandfather, Shoghi Effendi seems to have always been aware of what he called "the initial perturbations of the world-shaking catastrophe in store for an unbelieving humanity". Though he saw another war coming, he did not live in a constant state of false emergency. He reassured Martha Root, who in 1927 wrote to him from Europe about her fears: "As to the matter of an eventual war that may break out in Europe, do not feel in the least concerned or worried. The prospect is very remote, the danger for the near future is non-existent"—even though that same year he had stated the inevitability of another deadly conflict was becoming increasingly manifest. Over and over he prepared the minds of the Bahá'ís to face the fact that a world conflagration was coming. In 1938 he wrote, "The twin processes of internal disintegration and external chaos are being accelerated and every day are inexorably moving towards a climax. The rumblings that must precede the eruption of those forces that must cause 'the limbs of humanity to quake' can already be heard. 'The time of the end', 'the latter years', as foretold in the Scriptures, are at long last upon us." And in *The Advent of Divine Justice*, which he wrote at the end of December 1938, he clearly anticipated the war: "Who knows", he asked, "but that these few remaining, fast-fleeting years, may not be pregnant with . . . conflicts more devastating than any which have preceded them." And in April 1939 he had written: "the sands of a moribund civilization are inexorably running out".

As the long shadow of war descended on Europe I remember well the almost tangible feeling of catastrophe that enveloped me when Shoghi Effendi wrote, from the very heart of that continent, the poetic and powerful words that opened his cable of August 30, 1939: "shades night descending imperilled humanity inexorably deepening . . ." In July 1940 he had cabled that the fires of war ". . . now threaten devastation both Near East Far East respectively enshrining World Centre chief remaining citadel Faith Bahá'u'lláh . . ." It seems unbelievable that in the midst of so many anxieties the Guardian should have had the mental power and physical strength to sit down and write such a book as *The Promised Day Is Come*—a book in which he made it quite clear that the "retributory calamity" which had overtaken mankind, whatever its political and economic causes might be, was primarily due to its having ignored for a hundred years the Message of God for this day.

The dangers and problems which the war brought to us in Haifa and to the Bahá'í world in general were faced by Shoghi Effendi with remarkable calm. This does not mean he did not suffer from them. The burden of responsibility was always there, he could never lay it down for a single moment. I remember on one occasion, when I was frantic because he always had to have everything referred to him for decision, even when he was ill, he said that other leaders, even Prime Ministers, could delegate their powers for at least a short time if they were forced to, but that he could not delegate his for a single moment as long as he was alive. No one else was divinely guided to fulfill his function and he could not delegate his guidance to someone else.

Although World War II did not actually reach the Holy Land, for years we lived in the imminent danger that it might do so at any time.

In November 1941, Shoghi Effendi, in a cabled message had forecast the future and characterized the years immediately before us: ". . . as fury destructiveness tremendous world ordeal attains most intensive pitch . . ." In spite of what lay ahead of the world we in Palestine had already, during 1941, passed through what for us were the most agonizing months of the entire war which had caused the Guardian intense anxiety. It was during that year that the abortive revolution of the anti-ally Rashíd 'Alí took place in 'Iráq; the British forces were persistently driven back by General Rommel in

Libya and the Germans eventually (in 1942) reached the gates of Alexandria; the Nazi forces occupied Crete—a second springboard for their contemplated conquest of the Middle East; and British and French forces invaded the Lebanon and ousted the regime controlled by the Vichy Government in that country. In addition to these all too palpable dangers the Grand Muftí of Jerusalem, the enemy of both the Faith and the Guardian, was the firm ally of the Nazi Government. It does not require much imagination to picture what would have happened to Shoghi Effendi and the Shrines, the World Centre records and archives material, if a victorious German army, accompanied by the scheming and vituperative Muftí, had taken Palestine. Many times Shoghi Effendi said that it was not so much a question of what the Germans would do but the fact that there were so many local enemies who, combining with the Muftí, could completely poison the minds of the Germans against him and thus aggravate a situation already dangerous enough since our Bahá'í ideas were in many respects so inimical to the Nazi ideology.

Throughout the years of the war Shoghi Effendi was in a position to maintain his contact with the mass of the believers in those countries where some of the oldest and most populous Bahá'í communities existed, such as Persia, America, India and Great Britain, as well as the new and rapidly growing centres in Latin America. The relatively small communities in Japan, the European countries, Burma, and for a time 'Iráq, were the only ones cut off from him—a severance that grieved him and caused him much concern for their fate. Because of this little-short-of-miraculous manner in which contact was maintained with the body of believers throughout the Bahá'í world Shoghi Effendi was able not only to send his directives to the various National Assemblies, but to indicate what this great war signified to us as Bahá'ís. In his epistle known as *The Promised Day Is Come* he stated that "God's purpose is none other than to usher in, in ways He alone can bring about, and the full significance of which He alone can fathom, the Great, the Golden Age of a long-divided, a long-afflicted humanity. Its present state, indeed even its immediate future, is dark, distressingly dark. Its distant future, however, is radiant, gloriously radiant—so radiant that no eye can visualize it . . . The ages of its infancy and childhood are past, never again to return, while the Great Age, the consummation of all ages, which must signalize the coming of age of the entire human race, is yet to come. The convulsions of this transitional and most turbulent period in the annals of humanity are the essential prerequisites, and herald the inevitable approach, of that Age of Ages, 'the time of the end', in which the folly and tumult of strife that has, since the dawn of history, blackened the annals of mankind, will have been finally transmuted into the wisdom and the tranquility of an undisturbed, a universal, and lasting peace, in which the discord and separation of the children of men will have given way to the world-wide reconciliation, and the complete unification of the divers elements that constitute human society . . . It is this stage which humanity, willingly or unwillingly, is resistlessly approaching. It is for this stage that this vast, this fiery ordeal which humanity is experiencing is mysteriously paving the way."

So great was the relief and joy of the Guardian when the European phase of the war ended in May 1945 that he cabled America: "Followers Bahá'u'lláh throughout five continents unanimously rejoice partial emergence war torn humanity titanic upheaval" and expressed what lay so deeply in his heart: "gratefully acclaim signal evidence interposition divine Providence which during such perilous years enabled World Centre our Faith escape . . ." and went on to express an equal thanksgiving for the manner in which other communities had been miraculously preserved, recapitulating the truly extraordinary victories won for the Faith during and in spite of the war. On August 20, 1945, he again cabled: "Hearts uplifted thanksgiving complete cessation prolonged unprecedented world conflict" and urged the American believers to arise and carry on their work, hailing the removal of restrictions which would now enable them to launch the second stage of the Divine Plan. Nothing could provide a better example of the determination, the enthusiasm and the brilliant leadership of the Guardian than these messages sent on the morrow of the emergence of the world from the worst war in its entire history.

Whatever the state of the rest of the world, the internal situation in Palestine continued to worsen in every respect. The holocaust that had engulfed European Jewry; the bitterness induced amongst the Palestine Jews by British policy in regard to Jewish immigration, which was strictly limited and controlled; the burning resentment of the Arabs against that same policy—all served to increase local tensions and hatred. Many of the hardships from which other countries were beginning to slowly emerge, such as severe food rationing, we were now entering. Everything was difficult. We were no longer in danger of being invaded or bombed, but the outlook for this small but sacred country grew steadily blacker as we entered that period which was characterized by Shoghi Effendi as "the gravest turmoil rocking the Holy Land in modern times."

Shoghi Effendi was exhausted from the strain of the war years, years during which he had not only written *The Promised Day Is Come* and *God Passes By*, but during which he had prosecuted—for who can deny his was the ceaseless output of enthusiasm, encouragement and energy that galvanized the Bahá'ís into action?—five years of the first Seven Year Plan, during which he had comforted, inspired and held the Bahá'í world together, during which he had steadily enlarged the periphery of the Cause and deepened and expanded the life of its National communities, during which the unique project of building the superstructure of the Báb's Shrine had been initiated, and during which the family of 'Abdu'l-Bahá, including his own family, had been hopelessly lost to him. He was now approaching fifty, his hair whitening at the temples, his shoulders bent from so much stooping over his desk, his heart not only saddened by all he had gone through but, I firmly believe, wearing out because of it.

As the British Mandate approached its end on May 14, 1948 the situation in Palestine grew steadily worse. The entire country boiled with apprehension and hatred and acts of terrorism increased steadily. The Arabs, the Jews and the British were all involved; all three of them were well aware of the complete aloofness of the Guardian from the political issues at stake and it is no exaggeration to say he was universally respected—and let alone. This is a fact of major importance for during the years, and particularly the months, preceding the end of the Mandate there was practically no neutral ground left; Jews paid for the defense of the Jewish community and Arabs paid for the defense of the Arab community. That the Guardian should have been able to steer the small Bahá'í community safely through the dangerous rapids of those days, that he himself should not have been approached for funds to support the cause of his fellow Orientals (who all knew he had been born and bred in the country), testify to the high reputation he had established as a man of unbending principle and iron determination.

Many times Shoghi Effendi referred to the miraculous protection the World Centre received during the disturbed and dangerous period of the end of the British Mandate and the firm establishment of the Jewish State. The very list of the dangers avoided and the achievements witnessed during this period—which he enumerated in a cable sent to the American Bahá'í Convention on April 25,

1949—is sufficient to enable us to glimpse the keenness of the anxiety he had experienced and the gravity of the problems with which he had been faced. The published version of this cable pointed out how great had been the "evidences divine protection vouchsafed World Centre Faith course third year second Seven Year Plan" and went on to say: "Prolonged hostilities ravaging Holy Land providentially terminated. Bahá'í Holy Places unlike those belonging other faiths miraculously safeguarded. Perils no less grave than those threatened World Centre Faith under 'Abdu'l-Ḥamíd Jamál Páshá and through Hitler's intended capture Near East averted. Independent sovereign State within confines Holy Land established recognized marking termination twenty-century-long provincial status. Formal assurance protection Bahá'í holy sites continuation Bahá'í pilgrimage given by Prime Minister newly emerged State. Official invitation extended by its government historic occasion opening State's first parliament. Official record Bahá'í marriage endorsed Bahá'í endowments exempted responsible authorities same State. Best wishes future welfare Faith Bahá'u'lláh conveyed writing by newly elected Head State in reply congratulatory message addressed him assumption his office."

In the post-war years, as the victories the Bahá'ís were winning multiplied and the United Nations—the mightiest instrument for creating peace that men had ever devised—emerged, many of us no doubt hoped, and wishfully believed, that we had left the worst phase of humanity's long history of war behind us and that we could now discern the first light of that dawn we Bahá'ís are so firmly convinced lies ahead for the world. But the sober, guided mind of the Guardian did not see events in this light. Until the end of his life he continued to make the same remark, based on Bahá'u'lláh's own words, that he had so often made before the war: "The distant future is very bright, but the immediate future is very dark."

Among the encouraging messages he so frequently sent to the Bahá'ís all over the world, his praises of the wonderful services they were rendering, his plans which he devised in such detail for them to prosecute, ever and anon the note of foreboding and warning would recur. In 1947 he stated that the Bahá'ís had thus far been graciously aided to follow their course "undeflected by the crosscurrents and the tempestuous winds which must of necessity increasingly agitate human society ere the hour of its ultimate redemption approaches . . ." In that communication, urging the American Community to press forward with the supremely important work of its second Seven Year Plan, he spoke of the future: "As the international situation worsens, as the fortunes of mankind sink to a still lower ebb . . . As the fabric of present-day society heaves and cracks under the strain and stress of portentous events and calamities, as the fissures, accentuating the cleavage separating nation from nation, class from class, race from race, and creed from creed, multiply . . ." Far from having rounded the corner and turned our backs forever on our unhappy past, there was "a steadily deepening crisis". In March 1948 he went still further in a conversation I recorded in my diary: "Tonight Shoghi Effendi told me some very interesting things: roughly, he said that to say that there was not going to be another war, in the light of present conditions, was foolish, and to say that if there was another war the Atom Bomb would not be used was also foolish. So we must believe there probably will be a war and it will be used and there will be terrific destruction. But the Bahá'ís will, he felt, emerge to form the nucleus of the future world civilization. He said it was not right to say the good would perish with the bad because in a sense all are bad, all humanity is to blame, for ignoring and repudiating Bahá'u'lláh after He had repeatedly trumpeted to everyone His Message. He said the saints in the monasteries and the sinners in the worst flesh pots of Europe are all wicked because they have rejected the Truth. He said it was wrong to think, as some of the Bahá'ís do, that the good would perish with the evil, all men are evil because they have repudiated God in this day and turned from Him. He said we can only believe that in some mysterious way, in spite of the terrible destruction, enough will be left over to build the future."

In November of that same year, again encouraging the American believers to persevere with their Plan, he wrote: "As the threat of still more violent convulsions assailing a travailing age increases, and the wings of yet another conflict, destined to contribute a distinct, and perhaps a decisive, share to the birth of the new Order which must signalize the advent of the Lesser Peace, darken the international horizon . . . Rumblings of catastrophes yet more dreadful agitate with increasing frequency a sorely stressed and chaotic world . . . so must every aggravation in the state of a world still harassed by the ravages of a devastating conflict, and now hovering on the brink of a yet more crucial struggle, be accompanied by a still more ennobling manifestation of the spirit of this second crusade . . ." In that same month he referred to "The deepening crisis ominously threatening further to derange the equilibrium of a politically convulsed, economically disrupted, socially subverted, morally decadent and spiritually moribund society". He went on to speak of the "premonitory rumblings of a third ordeal threatening to engulf the Eastern and Western Hemispheres" and said, "the world outlook is steadily darkening." He urged the Bahá'ís to "forge ahead into the future serenely confident that the hour of their mightiest exertions, and the supreme opportunity for their greatest exploits, must coincide with the apocalyptic upheaval marking the lowest ebb in mankind's fast-declining fortunes."

It went on and on. The victories we won, the praise, the encouragement, joy of the Guardian—and the warnings. In 1950 he told the Bahá'ís they should be "undaunted" by the perils of a "progressively deteriorating international situation" and in 1951 informed the European Teaching Conference that the "perils" confronting that "sorely tried continent" were "steadily mounting". But it was really in a most grave and thought-provoking letter, written in 1954, that Shoghi Effendi expatiated on this subject of a future conflict, its causes, its course, its outcome, and its effect on America, in more detail and in a more forceful language than he had ever before used. He associates the "crass" and "cancerous materialism" prevalent in the world today with the warnings of Bahá'u'lláh and states He had compared it "to a devouring flame" and regarded it "as the chief factor in precipitating the dire ordeals and world-shaking crises that must necessarily involve the burning of cities and the spread of terror and consternation in the hearts of men". Shoghi Effendi goes on to say: "Indeed a foretaste of the devastation which this consuming fire will wreak upon the world, and with which it will lay waste the cities of the nations participating in this tragic world-engulfing contest, has been afforded by the last World War, marking the second stage in the global havoc which humanity, forgetful of its God and heedless of the clear warnings uttered by His appointed Messenger for this day, must, alas, inevitably experience."

The letter in which these appalling predictions are expressed was addressed to the American Bahá'ís and in it the Guardian points out that the general deterioration in the situation of a "distracted world" and the multiplication of increasingly destructive armaments, to which the two sides engaged in a world contest were contributing—"caught in a whirlpool of fear, suspicion and hatred" as they were—were ever-increasingly affecting their own country and were bound, if not remedied, "to involve the American nation in a catastrophe of undreamed-of dimensions and of untold consequences to the social structure, the standard and conception of the American people and government . . . The American nation . . . stands, indeed, from whichever angle one observes its immediate fortunes, in grave peril. The woes and tribulations which threaten it are partly avoidable, but mostly inevitable and God-sent . . ." He went on to point out the changes which these unavoidable afflictions must bring about in the "obsolescent doctrine of absolute sovereignty" to which its government and people still clung and which was so "manifestly at variance with the needs of a world already contracted into a neighbourhood and crying out for unity" and through which this nation will find itself purged of its anachronistic conceptions and prepared to play the great role 'Abdu'l-Bahá foretold for it in the establishment of the Lesser Peace. The "fiery tribulations" to come would not only "weld the American nation to its sister nations in both hemispheres" but would cleanse it of "the accumulated dross which ingrained racial prejudice, rampant materialism, widespread ungodliness and moral laxity have combined, in the course of successive generations, to produce, and which have prevented her thus far from assuming the role of world spiritual leadership forecast by 'Abdu'l-Bahá's unerring pen—a role which she is bound to fulfill through travail and sorrow."

If we, the generation of the twilight before the sun of this new day rises, ask ourselves why such catastrophes should be facing us in these times, the answers all are there, made crystal clear by the Guardian in his great expositions of the meaning and implications of our teachings. Two factors, he taught us, are involved. The first is contained in those words of Bahá'u'lláh, *"Soon will the present-day order be rolled up, and a new one spread out in its stead."* To tear off the time-honoured protective covering of innumerable societies, each embedded in its own customs, superstitions and prejudices, and apply to them a universal new frame of existence is an operation only Almighty God can perform and of necessity a very painful one. This is made even more painful by the state of men's souls and minds; some societies are the victims of "a flagrant secularism—the direct offspring of irreligion", some are in the grip of "a blatant materialism and racialism" which have, Shoghi Effendi stated, "usurped the rights of God Himself", but all—all the peoples of the earth—are guilty of having, for over a century, "refused to recognize the One Whose advent had been promised to all religions, and in Whose Faith alone, all nations can and must eventually, seek their true salvation." Fundamentally it was because of this new

Faith, the "priceless gem of Divine Revelation enshrining the Spirit of God and incarnating His Purpose for all mankind in this age" as Shoghi Effendi described it, that the world was "undergoing such agonies". Bahá'u'lláh Himself had said:

> *"The world's equilibrium hath been upset through the vibrating influence of this most great, this new World Order." "The signs of impending convulsions and chaos can now be discerned, inasmuch as the prevailing Order appeareth to be lamentably defective." "The world is in travail and its agitation waxeth day by day. Its face is turned towards waywardness and unbelief. Such shall be its plight that to disclose it now would not be meet and seemly. Its perversity will long continue. And when the appointed hour is come, there shall suddenly appear that which shall cause the limbs of mankind to quake. Then, and only then, will the Divine Standard be unfurled, and the Nightingale of Paradise warble its melody." "After a time, all the governments on earth will change. Oppression will envelop the world. And following a universal convulsion, the sun of justice will rise from the horizon of the unseen realm."*

So thrilling, however, is the vision of the future which Shoghi Effendi painted for us in his brilliant words, that it wipes away all fear and fills the heart of every Bahá'í with such confidence and joy that the prospect of any amount of suffering and deprivation cannot weaken his faith or crush his hopes. "The world is, in truth," Shoghi Effendi wrote, "moving on towards its destiny. The interdependence of the peoples and nations of the earth, whatever the leaders of the divisive forces of the world may say or do, is already an accomplished fact." The world commonwealth, "destined to emerge, sooner or later, out of the carnage, agony, and havoc of this great world confusion" was the assured consummation of the working of these forces. First would come the Lesser Peace, which the nations of the earth, as yet unconscious of Bahá'u'lláh's Revelation, would themselves establish; "This momentous and historic step, involving the reconstruction of mankind, as the result of the universal recognition of its oneness and wholeness, will bring in its wake the spiritualization of the masses, consequent to the recognition of the character, and the acknowledgement of the claims, of the Faith of Bahá'u'lláh—the essential condition to that ultimate fusion of all races, creeds, classes, and nations which must signalize the emergence of His New World Order." He goes on to state: "Then will the coming of age of the entire human race be proclaimed and celebrated by all the peoples and nations of the earth. Then will the banner of the Most Great Peace be hoisted. Then will the worldwide sovereignty of Bahá'u'lláh . . . be recognized, acclaimed, and firmly established. Then will a world civilization be born, flourish, and perpetuate itself, a civilization with a fullness of life such as the world has never seen nor can as yet conceive . . . Then will the planet, galvanized through the universal belief of its dwellers in one God, and their allegiance to one common Revelation, . . . be . . . acclaimed as the earthly heaven, capable of fulfilling that ineffable destiny fixed for it, from time immemorial, by the love and wisdom of its Creator."

SHOGHI EFFENDI WITH DR. J. E. ESSLEMONT
Taken at Dr. Esslemont's sanatorium in Bournemouth, England, during a visit of Shoghi Effendi; they were devoted friends

THE GUARDIAN AFTER HIS RETURN TO HAIFA
Shoghi Effendi with Ismail Aqa, the old gardener of 'Abdu'l-Bahá,

'ABDU'L-BAHÁ'S HOME

Showing the extra rooms (on the left) built on the roof for Shoghi Effendi's use by the Greatest Holy Leaf in 1923

THE TOMB OF THE BÁB

A photograph taken by Shoghi Effendi from his own room on the roof of the Master's home, showing the bright light he placed on the Shrine

VIII

THE WRITINGS OF SHOGHI EFFENDI

In an age when people play football with words, kicking them right and left indiscriminately with no respect for either their meaning or correct usage, the style of Shoghi Effendi stands out in dazzling beauty. His joy in words was one of his strongest personal characteristics, whether he wrote in English—the language he had given his heart to—or in the mixture of Persian and Arabic he used in his general letters to the East. Although he was so simple in his personal tastes he had an innate love of richness which is manifest in the way he arranged and decorated various Bahá'í Holy Places, in the style of the Shrine of the Báb, in his preferences in architecture and in his choice and combination of words. Of him it could be said, in the words of another great writer, Macaulay, that "he wrote in language . . . precise and luminous." Unlike so many people Shoghi Effendi wrote what he meant and meant exactly what he wrote. It is impossible to eliminate any word from one of his sentences without sacrificing part of the meaning, so concise, so pithy is his style. A book like *God Passes By* is a veritable essence of essences; from this single hundred-year history, fifty books could easily be written and none of them would be superficial or lacking in material, so rich is the source provided by the Guardian, so condensed his treatment of it.

The language in which Shoghi Effendi wrote, whether for the Bahá'ís of the West or the East, has set a standard which should effectively prevent them from descending to the level of illiterate literates which often so sadly characterizes the present generation as far as the usage and appreciation of words is concerned. He never compromised with the ignorance of his readers but expected them, in their thirst for knowledge, to overcome their ignorance. Shoghi Effendi chose, to the best of his great ability, the right vehicle for his thought and it made no difference to him whether the average person was going to know the word he used or not. After all, what one does not know one can find out. Although he had such a brilliant command of language, he frequently reinforced his knowledge by certainty through looking up the word he planned to use in Webster's big dictionary. In his translations of the Bahá'í writings, and above all in his own compositions, Shoghi Effendi set a standard that educates and raises the cultural level of the reader at the same time that it feeds his mind and soul with thoughts and truth.

I remember once Shoghi Effendi giving me an article to read from a British newspaper which called attention to the bureaucratic language which is developing, particularly in the United States, in which more and more words are used to convey less and less and merely produce confusion confounded. Shoghi Effendi heartily supported the article! Words were very precise instruments to him. I also recall a particularly beautiful distinction he made in speaking to some pilgrims in the Western Pilgrim House. He said: "we are orthodox, but not fanatical."

Many times the language of the Guardian soared to great poetic heights. Witness such passages as these that shine with the brilliance of cathedral glass: "We behold, as we survey the episodes of this first act of a sublime drama, the figure of its Master Hero, the Báb, arise meteor-like above the horizon of Shíráz, traverse the sombre sky of Persia from South to North, decline with tragic swiftness, and perish in a blaze of glory. We see His satellites, a galaxy of God-intoxicated heroes, mount above that same horizon, irradiate that same incandescent light, burn themselves out with that selfsame swiftness, and impart in their turn an added impetus to the steadily gathering momentum of God's nascent Faith." He called the Báb "that youthful Prince of Glory" and describes the scene of His entombment on Mt. Carmel: "when all was finished, and the earthly remains of the Martyr-Prophet of Shíráz were, at long last, safely deposited for their everlasting rest in the bosom of God's holy mountain, 'Abdu'l-Bahá, Who had cast aside His turban, removed His shoes and thrown off His cloak, bent low over the still open sarcophagus, His silver hair waving about His head and His face transfigured and luminous, rested His forehead on the border of the wooden casket, and, sobbing aloud, wept with such a weeping that all those who were present wept with Him." "The second period . . . derives its inspiration from the august figure of Bahá'u'lláh, pre-eminent in holiness, awesome in the majesty of His strength and power, unapproachable in the transcendent brightness of His glory." "Amidst the shadows that are increasingly gathering about us we can discern the glimmerings of Bahá'u'lláh's unearthly sovereignty appearing fitfully on the horizon of history." Or these words addressed to the Greatest Holy Leaf: "In the innermost recesses of our hearts, O Thou exalted Leaf of the Abhá Paradise, we have reared for thee a shining mansion that the hand of time can never undermine, a shrine which shall frame eternally the matchless beauty of thy countenance, an altar whereon the fire of thy consuming love shall burn for ever." Or these words painting a picture of the punishment of God in this day: "On the high seas, in the air, on land, in the forefront of battle, in the palaces of kings and the cottages of peasants, in the most hallowed sanctuaries, whether secular or religious, the evidences of God's retributive act and mysterious discipline are manifest. Its heavy toll is steadily mounting—a holocaust sparing neither prince nor peasant, neither man nor woman, neither young nor old." Or these words concerning the attitude of the true servants of the Cause: "Of such men and women it may be truly said that to them 'every foreign land is a fatherland, and every fatherland a foreign land'. For their citizenship . . . is in the Kingdom of Bahá'u'lláh. Though willing to share to the utmost the temporal benefits and the fleeting joys which this earthly life can confer, though eager to participate in whatever activity that conduces to the richness, the happiness and peace of that life, they can at no time forget that it constitutes no more than a transient, a very brief stage of their existence, that they who live it are but pilgrims and wayfarers whose goal is the Celestial City, and whose home the Country of never-failing joy and brightness."

There are so many aspects to Shoghi Effendi's literary life. I can name on one hand the books (other than his beloved Gibbon) he read for recreation during the twenty years I was with him, though he had read during his youth very extensively on many subjects. This is no doubt because of the fact that by 1937, when I took up my new life in Haifa, he was already overwhelmed by the ever-increasing amount of material he had to read in connection with his work, such as news-letters, National Assembly minutes, circulars and mail. By the end of his life if he did not read at least two or three hours a day he could no longer keep up with his work at all; he read on planes, trains, in gardens, at table when we were away from Haifa and in Haifa hour after hour at his desk, until he would get so tired he would go to bed and sit up reading there. He assiduously kept abreast of the political news and trends of the world.

The supreme importance of Shoghi Effendi's English translations and communications can never be sufficiently stressed because of his function as sole and authoritative interpreter of the Sacred Writings, appointed as such by 'Abdu'l-Bahá in His Will. There are many instances when, owing to the looseness of construction in Persian sentences, there could be an ambiguity in the mind of the reader regarding the meaning. Careful and correct English, not lending itself to ambiguity in the first place, became, when coupled with Shoghi Effendi's brilliant mind and his power as interpreter of the Holy Word, what we might well call the crystallizing vehicle of the teachings. Often by referring to Shoghi Effendi's translation into English the original meaning of the Báb, Bahá'u'lláh, or 'Abdu'l-Bahá becomes clear and is thus safeguarded against misinterpretation in the future. He was meticulous in translating and made absolutely sure that the words he was using in English conveyed and did not depart from the original thought nor the original words. One would have to have a mastery of Persian and Arabic to correctly understand what he did. For instance in reading the original one finds that one word in Arabic was susceptible of being translated into two or more words in English; thus Shoghi Effendi, in the construction of his English sentences, might use "power", "strength" and "might" alternatively to replace this one word, choosing the exact nuance of meaning that would fit best, do away with reiteration, and lend most colour to his translation without sacrificing the true meaning, indeed, thereby enhancing the true meaning. Once—only once, alas, in our busy, harassed life—Shoghi Effendi said to me that I now knew enough Persian to understand the original and he read a paragraph of one of Bahá'u'lláh's Tablets and said, "How can one translate that into English?" For about two hours we tried, that is he tried and I feebly followed him. When I would suggest a sentence, which did convey the meaning, Shoghi Effendi said "Ah, but that is not translation! You cannot change and leave out words in the original and just put what you think it means in English." He pointed out a translator must be absolutely faithful to his original text and that in some cases this meant that what came out in another language was ugly and even meaningless. As Bahá'u'lláh is always sublimely beautiful in His words this could not be done.

The Guardian was exceedingly cautious in everything that concerned the original Word and would never explain or comment on a text submitted to him in English (when it was not his own translation) until he had verified it with the original. He was very careful of the words he used in commenting on various events in the Faith, refusing, for instance, to designate a person a martyr—which is a station—just because they were slain, and sometimes designating as martyrs people who were not killed but the nature of whose death he associated with martyrdom.

Another highly important aspect of the divinely-conferred position Shoghi Effendi held of interpreter of the Teachings was that he had not only protected the Sacred Word from being misconstrued but that he also carefully preserved the relationship and importance of different aspects of the Teachings to each other and safeguarded the rightful station of each of the three Central Figures of the Faith. An interesting example of this is reflected in a letter of A. L. M. Nicolas, the French scholar who translated the *Bayán* of the Báb into French and who might correctly be described as a Bábí. For many years he was under the impression that the Bahá'ís had ignored the greatness and belittled the station of the Báb. When he discovered that Shoghi Effendi in his writings exalted the Báb, perpetuated His memory through a book such as *Nabíl's Narrative*, and repeatedly translated His words into English, his attitude completely changed. In a letter to one of the old believers in France he wrote: "Now I can die quietly . . . Glory to Shoghi Effendi who has calmed my torment and my anxiety, glory to him who recognizes the worth of Siyyid 'Alí Muḥammad called the Báb. I am so content that I kiss your hands which traced my address on the envelope which brought me the message of Shoghi. Thank you, Mademoiselle, thank you from the bottom of my heart."

One of the earliest acts of Shoghi Effendi's ministry was to begin circulating his translations of the holy Writings. One year and ten days after the reading of 'Abdu'l-Bahá's Will we find him writing to the American National Assembly: "It is a great pleasure for me to share with you the translation of some of the prayers and Tablets of our beloved Master . . ." and he goes on to add that he trusts "that in the course of time I will be enabled to send you regularly correct and reliable translations . . . which will unfold to your eyes a new vision of His Glorious Mission . . . and give you an insight into the character and meaning of His Divine Teachings."

The writing, translation and promulgation of Bahá'í books was one of the Guardian's major interests, one he never tired of and one he actively supported. The ideal situation is for local and national communities to pay for their own activities, but in this Formative

Age of our Faith the Guardian fully realized this was not always possible and from the funds at his disposal he assisted substantially throughout the years in financing the translation and publication of Bahá'í literature. In periods of emergency, when the attainment of cherished goals was at stake, Shoghi Effendi would fill the breach.

Literature in all languages the Guardian collected in Haifa, placing books in his own library, in the two Pilgrim House libraries, in the Mansion of Bahá'u'lláh in Bahjí, and in the International Archives. In this connection it is interesting to note how he placed them, for I never saw it done before: he would have, say, a lot of rather dull bindings, of some inexpensive edition, in grey and a lot more in blue or some other colour. With these he would fill his bookshelves in patterns, five red, two blue, five red and so on, using the variation in colour and number to add charm to the general effect of a book case that otherwise would have presented a monotonous and uninteresting appearance.

Facts and events are more or less useless unless seen in the proper perspective, unless vision is applied to their interpretation. One of the marked aspects of Shoghi Effendi's genius was the way he plucked the significance of an occurrence, an isolated phenomenon, from the welter of irrelevancies associated with the international development of the Cause and set it in its historical frame, focussing on it the light of his appraising mind and making us understand what was taking place and what it signified now and forever. This was not a static thing, a picture of shapes and forms, but rather a description of where a leviathan was moving in an ocean—the leviathan of the co-ordinated movements inside the Community of Bahá'u'lláh's followers moving in the ocean of His Dispensation. An Assembly was formed, someone died, a certificate was granted by some obscure governmental body—in themselves isolated facts and events—but to Shoghi Effendi's eyes they were part of a pattern and he made us see this pattern being woven before our eyes too. In the volumes of *The Bahá'í World* the Guardian did this not only for the believers, but for the public at large. He dramatized the progress of the Faith and a mass of scattered facts and unrelated photographs were made to testify to the reality of the claim of that Faith to be world-wide and all-inclusive.

It is interesting to note that the actual suggestion for a volume along the lines of *The Bahá'í World* came to Shoghi Effendi from Horace Holley in a letter he wrote in February 1924—though I have no doubt that it was the breadth of vision of the young Guardian and the shape he was already giving to the work of the Cause in his messages to the West that, working on Horace's own creative mind, stimulated him to this concept. Shoghi Effendi seized on this idea and from then on Horace became Shoghi Effendi's primary instrument, as a gifted writer, and in his capacity as Secretary of the American National Spiritual Assembly, in making of *The Bahá'í World* the remarkable and unique book it became. Volume One, published in 1925 and called *Bahá'í Year Book*—which covered the period from April 1925 to April 1926 and comprised 174 pages— received its permanent title, in Volume Two, of *The Bahá'í World, A Biennial International Record* suggested by that National Assembly and approved by Shoghi Effendi. At the time of the Guardian's passing twelve volumes had appeared, the largest running to over 1,000 pages. Although these were prepared under the supervision of the American National Assembly, published by its Publishing Committee, compiled by a staff of editors and dedicated to Shoghi Effendi, it would be more in conformity with the facts to call them Shoghi Effendi's Book. He himself acted as Editor-in-Chief; the tremendous amount of material comprised in each volume was sent to him by the American Assembly, with all photographs, before it appeared and his was the final decision as to what should go in and what be omitted. As six of these books were published during the period I was privileged to be with him I was able to observe how he edited them. With his infinite capacity for work Shoghi Effendi would go over the vast bundles of papers and photographs forwarded to him, eliminating the poorer and more irrelevant material; section by section, following the Table of Contents which he himself had arranged, would be prepared and set aside until the entire manuscript was ready to be mailed back to America for publication. He always deplored the fact that the material was not of a higher standard. It is due solely to his determination and perseverance that *The Bahá'í World* volumes are as brilliant and impressive as they are. The editors (some of whom he had nominated himself), struggling against the forces of inertia that beset any body trying to achieve its ends through correspondence with sources thousands of miles away, and seeking to work through often inexperienced and inefficient administrative organs, would never have been successful in assembling the material required without the drive and authority of the Guardian behind their efforts. An interesting side light on this work is that Shoghi Effendi, after the book was published, had all the original manuscripts returned to Haifa and stored at the World Centre.

As soon as one volume was published he began to himself collect material for the next one. In addition to the repeated reminders he sent to the American National Assembly to do likewise, he sent innumerable letters and cables to different Assemblies and individuals. In one day, for instance, he cabled three National Assemblies: "National Assembly photograph for Bahá'í World essential"; he cabled such an isolated and out-of-the-way outpost as Shanghai for material he wanted. "Bahá'í World manuscript mailed. Advise speedy careful publication" was not an unusual type of message for the American Assembly to receive. It was Shoghi Effendi who arranged the order of the volume, had typed in Haifa the entire Table of Contents, had all the photographs titled, chose all the frontispieces, decided on the colour of the binding of the volume to appear, and above all gave exact instructions, in long detailed letters to Horace Holley, whom he himself had chosen as the most gifted and informed person to write the International Survey of Current Bahá'í Activities, to which he attached great importance.

What Shoghi Effendi himself thought of *The Bahá'í World* he put down in writing. As early as 1927, when only one volume had been published, he wrote to a non-Bahá'í: "I would strongly advise you to procure a copy of the Bahá'í Year Book . . . which will give you a clear and authoritative statement of the purpose, the claim and the influence of the Faith." In a general letter addressed, in 1928, "To the beloved of the Lord and the hand-maids of the Merciful throughout the East and West", and entirely devoted to the subject of *The Bahá'í World*, Shoghi Effendi informs them: "I have ever since its inception taken a keen and sustained interest in its development, have personally participated in the collection of its material, the arrangement of its contents, and the close scrutiny of whatever data it contains. I confidently and emphatically recommend it to every thoughtful and eager follower of the Faith, whether in the East or in the West . . ." He wrote that its material is readable, attractive, comprehensive and authoritative; its treatment of the fundamentals of the Cause concise and persuasive, and its illustrations thoroughly representative; it is unexcelled and unapproached by any other Bahá'í publication of its kind. This book Shoghi Effendi always visualized as being—indeed he designed it to be—eminently suitable for the public, for scholars, to place in libraries and as a means, as he put it, of "removing the malicious misrepresentations and unfortunate misunderstandings that have so

THE TOMB OF THE BÁB ON MT. CARMEL

A very early photograph which shows the electric light placed by Shoghi Effendi on the roof of the Shrine

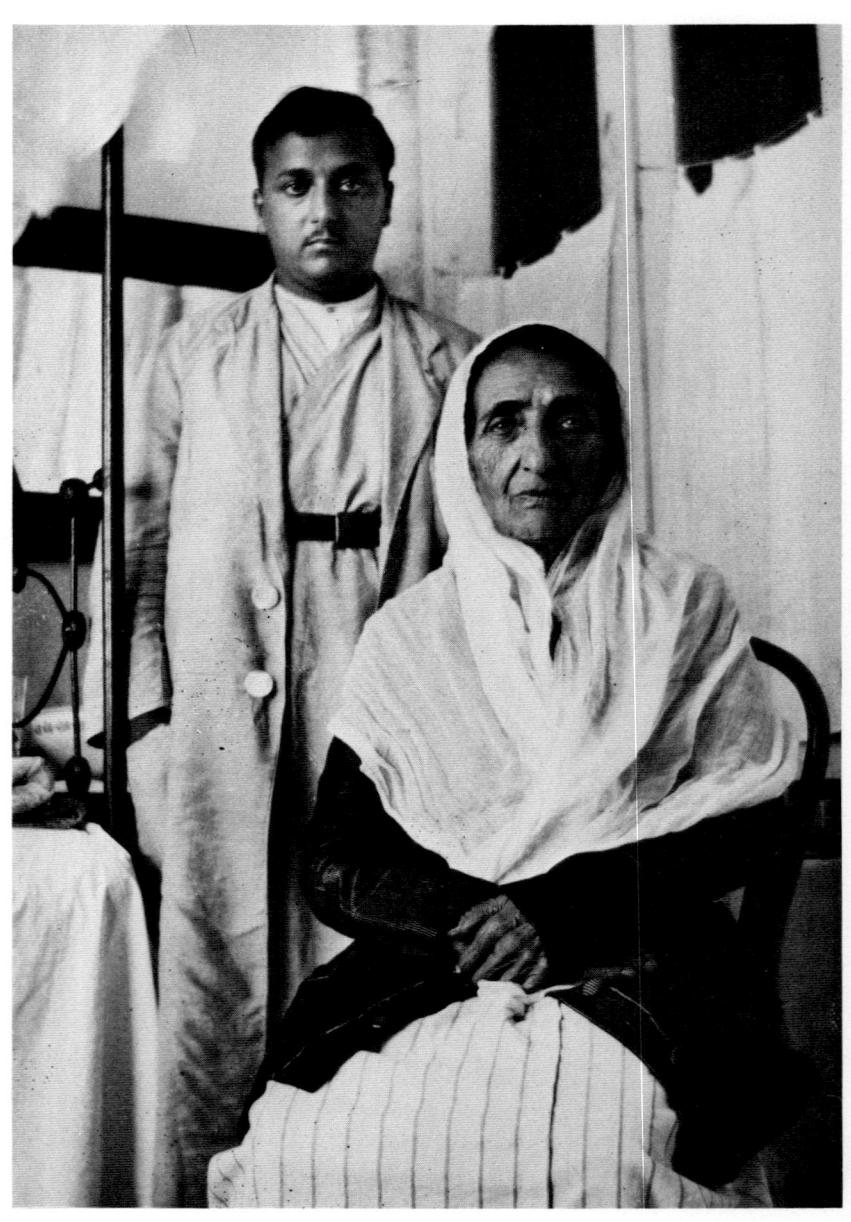

THE GUARDIAN AND BAHÍYYIH KHÁNUM
Probably taken in 1919, before Shoghi Effendi left to study in England

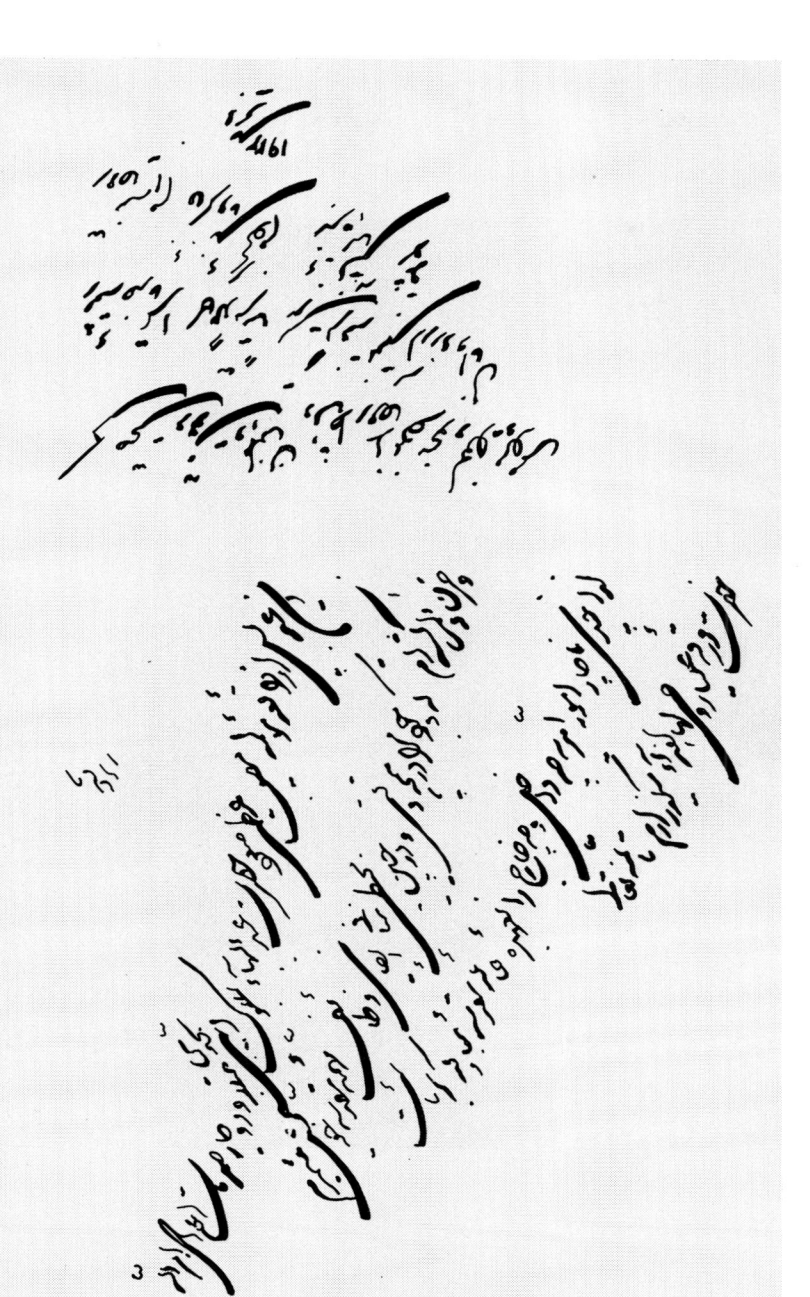

THE GUARDIAN'S HANDWRITING

Shoghi Effendi informs the Bahá'ís, through a letter to the *Star of the West*, that "unable to do otherwise, I have left for a time the affairs of the Cause both at home and abroad, under…the headship of the Greatest Holy Leaf". Circa April, 1922

SHOGHI EFFENDI IN THE EARLY 1920'S

long and so grievously clouded the luminous Faith of Bahá'u'lláh."

It was a book that he himself often gave as a gift to royalty, to statesmen, to professors, universities, newspaper editors and non-Bahá'ís in general, mailing it to them with his simple personal card "Shoghi Rabbani" enclosed.

It is difficult to realize, looking back upon Shoghi Effendi's achievements, that he actually wrote only one book of his own, as such, and this was *God Passes By* published in 1944. Even *The Promised Day Is Come*, written in 1941, is a 136-page-long general letter to the Bahá'ís of the West. This fact alone is a profound indication of the deeply modest character of the man. He communicated with the Bahá'ís because he had something to say that was important, because he was appointed to guide them, because he was the Custodian of the Faith of Bahá'u'lláh; he was impelled by forces stronger than himself over which he had no control.

Concurrent with the period when these first illuminating letters on such major subjects were streaming from the pen of Shoghi Effendi, he undertook the translation of two books. In a letter written on July 4, 1930, Shoghi Effendi says: "I feel exceedingly tired after a strenuous year of work particularly as I have managed to add to my labours the translation of the Íqán, which I have already sent to America." This was the first of his major translations, Bahá'u'lláh's great exposition on the station and role of the Manifestations of God, more particularly in the light of Islamic teachings and prophecies, known as the *Kitáb-i-Íqán* or *Book of Certitude*. It was an invaluable adjunct to the Western Bahá'ís in their study of the Faith they had embraced and infinitely enriched their understanding of Divine Revelation.

During that same year the Guardian began work on the second book published during this period, a work that was neither a translation of Bahá'u'lláh's words nor one of Shoghi Effendi's general letters, but which must be considered a literary masterpiece and one of his most priceless gifts for all time. This was the translation of the first part of the narrative compiled by a contemporary follower of both the Báb and Bahá'u'lláh known as Nabíl, which was published in 1932 under the title *The Dawn-Breakers*. If the critic and sceptic should be tempted to dismiss the literature of the Bahá'í Faith as typical of the better class of religious books designed for the initiate only, he could not for a moment so brush aside a volume of the quality of *Nabíl's Narrative*, which deserves to be counted as a classic among epic narratives in the English tongue. Although ostensibly a translation from the original Persian, Shoghi Effendi may be said to have recreated it in English, his translation being comparable to Fitzgerald's rendering of Omar Khayyam's *Rubaiyat* which gave the world a poem in a foreign language that in many ways exceeded the merits of the original. The best and most descriptive comments on this masterpiece of the Guardian are to be found in the words of prominent non-Bahá'ís. The playwright Gordon Bottomley wrote: ". . . living with it has been one of the salient experiences of a lifetime; but beyond that it was a moving experience both in itself and through the psychological light it throws on the New Testament narrative." The well-known scholar and humanitarian, Dr. Alfred W. Martin of the Ethical Culture Society, in his letter of thanks to Shoghi Effendi for sending him *Nabíl's Narrative* wrote: "Your magnificent and monumental work . . . will be a classic and a standard for all time to come. I marvel beyond measure at your ability to prepare such a work for the press over and above all the activities which your regular professional position devolves upon you." One of his old professors, Bayard Dodge of the American University of Beirut, after receiving the gift of *Nabíl's Narrative* from the Guardian wrote to him: "I have profited by the leisure of the summer to read *Nabíl's Narrative* . . . Everyone interested in religion and also in history owes you a very great debt of gratitude for publishing such a fine piece of work. The deeper side of the work is so impressive, that it seems hardly fitting to compliment you upon some of the practical matters connected with the translation. However, I cannot refrain from telling you how much I appreciate your taking the time from a busy life to accomplish such a large task."

The letter which Sir E. Denison Ross, the well-known Orientalist, wrote to him from the School of Oriental Studies of the University of London was the most highly prized tribute he received:

27th April, 1932

My dear Shoghi Effendi,

It was most kind of you to remember me and send me copies of your two latest works, which I am very proud to possess, especially as coming from such a quarter. The *Dawn Breakers* is really one of the most beautiful books I have seen for many years; the paper, printing, and illustrations are all exquisite, and as for your English style, it really could not be bettered, and never does it read like a translation. Allow me to convey my warmest congratulations on your most successful achievement of what you set out to do when you came to Oxford, namely, to attain a perfect command of our language.

Apart from this, Nabíl's narrative will be of the utmost service to me in the lectures I deliver here every Session on the Bab and the Baha.

Trusting you are in good health,
I remain,
Yours very sincerely,
E. Denison Ross
Director

In 1935 Shoghi Effendi again presented the western Bahá'ís with a magnificent gift, published under the title *Gleanings from the Writings of Bahá'u'lláh*, which the Guardian himself described as "consisting of a selection of the most characteristic and hitherto unpublished passages from the outstanding works of the Author of the Bahá'í Revelation." Remembering the scanty pages of the New Testament, the reputed words of Buddha, and the mere handful of sayings of some other Divine luminaries, which nevertheless have transfigured for centuries the lives of millions of men, the *Gleanings* alone seems to provide a source of guidance and inspiration sufficient for the spiritual Dispensation of any Prophet. The most treasured tribute to this book was that of Queen Marie of Rumania who told Martha Root: "even doubters would find a powerful strength in it, if they would read it alone, and would give their souls time to expand." To Shoghi Effendi himself the Queen wrote, in January 1936, after receiving from him a copy, "May I send you my most grateful thanks for the wonderful book, every word of which is precious to me, and doubly so in this time of anxiety and unrest."

This was followed by the translation in 1936–1937, of what might almost be termed a companion volume, comparable in richness and complementary in material, namely, *Prayers and Meditations by Bahá'u'lláh*.

Immediately after the publication of this diamond-mine of communion with God, unsurpassed in any religious literature of the world, Shoghi Effendi set to work on a longer general letter than he had ever before written, which appeared in 1939 under the title of *The Advent of Divine Justice*. With a kind but firm hand Shoghi Effendi held up before the face of the North American Community the mirror of the civilization by which they were surrounded and warned them, in terms that riveted the eye and chilled the heart, against its evils, pointing out to them a truth few of them had ever pondered, namely, that the very evils of that civilization were the mystic reason for their homeland having been chosen by God as the cradle of His World Order in this day. As the warnings contained in *The Advent of Divine Justice* are an integral part of the vision and guidance Shoghi Effendi gave to the faithful throughout his ministry, they cannot be passed over in silence if we are to obtain any correct understanding of his own mission. In no uncertain terms he castigated the moral laxity, political corruption, racial prejudice and corrosive materialism of their society, contrasting it with the exalted standards inculcated by Bahá'u'lláh in His Teachings, and enjoined by Him upon His followers. It warned them of the war so soon to come and admonished them to stand fast, in spite of every trial that might in future afflict them and their nations, and discharge their sacred trust by prosecuting to a triumphal outcome the Plan they had so recently inaugurated throughout the Western Hemisphere.

Another general letter—this time addressed to the body of the Bahá'ís throughout the West—appeared in print in 1941. It was called *The Promised Day Is Come* and, together with *The Advent of Divine Justice*, sets forth the root-decay of the present-day world. In it, written during the second year of the war, Shoghi Effendi thunders his denunciations of the perversity and sinfulness of this generation, using as his missiles quotations from the lips of Bahá'u'lláh Himself:

"The time for the destruction of the world and its people hath arrived"; "The promised day is come, the day when tormenting trials will have surged above your heads, and beneath your feet, saying: 'Taste ye what your hands have wrought!'"; "Soon shall the blasts of His chastisement beat upon you, and the dust of hell enshroud you."; "And when the appointed hour is come, there shall suddenly appear that which shall cause the limbs of mankind to quake."; "The day is approaching when its (civilization's) *flame will devour the cities, when the Tongue of Grandeur will proclaim: 'The Kingdom is God's, the Almighty, the All-Praised!'"; "The day will soon come, whereon they will cry out for help and receive no answer."; "We have fixed a time for you, O people! If ye fail, at the appointed hour, to turn towards God, He,*

verily, will lay violent hold on you, and will cause grievous afflictions to assail you from every direction. How severe indeed is the chastisement with which your Lord will then chastise you!"; "O ye peoples of the world! Know verily that an unforeseen calamity is following you and that grievous retribution awaiteth you. Think not the deeds ye have committed have been blotted from My sight. By My Beauty! All your doings hath My pen graven with open characters upon tablets of chrysolite."

The Guardian paints a terrible, terrifying and majestic picture of the plight to which the human race has been reduced through its steadfast rejection of Bahá'u'lláh. The "world-afflicting ordeal that has laid its grip upon mankind" is, he wrote, "primarily a judgment of God pronounced against the peoples of the earth, who, for a century, have refused to recognize the One Whose advent had been promised to all religions". Shoghi Effendi recapitulates the sufferings, the persecution, the calumny and cruelty to which the Báb, Bahá'u'lláh and 'Abdu'l-Bahá were subjected and recounts the tale of Their blamelessness, Their patience and fortitude in the face of these trials and Their final weariness with this world as They gathered Their skirts about Them and repaired to the Celestial Realms of Their Creator. Shoghi Effendi enumerates the sins of mankind against these Sinless Ones and points the finger of blame at the leaders of mankind, at its kings, its highest ecclesiastical personages and rulers to whom the Twin Manifestations of God had directed the full force of Their Message and because of whose neglect of their supreme duty to pay heed to the Call of God, Bahá'u'lláh Himself stated: *"From two ranks amongst men power hath been seized: kings and ecclesiastics."*

Between these two so-called general letters—*The Advent of Divine Justice* and *The Promised Day Is Come*—Shoghi Effendi gave the western believers his fifth and last book of translations of the Writings of Bahá'u'lláh, undertaken during the winter of 1939–1940, at another of the most difficult and hazardous periods of his life. *The Epistle to the Son of the Wolf* was Bahá'u'lláh's last major work and contains a selection from His own Writings, made by Himself (surely a unique occurrence in religious history!) during the last two years of His life and has therefore a special position of its own in the literature of our Faith.

God Passes By, the most brilliant and wondrous tale of a century that has ever been told, is truly a "Mother" of future histories, a book wherein every word counts, every sentence burgeons with thought, every thought leads the way to a field of its own. Packed with salient facts it has the range and precision of snow flake crystals, each design perfect in itself, each theme brilliant in outline, coordinated, balanced, self-contained, a matrix for those who follow on and study, evaluate and elaborate the Message and Order of Bahá'u'lláh. It was one of the most concentrated and stupendous achievements of Shoghi Effendi's life.

The method of Shoghi Effendi in writing *God Passes By* was to sit down for a year and read every book of the Bahá'í Writings in Persian and English, and every book written about the Faith by Bahá'ís, whether in manuscript form or published, and everything written by non-Bahá'ís that contained significant references to it. I think in all, this must have covered the equivalent of at least two hundred books. As he read he made notes and compiled and marshalled his facts. Anyone who has ever tackled a work of an historical nature knows how much research is involved, how often one has to decide, in the light of relevant material, between this date given in one place and that date given in another, how back-breaking the whole work is. How much more so then was such a work for the Guardian who had, at the same time, to prepare for the forthcoming Centenary of the Faith and make decisions regarding the design of the superstructure of the Báb's Shrine. When all the ingredients of his book had been assembled Shoghi Effendi commenced weaving them into the fabric of his picture of the significance of the first century of the Bahá'í Dispensation. It was not his purpose, he said, to write a detailed history of those hundred years, but rather to review the salient features of the birth and rise of the Faith, the establishment of its administrative institutions, and the series of crises which had propelled it forward in a mysterious manner, through the release of the Divine power within it, from victory to victory. He revealed to us the panorama of events which, he wrote, "the revolution of a hundred years . . . has unrolled before our eyes" and lifted the curtain on the opening acts of what he asserted was one "indivisible, stupendous and sublime drama, whose mystery no intellect can fathom, whose climax no eye can even dimly perceive, whose conclusion no mind can adequately foreshadow."

Not content with the history he had just completed in English, Shoghi Effendi now turned his thoughts to the loving and loyal Community of Bahá'u'lláh's long-suffering and persecuted fol'owers in His native land and began the composition of another memorial, written in Persian and Arabic, to the first hundred years of the Bahá'í Faith. This was a comparable, though shorter version of the same subject, different in nature but no less splendid in both the facts it presented and the brilliancy of its language.

For the next thirteen years Shoghi Effendi neither translated nor wrote any more books. It is our great loss that he no longer had the time to do so. The international community of the Faith he had been at such pains to build up since 1921 had now reached such proportions that it consumed his time and strength and left little of either for the intensely creative work he was so richly endowed by nature to produce.

Until the end of his days Shoghi Effendi continued to inspire the Bahá'í world with his instructions and thoughts; words of great power and significance, equal in bulk to a number of volumes, flowed from his pen. But an epoch had ended with the close of the war and the increase in administrative activity all over the world. Although his driving power never left him, and the hours of work he spent on the Cause of God each day never diminished until he passed away, Shoghi Effendi was deeply tired.

The life work of Shoghi Effendi might well be divided into four major aspects: his translations of the Words of Bahá'u'lláh, the Báb, 'Abdu'l-Bahá and Nabíl's narrative; his own writings such as the history of a century, published as *God Passes By*, as well as an uninterrupted stream of instructive communications from his pen which pointed out to the believers the significance, the time and the method of the building up of their administrative institutions; an unremitting programme to expand and consolidate the material assets of a world-wide Faith, which not only involved the completion, erection or beautification of the Bahá'í Holy Places at the World Centre, but the construction of Houses of Worship and the acquisition of national and local headquarters and endowments in various countries throughout the East and the West; and, above all, a masterly orientation of thought towards the concepts enshrined in the teachings of the Faith and orderly classification of those teachings into what might well be described as a vast panoramic view of the meaning, implications, destiny and purpose of the religion of Bahá'u'lláh, indeed of religious truth itself in its portrayal of man as the apogee of God's creation, evolving towards the consummation of his development—the establishment of the Kingdom of God on earth.

IX

CREATION OF A WORLD HEADQUARTERS

The development of the World Centre of the Faith under the aegis of the Guardian represents one of the major achievements of his life and can only be compared in importance to the spread and consolidation of the Cause itself throughout the entire globe. Of the unique significance of this Centre Shoghi Effendi wrote that it was: ". . . the Holy Land—the Qiblih of a world community, the heart from which the energizing influences of a vivifying Faith continually stream, and the seat and centre around which the diversified activities of a divinely appointed Administrative Order revolve—".

When in 1921 Shoghi Effendi assumed the responsibilities conferred upon him in the *Will and Testament* of 'Abdu'l-Bahá, the Bahá'í holdings in Haifa and 'Akká consisted of the Shrine of Bahá'u'lláh in Bahjí, which was situated in a house belonging to the Afnán heirs of the daughter of Bahá'u'lláh, in whose home He had been interred after His ascension; the Shrine of the Báb on Mt. Carmel, surrounded by a few plots of land, purchased during the lifetime of 'Abdu'l-Bahá, on one of which stood the Oriental Pilgrim House; the house of 'Abbúd, where Bahá'u'lláh had resided for many years in 'Akká and in which He revealed the *Kitáb-i-Aqdas*; and the house of 'Abdu'l-Bahá in Haifa. The Mansion of Bahá'u'lláh, adjoining His Shrine, was occupied by the Arch-Covenant-breaker Muḥammad 'Alí; and the title to almost all the Bahá'í properties was registered either in the names of various members of the family or those of a few Bahá'ís. So insecure was the entire legal position of the Faith and its properties that the work Shoghi Effendi accomplished during his ministry in safeguarding and adding to these Holy Places, in extending the lands surrounding them, in registering these lands, in many instances in the names of locally incorporated Palestine Branches of various National Bahá'í Assemblies, and in securing exemption from municipal and national taxes for them, is little short of miraculous. When we remember that his position in 1922 was so precarious that Muḥammad 'Alí was emboldened to seize the keys of Bahá'u'lláh's Holy Tomb, that many Muslim and Christian elements, jealous of the universal favour 'Abdu'l-Bahá had enjoyed at the end of His life, were only too anxious to discredit His young successor in the eyes of the authorities, and that Shoghi Effendi himself had been immediately overwhelmed by grave problems of every conceivable nature, within and without the Cause, we cannot but marvel anew at the wisdom and statesmanship that characterized his conduct of affairs at the World Centre.

The Heroic Age of the Faith had passed. What Shoghi Effendi termed the Formative Age dawned with his own ministry, and was shaped for all time by him. Fully realizing that neither his own station nor his capacities were the same as those of his beloved Master, Shoghi Effendi refused to imitate Him in any way, in dress, in habits, in manner. To do so would have been, he believed, completely lacking in both judgement and respect. A new day had come to the Cause, new methods were required. This was to be the era of emancipation of the Faith, of recognition of its independent status, of the establishment of its Order, of the up-building of its institutions. 'Abdu'l-Bahá had come to the Holy Land a prisoner and exile; although He could proclaim, during His travels in the West and through His letters, the independent character of the Cause of His Father, locally He could not, at the end of His life, break through the chrysalis of common custom that had bound Him so long to the predominantly Muslim community; to do things ungracefully and hurtfully was no part of the Bahá'í Teachings. But Shoghi Effendi, returning from his studies in England, young, western in training and habit, was now in a position to do this. However much loved and esteemed 'Abdu'l-Bahá had been, He was not viewed as the Head of an independent world religion but rather as the saintly protagonist of a great spiritual philosophy of universal brotherhood, a distinguished notable among other notables in Palestine. By sheer force of personality He had dominated those around Him. But Shoghi Effendi knew he could never do this in the circumstances surrounding him at the outset of his Guardianship, neither had he any desire to do so. His function everywhere—but particularly at the World Centre—was to win recognition for the Cause as a world religion entitled to the same status and prerogatives that other religions such as Christianity, Islám and Judaism, enjoyed.

During the first two decades of his ministry Shoghi Effendi had more or less close personal contact with various High Commissioners and District Commissioners and through this he was able to win back the keys of Bahá'u'lláh's Tomb and assert his undisputed right to its custody, to obtain possession of the Mansion of Bahá'u'lláh, to receive permission to bury 'Abdu'l-Bahá's closest relatives in the vicinity of the Báb's Shrine, in the centre of a residential district on Mt. Carmel, to have the Bahá'í Marriage Certificate accepted by the government on the same footing as that of Jews, Christians and Muslims, and above all, through his persistent efforts, to succeed in impressing upon the British authorities the sacred nature of the Bahá'í holdings in Palestine and in winning from them the exemption from taxes, both municipal and national, which he sought.

Bahjí was always Shoghi Effendi's first preoccupation and he was determined to safeguard not only the Shrine where Bahá'u'lláh lay buried but the last home He had occupied in this world and the buildings and lands that adjoined it. From the time Bahá'u'lláh passed away in 1892 until 1927 Muḥammad 'Alí and his relatives had been in possession of this home, known as the "Qasr" or "Palace" of 'Údí Khammár, a building unique in Palestine for its majestic style of architecture and which had been purchased for Bahá'u'lláh towards the end of His life.

By April 1932 the pilgrims were privileged to sleep overnight in this historic and Sacred Spot and its doors were opened to non-Bahá'í visitors as well, who wandered through its beautiful rooms and gazed on the impressive array of testimonials to the world-wide nature of the Cause, on the innumerable photostatic copies of Bahá'í Assembly incorporations, marriage licenses and other historical material as well as photographs of the martyrs and pioneers of the Faith.

Ever mindful of what was to him the deepest trust of his Guardianship—to fulfil to the letter insofar as lay within his power every wish and instruction of his beloved Master—Shoghi Effendi's second greatest concern at the World Centre was the Shrine of the Báb. The work connected with this second holiest Shrine of the Bahá'í Faith had two aspects: the completion of the building itself and the protection and preservation of its surroundings. The first involved the construction of three additional rooms as well as a superstructure—an entire building in itself—which is undoubtedly one of the most beautiful edifices on the shores of the Mediterranean Sea, and the second the gradual purchase, during a third of a century, of a great protective belt of land surrounding the Shrine and reaching from the top to the bottom of Mt. Carmel. This area of over fifty acres is best discerned at night, as it lies a huge unlighted "V" in the heart of the city, in whose centre seems pinned a golden brooch, the flood-lit Shrine of the Báb, resting majestically on the bosom of the mountain, set off on the velvety black space of its gardens and lands. For thirty-six years Shoghi Effendi devoted himself to the development of this Sacred Spot in the midst of God's Holy Mountain; so impressive, so unique and of such vast proportions was his work there that it seems to me some of his very essence must be incorporated in its stones and soil.

It took more than one hundred years for Bahá'u'lláh, 'Abdu'l-Bahá and Shoghi Effendi to finally discharge the sacred trust which the Báb's remains represented for them, a trust which lasted from the day of His martyrdom in 1850 until the final completion of His Shrine in 1953. From the moment when He was apprised of the execution of the Báb until He ascended in 1892 Bahá'u'lláh had watched over that Sacred Dust, supervising its removal from one place of concealment to another. During a visit to Mt. Carmel He had pointed out to 'Abdu'l-Bahá with His own hand where the Báb's body was to rest forever, instructing Him to purchase this piece of land and bring the hidden remains from Persia and inter them there. 'Abdu'l-Bahá, Himself a prisoner, succeeded in having the small wooden box containing the remains of the Báb and His martyred companion conveyed, by caravan and boat, from Persia to 'Akká. When the first group of western pilgrims visited the prison-city in the winter of 1898–1899, this precious casket was already concealed in the Master's home, its presence a carefully guarded secret.

One day in 1915, as 'Abdu'l-Bahá stood on the steps of His home and looked up at the Báb's Tomb, He remarked to one of His companions: "The sublime Shrine has remained unbuilt. Ten–twenty thousand pounds are required. God willing it will be accomplished. We have carried its construction to this stage." To a pilgrim He had said: "The Shrine of the Báb will be built in the most beautiful and majestic style", and had even gone so far as to order a Turk in Haifa to make him a sketch of how it would appear when completed. But in spite of the clear concept He had of the nature of the Shrine He desired so much to build for the Forerunner of the Faith, the ultimate task was to fall to Shoghi Effendi.

In everything Shoghi Effendi did he was guided by what he knew to be the desire of the Master. 'Abdu'l-Bahá had succeeded, by 1907, in completing only six of the nine rooms which would compose a square, in the centre of which the Body of the Báb would repose, and already during that year meetings were held in the ones facing the sea. In 1909, with His own hands He had laid the remains of the Martyr-Herald of the Faith away in their final resting-place. The next year He set out on His western journeys, the war ensued and He passed away. He had, however, expressed His concept of the finished structure: it should have an arcade surrounding the original nine rooms He had planned and be surmounted by a dome. The thought of this plan of the Master never left Shoghi Effendi but its realization seemed very indefinite. Where and when would he find the architect to design such a Shrine and the money to build it?

The answer came in a most unexpected way. In 1940 my mother died in Buenos Aires and my father was left entirely alone, as I was his only child. With that kindness of his which was so incomparable Shoghi Effendi said to me one day that now my mother was dead, my father's place was with us. He invited him to join us and in spite of the war, whose arena was rapidly spreading, my father was able to do so. This marked the beginning of a beautiful partnership. I have never known two people who had such a perfect sense of proportion as Shoghi Effendi and my father and of the two the Guardian's was the finer.

It seems to me, in looking back on Shoghi Effendi's life, that aside from the great sweep of the Faith, whose victories meant so much to him, Martha Root in one way and Sutherland Maxwell in another brought him more deep personal satisfaction than any other believers. They were very much alike in some ways, saintly and modest souls who adored Shoghi Effendi and gladly gave him the best they had in service and loyalty. Though Martha's services were far more important for the Cause, the talents of Sutherland became a medium through which Shoghi Effendi could express at last with ease the great creative and artistic side of his own nature and this gave him both satisfaction and happiness. Until the end of his life my father designed for him stairs, walls, pillars, lights and various entrances to the gardens on Mt. Carmel. In addition to being an experienced architect he drew and painted beautifully and could model and carve anything with his hands.

Having tried my father on various small projects and found him far from wanting, suddenly—I think it was towards the end of 1942—Shoghi Effendi told him he wished him to make a design for the superstructure of the Shrine of the Báb. The Builder had at last been given the vehicle whereby he could realize the plan of 'Abdu'l-Bahá.

In the Oriental Bahá'í Pilgrim House, during the afternoon meeting on May 23, 1944 when the Bahá'í men were gathered in the presence of the Guardian—including many visitors from neighbouring countries—to commemorate the dawn of their Faith a hundred years earlier, Shoghi Effendi had the model brought out and placed on a table for all to see. Two days later he cabled America: ". . . Announce friends joyful tidings hundredth anniversary Declaration Mission Martyred Herald Faith signalized by historic decision to complete structure His sepulchre erected by 'Abdu'l-Bahá site chosen by Bahá'u'lláh. Recently designed model dome unveiled presence assembled believers. Praying early removal obstacles consummation stupendous Plan conceived by Founder Faith and hopes cherished Centre His Covenant."

When this announcement was made the world was approaching the end of the most terrible war in history; the Bahá'ís of the Western Hemisphere had strained themselves to the utmost in order to win the goals of their first Seven Year Plan; the believers were affected by the general economic depletion prevailing in most countries. It was no doubt because of this, and because the Guardian made no effort to inaugurate a Shrine fund, that this project slipped relatively noiselessly into existence and no more was heard of it until on April 11, 1946, Shoghi Effendi instructed Mr. Maxwell to set plans in motion for building the first unit of the Shrine and later himself wrote to the municipal authorities:

Haifa,
Dec. 7th, 1947.

Haifa Local Building and
  Town Planning Commission.
To the Chairman

Dear Sir:
  In connection with the accompanying drawings and application for permission to build, I wish to add a word of explanation.
  The Tomb of the Báb, and of 'Abdu'l-Bahá, so well known to the people of Haifa as Abbas Effendi, is already in existence on Mt.

Carmel in an incomplete form. In its present state, in spite of the extensive gardens surrounding it, it is a homely building with a fortress-like appearance.

It is my intention to now begin the completion of this building by preserving the original structure and at the same time embellishing it with a monumental building of great beauty, thus adding to the general improvement in the appearance of the slopes of Mt. Carmel.

The purpose of this building will, when completed, remain the same as at present. In other words it will be used exclusively as a Shrine entombing the remains of the Báb.

As you will see from the accompanying drawings the completed structure will comprise an arcade of twenty-four marble or other monolith columns surmounted by an ornamental balustrade, on the first floor or ground floor of the building. It is this part of the building that we wish to begin work on at once, leaving the intermediary section and the dome, which will surmount the whole edifice when completed, to be carried on in the future, if possible at an early date after the completion of the ground floor arcade.

The Architect of this monumental building is Mr. W. S. Maxwell, F.R.I.B.A., F.R.A.I.C., R.C.A., the well-known Canadian architect, whose firm built the Chateau Frontenac Hotel in Quebec, the House of Parliament in Regina, the Art Gallery, Church of the Messiah, various Bank buildings, etc., in Montreal. I feel the beauty of his design for the completion of the Báb's Tomb will add greatly to the appearance of our city and be an added attraction for visitors.

Yours truly,
Shoghi Rabbani

The first historic steps had been taken but the obstacles in the way of the realization of this plan grew to what seemed insurmountable proportions. The British Mandate was nearing its end; Palestine was rocked by civil strife and was soon to be engulfed in a local war. Enquiries showed that the quarries from which suitable stone could be procured for the Shrine locally lay so near the Lebanese frontier that the owners could give no idea of when they could start deliveries. In addition to this the tremendous amount of carved material on the building would require a corps of expert workers and such labour was practically unavailable in the country. In view of this Shoghi Effendi came to another decision which was typical of his practical and audacious mind: he would see if part of the work could be done in Italy.

A letter, dated April 6, 1948, which I wrote on behalf of the Guardian to Dr. Ugo Giachery conveys very clearly the situation at that time: ". . . Mr. Maxwell . . . because of various difficulties . . . has not been able to place any contracts for the actual work to be carried out here in Palestine. However, he has been in touch with an Italian firm in Carrara about placing contracts for the granite columns which will surround the building on the first floor. He is now proceeding to Italy primarily to place the contract for these, and, if suitable stone, matching the Palestinian stone which will be used here can be found, to also place additional contracts for the capitals and certain pieces of the carved ornamentation . . . as Mr. Maxwell is now 74, though in the best of health, we hope you will take good care of him . . . Things are so acute here that it is extremely important that they get through with their business and return to Palestine . . ."

In such a storm yet another step in the unbelievably troubled history of the Báb's remains and the building of His Tomb was undertaken.

When the Shrine he had erected with so much love and care was completed, Shoghi Effendi, recognizing in it an essentially feminine quality of beauty and purity, called it the "Queen of Carmel". He described it as "enthroned on God's Holy Mountain, crowned with glowing gold, robed in shimmering white and girdled with emerald green, a sight enchanting every eye, whether viewed from the air, the sea, the plain or the hill."

There can be little doubt that upon reading the *Will and Testament* of 'Abdu'l-Bahá Shoghi Effendi's first thought was the speedy establishment of the Supreme Administrative Body of the Bahá'í Faith, the Universal House of Justice. One of his earliest acts, in 1922, had been to summon to Haifa old and key believers to discuss this matter with him. He repeatedly mentioned it in his communications—indeed in his first letter to Persia, written on January 16, 1922 he refers to it and states that he will announce to the friends later the preliminary arrangements for its election. There was never any question in his mind as to its function and significance; in March 1923 he had described it as "that Supreme Council that will guide, organize and unify the affairs of the Movement throughout the world". There can be no doubt that two forces were at work in the Guardian in those first days of his ministry; one was his youthful eagerness to speedily carry out all the instructions of his beloved Master, which included the establishment of the Universal House of Justice; and the other was the Divine guidance and protection promised him in the Will; the latter modified the former. Over and over again Shoghi Effendi essayed to put in motion at least the preliminaries for electing this Supreme Body—and over and over again the Hand of Providence manipulated events in such a way that premature action became impossible. At the consultations he held in 1922 it must have suddenly become apparent to him that however highly desirable even a preliminary stage in the formation of the Universal House of Justice might be, it was dangerous to take such a step at that time. The firm administrative foundation required to elect and support it was lacking as well as a sufficient reservoir of qualified and well-informed believers to draw from.

From an Indian pilgrim's notes in a letter to a friend, written in Haifa on June 15, 1929, we find the following: "Shoghi Effendi says . . . so long as the various National Assemblies do not have stabilized, well organized positions, it would be impossible to establish even an informal House of Justice. He wants us to at once draw up a constitution of the National Assembly on the lines of the American Trust and get it registered with the Government of India, if possible as a religious body, otherwise as a commercial body . . . Shoghi Effendi has urged in his recent letters to Eastern countries to have National Assemblies recognized as Religious Courts of Justice by local Governments . . ."

It is of interest to note that in a letter to Mrs. Stannard, who was in charge of the International Bahá'í Bureau in Geneva—an office designed to promote in Europe the affairs of the Faith as well as to stimulate its international functions throughout the world and which was constantly encouraged and directed by the Guardian in its work—Shoghi Effendi writes, in August 1926, that he wishes the Bahá'í Bulletin it publishes to be "in the three dominant languages in Europe, i.e., English, French and German . . . I have expressed in my cable to you my readiness to extend regular and financial assistance to you in order to ensure that the proposed circular will be published in the three recognized official languages of the western section of the Bahá'í world . . . Your Centre in Switzerland and the Bahá'í Esperanto Magazine published at Hamburg are both destined to shoulder some of the functions and responsibilities which will in future be undertaken by the International Bahá'í Assembly when formed."

In many such references, particularly in the first ten years of his ministry, Shoghi Effendi reveals that he is constantly anticipating the formation of some kind of International Secretariat or Council pending the election of the Universal House of Justice itself, the functions, significance and importance of which were growing in his mind.

From the very beginning Shoghi Effendi concentrated on multiplying and strengthening the "various Assemblies, local and National". As early as 1924, he stated they constituted "the bedrock upon the strength of which the Universal House is in future to be firmly established and raised." Almost invariably, in later years, when he called for the formation of new national bodies, the Guardian used phrases such as the following in his cable to the Fourth European Teaching Conference in 1951: ". . . Future edifice Universal House of Justice depending for its stability on sustaining strength pillars erected diversified communities East West, destined derive added power through emergence three National Assemblies . . . awaits rise establishment similar institutions European mainland . . ." In anticipation of the election of that august Body Shoghi Effendi made statements that, added to the words of its Founder, Bahá'u'lláh, and the clear and unmistakable powers and prerogatives conferred upon it by 'Abdu'l-Bahá in His *Will and Testament*, cannot but buttress the strength and facilitate the tasks of that Universal House for at least a thousand years. Shoghi Effendi said the Universal House of Justice would be the "nucleus and forerunner" of the New World Order; he said "that future House" was a House "posterity will regard as the last refuge of a tottering civilization"; it would be "the last unit crowning the structure of the embryonic World Order of Bahá'u'lláh"; it was "the highest legislative body in the administrative hierarchy of the Faith" and its "supreme elective institution". The Guardian stated: "To the Trustees of the House of Justice" Bahá'u'lláh "assigns the duty of legislating on matters not expressly provided in His Writings, and promises that God will *'inspire them with whatsoever He willeth,'*" and wrote that: ". . . the powers and prerogatives of the Universal House of Justice, possessing the exclusive right to legislate on matters not explicitly revealed in the Most Holy Book; the ordinance exempting its members from any responsibility to those whom they represent, and from the obligation to conform to their views, convictions or sentiments; the specific provisions requiring the free and democratic election by the mass of the faithful of the Body that constitutes the sole legislative organ in the world-wide Bahá'í Community—these are among the features which combine to set apart the Order identified with the Revelation of Bahá'u'lláh from any of the existing systems of human government."

In November 1950 the Guardian sent cables inviting the first of that group who later became members of the International Bahá'í Council to come to Haifa. Like almost everything he did, first it began to dawn and later the sun of the finished concept rose above the horizon. When Luṭfu'lláh Ḥakim (the first to arrive), Jessie and Ethel Revell, followed by Amelia Collins and Mason Remey were all gathered at table one day in the Western Pilgrim House, with Gladys Weeden and her husband Ben who were already living there, the Guardian announced to us his intention of constituting, out of that group, an International Council, we were all overcome by the unprecedented nature of this step he was taking and the infinite bounty it conferred upon those present as well as the entire Bahá'í world. It was not, however, until January 9, 1951 that he released this news through an historic cable: "Proclaim National Assemblies East West weighty epoch making decision formation first International Bahá'í Council forerunner supreme administrative institution destined emerge fullness time within precincts beneath shadow World Spiritual Centre Faith already established twin cities 'Akká Haifa."

The fulfilment of the prophecies of both Bahá'u'lláh and 'Abdu'l-Bahá, through the establishment of an independent Jewish State after the lapse of two thousand years, the unfoldment of the portentous historic undertaking associated with the construction of the superstructure of the Báb's Shrine, the now adequate maturity of the nine vigorously functioning National Assemblies, had all combined to induce him to make this historic decision, which was the most significant milestone in the evolution of the Administrative Order during thirty years. In that cable Shoghi Effendi went on to say that this new institution had a three-fold function: to forge links with the authorities in the newly-emerged State; to assist him in building the Shrine (only the arcade of which had then been completed); and to conduct negotiations with the civil authorities as regards matters of personal status. Further functions would be added as this first "embryonic International Institution" developed into an officially recognized Bahá'í Court, was transformed into an elected body and reached its final efflorescence in the Universal House of Justice; this in turn would find its fruition in the erection of many auxiliary institutions, constituting the World Administrative Centre. This message, so thrilling in portent, burst upon the Bahá'í world like a clap of thunder. Like a skilled engineer, locking the component parts of his machine together, Shoghi Effendi had now buckled into place the frame that would eventually support the crowning unit—the Universal House of Justice.

Fourteen months later, on March 8, 1952, Shoghi Effendi, in a long cable to the Bahá'í world, announced the enlargement of the International Bahá'í Council: "Present membership now comprises Amatu'l-Bahá Rúḥíyyih chosen liaison between me and Council. Hands Cause Mason Remey, Amelia Collins, Ugo Giachery, Leroy Ioas, President, Vice-President, Member-at-Large, Secretary-General respectively. Jessie Revell, Ethel Revell, Lotfullah Hakim, Treasurer, Western and Eastern Assistant Secretaries." The original membership had been changed through the departure of Mr. and Mrs. Weeden, for reasons of health, the arrival of Mr. Ioas, who had offered his services to the Guardian, and the inclusion of Dr. Giachery, who continued to reside in Italy and supervise the construction of the Shrine—every single stone of which was quarried, cut, and carved in that country and then shipped to Haifa and the golden tiles of whose dome were ordered in Holland—and to act as the agent of Shoghi Effendi in ordering and purchasing many other things required in the Holy Land. In May 1955 the Guardian announced that he had raised the number of members of the International Bahá'í Council to nine through the appointment of Sylvia Ioas.

Between the first and second messages Shoghi Effendi sent informing the Bahá'í world of the formation and membership of the International Bahá'í Council, he took another fundamental step in the historic development of the World Centre of the Faith through the official announcement of the appointment, on December 24, 1951, of the first contingent of the Hands of the Cause of God, twelve in number, and equally allocated between the Holy Land, the Asiatic, American and European continents. The people raised by the Guardian at that time to this illustrious rank were Sutherland Maxwell, Mason Remey and Amelia Collins who became Hands of the Cause of God in the Holy Land; Valíyu'lláh Varqá, Ṭarázu'lláh Samandarí and 'Alí Akbar Furútan in Asia; Horace Holley, Dorothy Baker and Leroy Ioas in America; George Townshend,

Hermann Grossmann and Ugo Giachery in Europe. Two months later, on February 29, 1952, Shoghi Effendi announced to the friends in East and West that he had raised the number of the Hands of the Cause of God to nineteen through nominating Fred Schopflocher in Canada, Corinne True in the United States, Dhikru'lláh Khádem and Shu'á'u'lláh 'Alá'í in Persia, Adelbert Mühlschlegel in Germany, Músá Banání in Africa and Clara Dunn in Australia. In making these two appointments of Hands of the Cause Shoghi Effendi said that the hour was now ripe for him to take this step in accordance with the provisions of 'Abdu'l-Bahá's Testament and that it was paralleled by the preliminary measure of the formation of the International Bahá'í Council, destined to culminate in the emergence of the Universal House of Justice. He announced that the august body of the Hands was invested, in conformity with 'Abdu'l-Bahá's Testament, with the two-fold sacred function of the propagation of the Faith and the preservation of its unity.

In Shoghi Effendi's last message to the Bahá'í world, dated October 1957, he announced he had designated "yet another contingent of the Hands of the Cause of God . . . The eight now elevated to this exalted rank are: Enoch Olinga, William Sears and John Robarts, in West and South Africa; Hasan Balyuzi and John Ferraby in the British Isles; Collis Featherstone and Rahmatu'lláh Muhájir, in the Pacific area; and Abú'l-Qásim Faizí in the Arabian Peninsula—a group chosen from four continents of the globe, and representing the Afnán, as well as the black and white races and whose members are derived from Christian, Muslim, Jewish and Pagan backgrounds."

The Guardian, in a two-month period in 1952, created a body of one Váhid (Nineteen) of the Hands of the Cause and he kept them at this number until 1957, when he added eight more, thus bringing them to three multiples of nine. Whenever one of the original nineteen passed away, Shoghi Effendi appointed another Hand. Two of the Hands thus appointed were raised to the position occupied by their fathers, thus the "mantle" of my father fell on my shoulders on March 26, 1952, after the death of Sutherland Maxwell; and 'Alí Muhammad Varqá was appointed to succeed his father on November 15, 1955 and also became the Trustee of the Huqúq in his place. After Dorothy Baker was killed in an accident, Paul Haney was made a Hand of the Cause on March 19, 1954 and following the passing of Fred Schopflocher, Jalál Kházeh was elevated to the same rank on December 7, 1953; not long after George Townshend's death the Guardian appointed Agnes Alexander on March 27, 1957; thus the number of nineteen was maintained by him until the third contingent of Hands was nominated in his last great message at the midway point of the World Crusade.

Between January 9, 1951 and March 8, 1952, remarkable and far-reaching changes took place in the Administrative Order of the Faith at its World Centre, changes which, Shoghi Effendi wrote, at long last signified the erection of the "machinery of its highest institutions", "the supreme Organs of its unfolding Order" which were now, in their "embryonic form" developing around the Holy Shrines. In his writings he had pointed out to the believers that the progress and unfoldment of Bahá'u'lláh's World Order was guided by the directives and the spiritual powers released through three mighty "charters", which he said had set in motion three distinct processes, the first given to us by Bahá'u'lláh Himself in the *Tablet of Carmel*, and the other two from the pen of the Master, namely, His *Will and Testament* and His *Tablets of the Divine Plan*. The first operated "in a land which", Shoghi Effendi stated, "geographically, spiritually and administratively, constitutes the heart of the entire planet", "the Holy Land, the Centre and Pivot round which the divinely appointed, fast multiplying institutions of a world-encircling, relentlessly marching Faith revolve", "the Holy Land, the Qiblih of a world community, the heart from which the energizing influences of a vivifying Faith continuously stream, and the seat and centre around which the diversified activities of a divinely appointed Administrative Order revolve". The hub of this *Tablet of Carmel* was those words of Bahá'u'lláh that *"ere long will God sail His Ark upon thee and will manifest the people of Bahá who have been mentioned in the Book of Names"*; the *"people of Bahá"*, Shoghi Effendi explained, signified the members of the Universal House of Justice.

Whereas the Charter of the *Will and Testament* of the Master operated throughout the world through the erection of those administrative institutions He had so clearly defined in it, and the Charter of His *Tablets of the Divine Plan* was concerned with the spiritual conquest of the entire planet through the teachings of Bahá'u'lláh and likewise had the globe itself as its theatre of operations, the *Tablet of Carmel* cast its illumination and its bounties literally upon Mt. Carmel, upon "that consecrated Spot which," Shoghi Effendi wrote, "under the wings of the Báb's overshadowing Sepulchre . . . is destined to evolve into the focal Centre of those world-shaking, world-embracing, world-directing administrative institutions, ordained by Bahá'u'lláh and anticipated by 'Abdu'l-Bahá, and which are to function in consonance with the principles that govern the twin institutions of the Guardianship and the Universal House of Justice."

The significance of the "unfolding glory" of these institutions at the World Centre was reflected in many messages sent by Shoghi Effendi during the last years of his life, messages which stirred a man like George Townshend to write to him in a letter dated January 14, 1952, sent at the time he thanked the Guardian for the bounty of being made a Hand: "Permit me to pay you a humble tribute of the utmost admiration and gratitude for the nearing vision of the Victory of God which you almost by your sole might now have spread before the astonished Bahá'í world."

In the course of these messages Shoghi Effendi revealed both the station and some of the functions of his newly-created body of Hands. He hailed the unfoldment, during the "opening years" of the second epoch of the Formative Age of this Dispensation, of that "august institution" which Bahá'u'lláh Himself had not only foreshadowed but a few members of which He had already appointed during His own lifetime and which 'Abdu'l-Bahá had formally established in His *Will and Testament*. In addition to the support the Hands of the Cause in the Holy Land had already given him, through erecting the Báb's Shrine, reinforcing the ties with the State of Israel, extending the international endowments in the Holy Land, and initiating preliminary measures for the establishment of the Bahá'í World Administrative Centre, they had also taken part in the four great Intercontinental Teaching Conferences held during the Holy Year, from October 1952 to October 1953, at which they represented the Guardian of the Faith, and after which, at his request, they had travelled extensively in North, Central and South America, Europe, Asia and Australia. This body, Shoghi Effendi said in April 1954, was now entering upon the second phase of its evolution, signalized by the forging of ties between it and the National Spiritual Assemblies engaged in the prosecution of the Ten Year Plan; the fifteen Hands who resided outside the Holy Land should, during the Riḍván period, appoint in each continent separately, from among the believers of that continent, Auxiliary Boards whose members would act as "deputies", "assistants" and "advisers" to the Hands and increasingly assist in the promotion of the Ten Year Crusade. These Boards were to consist of nine members each in America, Europe and Africa, seven in Asia and two in Australia. The Boards were responsible to the Hands of their respective continents; the Hands, on their part, were to keep in close contact with the National Assemblies in their areas and inform them of the activities of their Boards; they were also to keep in close touch with the Hands of the Cause in the Holy Land, who were destined to act as the liaison between them and the Guardian. At this time Shoghi Effendi inaugurated Continental Bahá'í Funds for the work of the Hands, opening these Funds by himself contributing one thousand pounds to each.

A year later Shoghi Effendi nominated the thirteen Hands of the Cause he wished to attend as his representatives the thirteen conventions to be held in 1957 to elect new National Assemblies; from the time he formally appointed Hands of the Cause until his death he constantly used them for this purpose. In 1957, exactly four months before he passed away, Shoghi Effendi, in a lengthy cable, informed the believers that the "triumphant consummation series historic enterprises" and the "evidences increasing hostility without" and "persistent machinations within" foreshadowing "dire contests destined range Army Light forces darkness both secular religious" necessitated a closer association between the Hands in five continents and the National Assemblies to jointly investigate the "nefarious activities internal enemies adoption wise effective measures counteract their treacherous schemes" in order to protect the mass of the believers and to arrest the spread of the evil influence of these enemies. At the beginning of this cable Shoghi Effendi points out that the Hands, in addition to their newly-assumed responsibility of assisting the National Spiritual Assemblies in the prosecution of the World Spiritual Crusade, must now fulfil their "primary obligation" of watching over and protecting the Bahá'í World Community, in close collaboration with the National Assemblies. He ends this portentous message with these words: "Call upon Hands National Assemblies each continent separately establish henceforth direct contact deliberate whenever feasible frequently as possible exchange reports to be submitted by their respective Auxiliary Boards National Committees exercise unrelaxing vigilance carry out unflinchingly sacred inescapable duties. Security precious Faith preservation spiritual health Bahá'í Communities vitality faith its individual members proper functioning its laboriously erected institutions fruition its worldwide enterprises fulfilment its ultimate destiny all directly dependent befitting discharge weighty responsibilities now resting members these two institutions occupying with Universal House Justice next institution Guardianship foremost rank divinely ordained administrative hierarchy World Order Bahá'u'lláh."

The last great message of Shoghi Effendi's life—dated October, but actually conceived in August—again reinforced the significance and importance of the institution of the Hands of the Cause. In it Shoghi Effendi not only appointed his last contingent of Hands but took the highly significant step of inaugurating a further Auxiliary Board in each continent: "This latest addition to the band of the high-ranking officers of a fast evolving World Administrative Order, involving a further expansion of the august institution of the Hands of the Cause of God, calls for, in view of the recent assumption by them of their sacred responsibility as protectors of the Faith, the appointment by these same Hands, in each continent separately, of an additional Auxiliary Board, equal in membership to the existing one, and charged with the specific duty of watching over the security of the Faith, thereby complementing the function of the original Board, whose duty will henceforth be exclusively concerned with assisting the prosecution of the Ten Year Plan."

It is almost inconceivable to imagine what state the Bahá'í world would have been plunged into after Shoghi Effendi's death if he had not referred in these terms to the Hands of the Cause, and if he had not so clearly charged the National Assemblies to collaborate with the Hands in their primary function as protectors of the Faith. Can we not discern, in these last messages, a black cloud the size of a man's hand on the horizon?

It was the duty and right of Shoghi Effendi, explicitly stated in the Master's Will, to appoint the Hands of the Cause. With one exception he made only posthumous appointments during the first thirty years of his ministry. It was the highest honour he could confer on a believer, living or dead, and he so named many Bahá'ís, East and West, after their death; the most outstanding of these was Martha Root, whom he characterized as the foremost Hand raised up in the first century of the Faith since the inception of its Formative Age. The one exception was Amelia Collins. He cabled her on November 22, 1946: "Your magnificent international services exemplary devotion and now this signal service impel me to inform you your elevation rank Hand Cause Bahá'u'lláh. You are first be told this honour in lifetime. As to time announcement leave it my discretion". It was the custom of Shoghi Effendi to inform each Hand of his elevation to this position at the time he made public his choice. Three of them, Fred Schopflocher and Músá Banání, who were in Haifa as pilgrims at the time he made his announcement, and myself, he informed to our faces. To try to describe with what feelings of stupefaction, of unworthiness and awe the news of this honour overwhelmed the recipients of it would be impossible. Each heart received it as a shaft that aroused an even greater love for and loyalty to the Guardian than that heart had ever held before.

The long years of preparation—outside in the body of the Bahá'í world through the erection of the machinery of the Administrative Order, inside its heart through the erection of the superstructure of the Shrine of the Báb and the general consolidation of the World Centre—had involved the creation of a Spot suitable to form the "focal centre", as Shoghi Effendi termed it, of the mightiest institutions of the Faith. This Spot was no less than the resting-places of the mother, sister and brother of 'Abdu'l-Bahá, those "three incomparably precious souls", as he called them, "who, next to the three Central Figures of our Faith, tower in rank above the vast multitude of the heroes, Letters, martyrs, hands, teachers and administrators of the Cause of Bahá'u'lláh."

It had long been the desire of the Greatest Holy Leaf to lie near her mother, who was buried in 'Akká, as was her brother, Midhí. But when Bahíyyih Khánum passed away in 1932 she had been befittingly interred on Mt. Carmel near the Shrine of the Báb. Shoghi Effendi conceived the idea of transferring the remains of her mother and brother, so unsuitably buried in 'Akká, to the vicinity of her resting-place and in 1939 he ordered in Italy twin marble monuments, similar in style to the one he had erected over her own grave.

The American Assembly, on December 5th, received the following cable from Shoghi Effendi: "Blessed remains Purest Branch and Master's mother safely transferred hallowed precincts Shrines Mount Carmel. Long inflicted humiliation wiped away. Machinations Covenant-breakers frustrate plan defeated. Cherished wish Greatest Holy Leaf fulfilled. Sister brother mother wife 'Abdu'l-Bahá reunited one spot designed constitute focal centre Bahá'í Administrative Institutions at Faith's World Centre. Share joyful news entire body American believers. Shoghi Rabbani." The signing of the Guardian's full name was required as we were at war and all correspondence was censored.

The exquisite taste and sense of proportion, so characteristic of everything the Guardian created, is nowhere better reflected than in the marble monuments he erected over the four graves of those close relatives of 'Abdu'l-Bahá. Designed in Italy according to Shoghi Effendi's own instructions and executed there in white Carrara marble, they were shipped to Haifa and placed, in the decade between 1932 and 1942, in their predestined positions, around which he constructed the beautiful gardens which are commonly referred to as the "Monument Gardens" and which he evolved into the fulcrum of that arc on Mt. Carmel about which are to cluster in future the International Institutions of the Faith.

At last Shoghi Effendi, so powerfully guided from on high, had succeeded in establishing his "focal Centre". But it was not until over fourteen years later that he was in a position to inform the Bahá'í world that he was now taking a step which would "usher in the establishment of the World Administrative Centre of the Faith on Mt. Carmel—the Ark referred to by Bahá'u'lláh in the closing passages of His Tablet of Carmel". This step was none other than the erection of an international Bahá'í Archives.

Shortly after the addition of three rooms to the Báb's Shrine, in the early thirties, Shoghi Effendi had established an Archives at the World Centre, housed temporarily in these quarters and based on the precious relics of both Bahá'u'lláh and 'Abdu'l-Bahá which were already in the possession of the Master's family and many of the old Bahá'ís living in Palestine.

As the Bahá'ís learned more about these Archives and the pilgrims visited them in increasing numbers and saw how safely historic and sacred material was preserved, how beautifully exhibited, how reverently displayed, they began to send from Persia truly priceless articles associated with the three Central Figures of the Faith as well as its martyrs and heroes. Amongst these most welcome additions were objects belonging to the Báb, contributed by the Afnáns, which greatly enriched the collection.

It was in 1954, during the first year of the World Crusade, that Shoghi Effendi decided to start on what he said was "the first of the major edifices destined to constitute the seat of the World Bahá'í Administrative Centre to be established on Mt. Carmel". His choice fell on a building he considered both urgently needed and feasible, namely, one to house the sacred and historic relics collected in the Holy Land which were dispersed at that time throughout six rooms in two separate buildings. By Naw-Rúz 1954, the excavation for its foundations had begun. Shoghi Effendi was, in choosing his initial design for buildings of the importance he had in mind, guided by three things: it must be beautiful, it must be dignified, and it must have a lasting value and not reflect the transient (and to him for the most part very ugly) style of modern buildings being erected in an age of experimentation and groping after new forms. He was a great admirer of Greek architecture and considered the Parthenon in Athens one of the most beautiful buildings ever created; he chose the proportions of the Parthenon as his model, but changed the order of the capitals from Doric to Ionic. After his many suggestions had been incorporated in the final design Shoghi Effendi approved it and what he described as "this imposing and strikingly beautiful edifice" was completed in 1957. It had cost approximately a quarter of a million dollars and was, like the Shrine of the Báb, ordered in Italy, entirely carved and completed there, and shipped to Haifa for erection; not only was each separate stone numbered, but charts showing where each one went facilitated its being placed in its proper position. Except for the foundations and reinforced cement work of floor, walls and ceiling, it would not be incorrect to say it was a building fabricated almost entirely abroad and erected locally.

In his last Riḍván Message to the Bahá'í World Shoghi Effendi's satisfaction with the Archives building he had chosen and erected is clearly reflected; after announcing its completion he wrote that it is "contributing, to an unprecedented degree, through its colourfulness, its classic style and graceful proportions, and in conjunction with the stately, golden-crowned Mausoleum rising beyond it, to the unfolding glory of the central institutions of a World Faith nestling in the heart of God's holy Mountain."

In a message addressed to the Bahá'í world on November 27, 1954—linked by the Guardian once again to the anniversary of his beloved Master's passing—Shoghi Effendi dwelt on the significance of this building: "The raising of this Edifice will in turn," he goes on to say, "herald the construction, in the course of successive epochs of the Formative Age of the Faith, of several other structures, which will serve as the administrative seats of such divinely appointed institutions as the Guardianship, the Hands of the Cause and the Universal House of Justice. These Edifices will, in the shape of a far-flung arc, and following a harmonizing style of architecture, surround the resting-places of the Greatest Holy Leaf, . . . of her brother, . . . and of their mother . . ."

So great was the importance Shoghi Effendi attached to this "arc", the lines of which he had studied very carefully on the ground and which sweeps around on the mountain in the form of a gigantic bow, arched above the resting-places of 'Abdu'l-Bahá's closest relatives, and on the right side of which now stands the Archives, that he announced its completion in his last Riḍván Message in 1957: "the plan designed to insure the extension and completion of the arc serving as a base for the erection of future edifices constituting the World Bahá'í Administrative Centre, has been successfully carried out."

X

THE HEART AND NERVE CENTRE

Underlying, reinforcing, and indeed often making possible such major undertakings as the erection of the superstructure of the Báb's Shrine, the construction of the Archives, the building of the terraces on Mt. Carmel, and many other activities, was the purchase of land, both in Haifa and Bahjí; it was a task to which the Guardian attached great importance and which he pursued throughout all the years of his ministry. Before he passed away he had succeeded in creating great protective rings of land around the holiest of all Shrines, Bahá'u'lláh's Tomb, and around the resting-places of the Báb, 'Abdu'l-Bahá, His mother, sister and brother. In addition to this he had chosen and directed the purchase of the land on Mt. Carmel which would serve as the site of the future Bahá'í Temple to be erected in the Holy Land. If we consider that at the time of 'Abdu'l-Bahá's passing the area of Bahá'í properties on Mt. Carmel probably did not exceed 10,000 square metres, and that Shoghi Effendi had, by 1957, raised this to 230,000 square metres, and that in Bahjí the comparable figures would be 1,000 square metres for 1921 and 257,000 square metres for 1957, we get an idea of his accomplishments in this one field alone. Through the generosity of individual Bahá'ís, through their bequests, through their response to his appeals in times of crisis, through the use of funds he held at the World Centre, Shoghi Effendi succeeded in purchasing land on the scale reflected by these figures and thus metamorphosed the situation of the Faith at its World Centre.

In May 1931 the Guardian cabled the National Spiritual Assembly of the Bahá'ís of the United States and Canada: "American Assembly incorporated as recognized religious body in Palestine entitled hold property as trustees American believers. Mailing title deed property already transferred their name. Prestige Faith greatly enhanced its foundations consolidated love". This was the first step in constituting Palestine Branches—which were later changed to Israel Branches—of various National Assemblies and registering in their names properties in the Holy Land. Although the power of disposing of these properties was entirely vested locally at the World Centre, the prestige of the Faith was greatly enhanced by this move, its Holy Places were buttressed and safeguarded, its world character emphasized in the eyes of the authorities, and national Bahá'í communities were encouraged and strengthened.

At the time of Shoghi Effendi's passing he had already established nine of these Branches, namely, the United States, Canada, Australia, New Zealand, the British Isles, Írán, Pákistán, Alaska and that of the National Spiritual Assembly of the Bahá'ís of India and Burma.

When Shoghi Effendi had built the three additional rooms of the Shrine of the Báb and completed the restoration of the Mansion of Bahá'u'lláh, thus producing local, tangible evidences of the strength of the Bahá'í Community, and had demonstrated to the British authorities, through the victories won over the Covenant-breakers, that he had the solid backing of Bahá'ís all over the world, he set about procuring for the Bahá'í Holy Places exemption from both municipal and government taxes. It was not as difficult to get a building, obviously a place of sacred association and visited by pilgrims, exempted from taxes as it was to secure similar exemptions for the steadily increasing area of land owned by the Faith, most of which was registered in the names of individuals. Because of this the ultimate exemption from all forms of taxation, including customs duty, which Shoghi Effendi obtained for the Bahá'í buildings and holdings throughout the country, was truly a great achievement. The victories in this field were all won in the days of the British Mandate, the Israeli Government accepting the status achieved by the Bahá'ís before the new State was formed in 1948.

On May 10, 1934, Shoghi Effendi cabled America: "Prolonged negotiations Palestine authorities resulted exemption from taxation entire area surrounding dedicated Shrines Mount Carmel" and indicated that he considered this step tantamount to "securing indirect recognition sacredness Faith International Centre . . ."

By thus reading the pleasant tail end of events one does not get any idea of what Shoghi Effendi went through in connection with purchasing, exempting from taxes and safeguarding the properties at the World Centre. In a cable to the American National Assem-

THE YOUNG GUARDIAN IN SWITZERLAND

Shoghi Effendi enjoying the famous springtime fields of wild narcissus flowers above Lac Léman

INTERLAKEN, SWITZERLAND

The weary Guardian, who often spent 10 hours walking in the mountains, surveys his beloved Alpine scenery

SHOGHI EFFENDI IN THE ALPS

The Guardian surveying one of Switzerland's greatest glaciers

RIVERS, MOUNTAINS AND GLACIERS
Shoghi Effendi had all the love of scenic beauty characteristic of his ancestors

THE GUARDIAN BECAME A MOUNTAINEER
Shoghi Effendi (wearing goggles) with a party of climbers and their guides in the Swiss Alps

THE INDOMITABLE ENTHUSIAST
Shoghi Effendi straddling an ice ridge on one of his climbs in the Swiss Alps

THE TOP OF THE MOUNTAIN
Shoghi Effendi (right) at the summit of one of his Swiss Alpine climbs with his guide

SHOGHI EFFENDI AND HIS GUIDE

A very happy young Guardian on top of a Swiss Alp with his guide; Shoghi Effendi carried his own camera with him, no doubt a member of the climb took this photograph

bly, of March 28, 1935, one of innumerable examples of what took place is given: "Contract for purchase and transfer to Palestine Branch American Assembly Dumits property situated centre area dedicated to Shrines on Mount Carmel signed. Four year litigation involving Bahá'í World's petitions Palestine High Commissioner abandoned. Owners require four thousand pounds. Half sum available. Will American believers unitedly contribute one thousand pounds before end of May and remaining one thousand within nine months. Am compelled appeal entire body American Community subordinate national interests of Faith to its urgent paramount requirements at its World Centre," to which the American Assembly replied, two days later, that the American Bahá'í Community "will with one heart fulfil glorious privilege conferred upon it by beloved Guardian".

So many times Shoghi Effendi referred to the Holy Land as the "heart and nerve centre" of the Faith. To protect it, develop it, and noise abroad its glory was part of his function as its Guardian. In addition to his official contacts with government and municipal authorities he maintained courteous and friendly relations with many non-Bahá'ís, of prominence and otherwise. The catholicity of spirit which so strongly characterized the Guardian, his complete lack of any breath of prejudice or fanaticism, the sympathy and courtesy that distinguished him so strongly, are all reflected in his letters and messages to such people. He carried on a lengthy correspondence, during the earliest years of his ministry, with Grand Duke Alexander of Russia, whom it was obvious, from the tone of his letters, he liked. He addresses him as: "My true brother in the service of God!", "My dear brother in the love of God!" The Grand Duke was very interested in a movement called the "Unity of Souls" and Shoghi Effendi encouraged him: "I am more and more impressed", he writes, "by the striking similarity of our aims and principles and I beseech the Almighty to bless His servants in their service to the cause of suffering humanity." The Grand Duke, in a letter to the Guardian writes: ". . . I must confess to you, my dear brother and fellow worker, that in my modest work occasionally I feel discouraged . . . the power of evil forces under the influence of which the majority of humanity is living, is appalling." Shoghi Effendi answers this most beautifully: ". . . I assure my dear fellow-worker in the service of God, that I too feel oftentimes overwhelmed by the rising wave of selfish, gross materialism that threatens to engulf the world, and I feel that however arduous be our common task we must persevere to the very end and pray continually and ardently that the ever-living spirit of God may so fill the souls of men as to cause them to arise with new vision for the service and salvation of humanity. Prayer and individual persistent effort, I feel, must be given greater and wider prominence in these days of stress and gloom . . ."

Shoghi Effendi was in touch not only with Queen Marie of Rumania and a number of her relatives, but with other people of royal lineage, such as Princess Marina of Greece who later became Duchess of Kent, and Princess Kadria of Egypt. To many of these, as well as to men of such prominence as Lord Lamington, a number of former High Commissioners for Palestine, Orientalists, university professors, educators and others, Shoghi Effendi was wont to send copies of the latest *Bahá'í World* volumes or one of his own recently published translations, with his visiting card enclosed. He was always very meticulous—as long as the relationship was one of mutual courtesy and esteem—to send messages of condolence to acquaintances who had suffered a bereavement, expressing his "heartfelt sympathy' at that person's "great loss". Such messages, often sent as cables or wires, deeply touched those who received them and gave him a reputation among them which belied the picture of him the Covenant-breakers did their best to create. He also often congratulated people on the occasion of a marriage or a promotion.

In addition to these personal relationships Shoghi Effendi had far more contact with certain non-Bahá'í organizations than is commonly supposed. This was particularly true of the Esperantists, whose whole object was to bring about the fulfilment of the Bahá'í principle that a universal auxiliary language must be adopted in the interests of World Peace. We have copies of his personal messages to the Universal Congress of Esperantists held in 1927, 1928, 1929, 1930 and 1931, and he no doubt sent many messages of a similar nature at other times. Shoghi Effendi not only responded warmly when there was any overture made to him, but often took the initiative himself in sending Bahá'í representatives, chosen by him, to various conferences whose interests coincided with those of the Bahá'ís. We thus find him writing to the Universal Esperantist Association, in 1927, that Martha Root and Julia Goldman will attend their Danzig Congress as official Bahá'í representatives, and that he trusts this "will serve to strengthen the ties of fellowship that bind the Esperantists and the followers of Bahá'u'lláh, one of whose cardinal principles . . . is the adoption of an international auxiliary language for all humanity." In his letter addressed to the delegates and friends attending this nineteenth Universal Congress of Esperantists he writes:

> My dear fellow workers in the service of humanity,
> I take great pleasure in addressing you and wishing you . . . from all my heart the fullest success in the work you are doing for the promotion of the good of humanity.
> It will interest you, I am sure, to learn that as the result of the repeated and emphatic admonitions of 'Abdu'l-Bahá His many followers even in the most distant villages and hamlets of Persia, where the light of Western civilization has hardly penetrated as yet, as well as in other lands throughout the East, are strenuously and enthusiastically engaged in the study and teaching of Esperanto, for whose future they cherish the highest hopes . . .

The Guardian himself was held in high esteem by many people working for ideals similar to those the Bahá'ís cherish. Sir Francis Younghusband, in 1926, wrote to him in connection with the "World Congress of Faiths": "Now I wish to ask a great favour of you. Once more I want to try and persuade you to come to England to attend the Congress. Your presence here would carry great influence and would be highly appreciated. And we would most willingly defray the expenses you might be put to." The Guardian declined this invitation, but arranged for a Bahá'í paper to be presented. His own plans and work precluded him, he felt, from opening such a door.

In 1925 the Zionist Executive in Jerusalem invited him to attend an event in connection with the establishment of a university there. Shoghi Effendi wired them, on April 1st: "Appreciate kind invitation regret inability to be present. Bahá'ís hope and pray the establishment of this seat of learning may contribute to the revival of a land of hallowed memories for us all and for which 'Abdu'l-Bahá cherished the highest hopes." To this message they replied in cordial terms: "Zionist Executive much appreciate your friendly message and good wishes we trust that newly established university may contribute not only advancement of science and learning but also to better understanding between men which ideal is so well served by Bahá'ís." Twenty-five years later the tie established is still there: "The Hebrew University was very gratified indeed to receive your check for £100.- as the contribution from His Eminence

Shoghi Effendi Rabbani towards the work of this institution . . . We were happy to know that His Eminence is aware of the important work that the University is doing and to receive this generous token of appreciation from him . . ."

A cable of Shoghi Effendi, sent to India in December 1930, is of particular interest because it shows how, up to the very end of her life, he would tenderly include the Greatest Holy Leaf in messages that seemed particularly suitable: "Convey to Indian Asian Women's Conference behalf Greatest Holy Leaf 'Abdu'l-Bahá's sister and myself our genuine profound interest their deliberations. May Almighty guide bless their high endeavours."

Aside from this wide correspondence with prominent individuals as well as various Societies, Shoghi Effendi was wont to receive in his home the visits of many distinguished people, such as Lord and Lady Samuel; Sir Ronald Storrs, another friend of 'Abdu'l-Bahá; Moshe Sharett, later to become one of Israel's most loved and prominent officials; Professor Norman Bentwich and many writers, journalists and notables.

However important were such contacts and exchanges as these, undoubtedly the most important of all such relations was that which the Guardian had with officials at the World Centre, whether under British rule during the Mandate in Palestine or later after the War of Independence and the establishment of the State of Israel.

In all his relationships with both government and municipal officials Shoghi Effendi sought from the very beginning to impress upon them that the Faith was an independent religion, universal in character, and that its permanent World Spiritual and Administrative Centre was situated in the Holy Land. He spent thirty-six years winning from the authorities the recognition and rights that such a status entitled the Bahá'í Faith to enjoy, one aspect of which was that he himself should receive the treatment on official occasions which was his due as the hereditary Head of such a Faith.

The Guardian was on very friendly terms with Colonel Symes, who was none other than that Governor of Phoenicia who spoke at the Master's funeral and attended the fortieth-day meeting in His home. It had been to Colonel Symes that Shoghi Effendi had written, on April 5, 1922, at the time of his withdrawal: "As I am compelled to leave Haifa for reasons of health, I have named as my representative during my absence, the sister of 'Abdu'l-Bahá, Bahíyyih Khánum," and goes on to say: "To assist her to conduct the affairs of the Bahá'í Movement in this country and elsewhere, I have also appointed a committee of the following Bahá'ís [eight men of the local community, three of them the sons-in-law of 'Abdu'l-Bahá] . . . The Chairman of this Committee, to be soon elected by its members, with the signature of Bahíyyih Khánum has my authority to transact any affairs that may need to be considered and decided during my absence. I regret exceedingly to be unable to see you before my departure, that I may express more adequately the satisfaction that I feel to know that your sense of justice will safeguard the interests of the Cause of Bahá'u'lláh whenever called upon to act."

The cordial relations between Symes and Shoghi Effendi and the esteem he evidently had for the character of the Governor are reflected in the letter he wrote to him upon his return: "It is my pleasant duty to inform you of my return to the Holy Land after a prolonged period of rest and meditation and of my assumption of my official functions", and goes on to say: "I had felt after the passing of my beloved Grandfather too exhausted, overwhelmed and sorrowful to be able to conduct efficiently the affairs of the Bahá'í Movement. Now that I feel again restored and refreshed and in a position to resume my arduous duties, I wish to express to you on this occasion my heartfelt gratitude and appreciation for the sympathetic consideration you have shown towards the Movement during my absence." The letter contains, in the next paragraph, an unusual warmth of feeling: "It is a great pleasure and privilege for me to be enabled to renew my acquaintance with you and Mrs. Symes which I am confident will in the course of time grow into warm and abiding friendship." Shoghi Effendi ended it with his "kind regards and best wishes" and simply signed it "Shoghi". The exchange of correspondence with Colonel Symes—who later was knighted, and became Governor-General of the Súdán before and during the second World War—went on for many years, even after his retirement.

Another official, whose position, though not so high, involved directly the affairs of the Bahá'í Community at its World Centre was the District Commissioner. During those years when Shoghi Effendi was beginning to seek recognition for the Faith in tangible privileges, Edward Keith-Roach, O.B.E., held this office. Although a man of an entirely different calibre from Colonel Symes he was nevertheless friendly and helpful and seemed to be fond of Shoghi Effendi, whose correspondence with him runs from 1925 to 1939. Keith-Roach, undoubtedly because he knew the higher authorities would approve, was at times very co-operative not only in facilitating and expediting Shoghi Effendi's work, but in making suggestions which the Guardian sometimes carried out. The first copy we find of a letter from Shoghi Effendi to him is so simple and yet so typical of the warmth with which the Guardian invariably responded to other people's overtures when they were made in the right spirit, that I cannot refrain from quoting it. It was dated simply "Haifa, 25–12–25" and said: "My dear Mr. Keith-Roach: I am touched by your welcome message of good-will and greeting and I hasten to assure you that I fully reciprocate the sentiments expressed in your letter. With best wishes for a happy Christmas, I am yours very sincerely, Shoghi Rabbani".

Throughout Shoghi Effendi's correspondence with both Keith-Roach and Symes there are invitations for them to have tea with him in the gardens on Mt. Carmel, in Colonel Symes's case the invitation sometimes included Mrs. Symes. It was not only Shoghi Effendi's way of extending some hospitality to these officials, but served to show them, by bringing them into the midst of the Bahá'í property, the latest developments and the most recent extension of the gardens and, I have no doubt, he made use of their presence to point out to them his future plans and seek their sympathetic support.

Immediately upon his return to the Holy Land after the Master's passing, Shoghi Effendi pursued the policy of keeping the authorities informed, locally and particularly at the seat of Government in Jerusalem, not only of his plans but his problems and various crises that arose, such as the seizure of the keys of Bahá'u'lláh's Shrine in Bahjí and His House in Baghdád, as well as the persecutions and injustices the Faith was suffering. Commencing with his first letter to the High Commissioner, Sir Herbert Samuel, the friend of 'Abdu'l-Bahá, written on January 16, 1922, Shoghi Effendi maintained this contact with the government until the end of his life, first with the British and later with the Jewish representatives. When Shoghi Effendi left Palestine, so crushed and ill, in the spring of 1922, he had informed Sir Herbert of the measures he had taken to protect the Cause during his absence; after his return to Haifa on December 15th of that same year, he had wired Sir Herbert, on the 19th: "Pray accept my best wishes and kind regards on my return to Holy Land and resumption of my official duties."

In May 1923 we find Shoghi Effendi keeping both the Governor of Haifa and the High Commissioner informed of events, for in a letter to the former he writes that the "Haifa Bahá'í Spiritual Assembly" has been "officially reconstituted and will, in conjunction with me, direct all local affairs in this region . . . I have lately informed H. E. the High Commissioner of this matter . . ." The letter he referred to, dated April 21st, had stated that he enclosed a copy of his recent circular letter to the Bahá'í communities in the West, similar to one written in Persian to the Bahá'í communities in the East, "As you had expressed in your last letter to me the desire to learn of the measures that have been taken to provide for the stable organization of the Bahá'í Movement . . . I shall be only too glad to throw further light on any point which your Excellency might desire to raise in connection with the enclosed letter, or regarding any other matter bearing upon the interests of the Movement in general."

It is impossible to go into the details of the thirty-six years of Shoghi Effendi's relations with the authorities, first of Palestine and later of Israel. That he succeeded in winning and maintaining their good will, their co-operation in his various undertakings at the World Centre, and their recognition of that Centre as the historic heart of the Bahá'í Faith entitled to enjoy the same rights as other Faiths in the Holy Land—indeed, in some respects to enjoy greater rights—all this in the face of the continuous mischief stirred up by various enemies who, whether overtly or covertly, consistently opposed every step he took is a tribute to the extraordinary wisdom and patience that characterized Shoghi Effendi's leadership of the Cause of God.

When Sir Herbert Samuel's term of office was drawing to a close the Guardian sent to him, on June 15, 1925, one of those messages that so effectively forged links of good will with the government, expressing his own and the Bahá'ís abiding sense of gratitude and deep appreciation of the "kind and noble attitude which Your Excellency has taken towards the various problems that have beset them since the passing of 'Abdu'l-Bahá . . . The Bahá'ís . . . remembering the acts of sympathy and good will which the Palestine Administration under your guidance has shown them in the past, will confidently endeavour to contribute their full share to the material prosperity as well as the spiritual advancement of a land so sacred and precious to them all." Sir Herbert replied to this letter in the following terms: ". . . I have been happy during my five years of office to maintain very friendly relations with the Bahá'í Community in Palestine and much appreciate the good will which they have always shown towards the Administration and to myself."

When, in 1929, there was an outbreak of trouble in Palestine, we find the Guardian writing to the then High Commissioner, Sir John Chancellor, on September 10th, a highly significant letter:

> Your Excellency:
>
> I have learned with profound regret of the lamentable occurrences in Palestine, and hasten, while away from home, to offer Your Excellency my heartfelt sympathy in the difficult task with which you are faced.
>
> The Bahá'í Community of Palestine, who, by reason of their Faith, are deeply attached to its soil truly deplore these violent outbursts of religious fanaticism, and venture to hope that, as the influence of Bahá'í ideals extends and deepens, they may be enabled in the days to come to lend increasing assistance to your Administration for the promotion of the spirit of good will and toleration among the religious communities in the Holy Land.
>
> I feel moved to offer Your Excellency in their behalf the enclosed sum as their contribution for the relief of the suffering and needy, irrespective of race or creed . . .

It was during that same year of 1929, that Shoghi Effendi, through the instrumentality of a formal petition to the government made by the Bahá'í Community of Haifa on May 4th, succeeded in obtaining for it permission to administer according to Bahá'í law the affairs of the Community in such matters of personal status as marriage, thus placing it, in this regard, on an equal footing with the Jewish, Muslim and Christian Communities in Palestine. Shoghi Effendi hailed this as "an act of tremendous significance and wholly unprecedented in the history of the Faith in any country". The Guardian's own exclusively Bahá'í marriage was registered and became legal as a result of this recognition he had won for the Faith.

One of the men who occupied the important office of High Commissioner during these years when the Cause was beginning to win in such tangible ways recognition for its independent status, was Sir Arthur Wauchope, a man who, like Colonel Symes, had a personal liking for Shoghi Effendi and who, one suspects, understood how heavy the burden was that rested on the shoulders of the young man who was the Head of the Bahá'í Faith. It was during the period of his administration—which partly coincided with the time Keith-Roach was District Commissioner in Haifa—that some of the greatest victories in winning concessions from the authorities took place, the most important of these, next to the right of the Community to obey some of its own laws governing personal status, being the exemption from taxation of the entire area surrounding the Shrine of the Báb on Mt. Carmel. Unlike most High Commissioners, Sir Arthur seems to have met Shoghi Effendi personally as he refers to this in some of his letters.

In one of them, dated June 26, 1933, Sir Arthur states: "I have received your letter of the 21st June and I hasten to write to thank you for it and to assure you that when the case you mention is referred to me for a decision under the Palestine (Holy Places) Order in Council, it will receive a most careful consideration. I have also received the 'Bahá'í World' for 1930–32. I am most grateful to you for this extremely interesting book . . . I hope to have the pleasure of another visit to the beautiful Gardens on the hillside outside Haifa."

On March 13, 1934, Shoghi Effendi wrote to him: ". . . As the case recently referred to Your Excellency concerning the Bahá'í Shrines on Mt. Carmel has vital international importance, I have asked Mr. ——— to come to Palestine to confer with me about it. I would greatly appreciate Your Excellency's kindly according him an interview in order to clarify one or two points which I do not quite understand and upon which my future action in this matter depends." On May 1st of that same year Shoghi Effendi again wrote to him: "I deeply appreciated the kind message of sympathy and support for the projected plan of the Bahá'í Community to beautify the slopes of Mt. Carmel which you sent to me through Mr. ———. It greatly encouraged me. Unfortunately there are strong and influential interests that are seeking to obstruct the plan. These are in part merely real estate speculators who, in their short-sightedness, are doing their utmost to develop the northern slope of Mt. Carmel for their immediate benefit. More difficult and dangerous for our plan however are those who definitely seek to frustrate the efforts of the followers of Bahá'u'lláh in anything that they may undertake. We believe that these people were back of the case brought against us by the Domets [Dumits], for example, and it was for that reason that we felt justified in our endeavour to have it withdrawn from the jurisdiction of the courts and submitted to Your Excellency's personal consideration . . . With kind regards and renewed expression of my warm appreciation of Your Excellency's sympathy and support . . ." The case in question, which involved four years of litigation, was finally abandoned and in 1935 a contract for the purchase of the Dumit land was signed and Shoghi Effendi cabled the National Assembly in America that he was planning to register it in the name of their Palestine Branch. It is interesting to note that to the Bahá'ís he transliterated the name, but not to the High Commissioner.

Shoghi Effendi had been endeavouring for some time to obtain exemption from taxation on Bahá'í properties surrounding the Báb's Shrine and had finally received news this had been granted. Behind the formal lines of this letter to Sir Arthur, written on May 11, 1934, his inner jubilation over this victory can be sensed:

> Your Excellency,
> The gratifying news has just come to me from the District Commissioner of Haifa that the petition for exemption from taxation of the Bahá'í property holdings on Mt. Carmel has been granted by the Government.
> I hasten to express to Your Excellency for the World Bahá'í Community and myself our deep appreciation of the sympathetic and effective interest which Your Excellency has taken in the matter and which I know must have contributed in large measure to this outcome. And I venture to hope for the continuation of Your Excellency's sympathetic support in our plan to gradually beautify this property for the use and enjoyment of the people of Haifa, for which this action of the Government now opens the way.

To this letter Sir Arthur replied in person, five days later:

> Dear Shoghi Effendi,
> Thank you for your letter of May 11th and the kind words it contains. I have always had great sympathy with your project for beautifying the slopes of Mt. Carmel and I hope this exemption will help you in carrying on your fine work.
>   Yours very sincerely,
>   Arthur Wauchope

In another letter the High Commissioner wrote: "I am most grateful to you for your kind present of the 'Dawn Breakers'. I shall read the book with much interest, for you know how the wonderful story stirred me when I first heard it in Persia. The book is charmingly produced and the illustrations and reproductions add to its attraction. Again with very many thanks for your kind thoughts and welcome gift . . ." There are similar letters thanking the Guardian for *Gleanings* and *Bahá'í World*. The last letter, written in February 1938, by this man, who through his high office assisted Shoghi Effendi in winning a major victory at the World Centre of the Faith, was typical of his courteous kindness: ". . . I had every intention of visiting you in Haifa, where I hoped to see the progress you had made with your garden and say good-bye in person. Unfortunately the many calls on my time . . . made this impossible, so I take this opportunity of bidding you farewell and expressing my best wishes to the Bahá'í Community." At the bottom of the letter he added by hand, "I hear your garden is growing more beautiful every year."

At the time when the Mandate drew to its close and the troubled people of Palestine were preparing to fight it out, the United Nations appointed a Special Committee on Palestine, headed by Justice Emil Sandstrom. On July 9th he wrote to Shoghi Effendi from Jerusalem, stating that under the terms of reference of this committee it was charged with giving most careful consideration to the religious interests in Palestine of Islám, Judaism and Christianity, and goes on to say: "I should appreciate it if you would advise me whether you wish to submit evidence—in a written statement on the religious interests of your Community in Palestine." Because of the historic importance to Bahá'ís of Shoghi Effendi's reply to this letter, I quote it in full:

Mr. Justice Emil Sandstrom,
Chairman,
United Nations Special Committee on Palestine.
Sir:
  Your kind letter of July 9th reached me and I wish to thank you for affording me the opportunity of presenting to you and your esteemed colleagues a statement of the relationship which the Bahá'í Faith has to Palestine and our attitude towards any future changes in the status of this sacred and much disputed land.
  I am enclosing with this letter, for your information, a brief sketch of the history, aims and significance of the Bahá'í Faith, as well as a small pamphlet setting forth its views towards the present state of the world and the lines on which we hope and believe it must and will develop.
  The position of the Bahá'ís in this country is in a certain

measure unique: whereas Jerusalem is the spiritual center of Christendom it is not the administrative center of either the Church of Rome or any other Christian denomination. Likewise although it is regarded by Moslems as the spot where one of its most sacred shrines is situated, the Holy Sites of the Muḥammadan Faith, and the center of its pilgrimages, are to be found in Arabia, not in Palestine. The Jews alone offer somewhat of a parallel to the attachment which the Bahá'ís have for this country inasmuch as Jerusalem holds the remains of their Holy Temple and was the seat of both the religious and political institutions associated with their past history. But even their case differs in one respect from that of the Bahá'ís, for it is in the soil of Palestine that the three central Figures of our religion are buried, and it is not only the center of Bahá'í pilgrimages from all over the world but also the permanent seat of our Administrative Order, of which I have the honor to be the Head.

The Bahá'í Faith is entirely non-political and we neither take sides in the present tragic dispute going on over the future of the Holy Land and its peoples nor have we any statement to make or advice to give as to what the nature of the political future of this country should be. Our aim is the establishment of universal peace in this world and our desire to see justice prevail in every domain of human society, including the domain of politics. As many of the adherents of our Faith are of Jewish and Moslem extraction we have no prejudice towards either of these groups and are most anxious to reconcile them for their mutual benefit and for the good of the country.

What does concern us, however, in any decisions made affecting the future of Palestine, is that the fact be recognized by whoever exercises sovereignty over Haifa and Acre, that within this area exists the spiritual and administrative center of a world Faith, and that the independence of that Faith, its right to manage its international affairs from this source, the right of Bahá'ís from any and every country of the globe to visit it as pilgrims (enjoying the same privilege in this respect as Jews, Moslems and Christians do in regard to visiting Jerusalem), be acknowledged and permanently safeguarded.

The Sepulchre of the Báb on Mt. Carmel, the Tomb of 'Abdu'l-Bahá in that same spot, the Pilgrim Hostel for oriental Bahá'ís in its vicinity, the large gardens and terraces which surround these places (all of which are open to visits by the public of all denominations), the Pilgrim Hostel for western Bahá'ís at the foot of Mt Carmel, the residence of the Head of the Community, various houses and gardens in Acre and its vicinity associated with Bahá'u'lláh's incarceration in that city, His Holy Tomb at Bahjí, near Acre, with His Mansion which is now preserved as a historic site and a museum (both likewise accessible to the public of all denominations), as well as holdings in the plain of Acre—all these comprise the bulk of Bahá'í properties in the Holy Land. It should also be noted that practically all of these properties have been exempted from both Government and Municipal taxes owing to their religious nature. Some of these extensive holdings are the property of the Palestine Branch of the National Spiritual Assembly of the United States and Canada, incorporated as a religious society according to the laws of the country. In future various other Bahá'í National Assemblies will hold, through their Palestine Branches, part of the International Endowments of the Faith in the Holy Land.

In view of the above information I would request you and the members of your Committee to take into consideration the safeguarding of Bahá'í rights in any recommendation which you may make to the United Nations concerning the future of Palestine.

May I take this opportunity of assuring you of my deep appreciation of the spirit in which you and your colleagues have conducted your investigations into the troubled conditions of this Sacred Land. I trust and pray that the outcome of your deliberations will produce an equitable and speedy solution of the very thorny problems which have arisen in Palestine.

Yours faithfully,
Shoghi Rabbani

Haifa, Palestine
July 14, 1947

It must be remembered that the only oriental notable of any standing whatsoever who had not fled from Palestine before the War of Independence, was Shoghi Effendi. This fact was not lost upon the authorities of the new State. By acts such as this, the Guardian had succeeded in impressing upon non-Bahá'ís, who had no reason whatever to take him on faith alone, the sterling personal integrity and strict adherence to what he believed was the right course that characterized his leadership of the Faith of Bahá'u'lláh.

Largely because of this, and a knowledge of what the Bahá'í Teachings represented, of which the *avant garde* of the Jewish Movement for independence were well aware, the new authorities were extremely co-operative in every way. One of their first acts, when the fighting was still going on, had been to place a notice on the Shrine of Bahá'u'lláh—much more isolated than the Shrines in Haifa—stating that it was a *Lieu Sainte* or "Holy Place", thus ensuring that it would be treated with respect by all Jews.

In January 1949 Mr. Ben Gurion, the Prime Minister of the Provisional Government, came to Haifa on his first official visit and the Mayor naturally invited Shoghi Effendi to attend the reception being given in his honour by the Municipality. The dilemma was acute, for if the Guardian did not go, it would, with every reason, be taken as an affront to the new Government, and if he did go he would inevitably be submerged in a sea of people where any pretence at protocol would be swept away (this was indeed the case, as my father, Shoghi Effendi's representative, reported after he returned from this reception). The Guardian therefore decided that as he would not be attending, but was more than willing to show courtesy to the Prime Minister of the new State, he would call upon him in person. With great difficulty this was arranged through the good offices of the Mayor of Haifa, Shabatay Levy, as Mr. Ben Gurion's time in Haifa was very short and it was only two days before the first general election in the new State.

The interview took place on Friday evening, January 21st, in the private home the Prime Minister was staying in on Mt. Carmel and lasted about fifteen minutes. Ben Gurion enquired about the Faith and Shoghi Effendi's relation to it and asked if there was a book he could read; Shoghi Effendi answered his questions and assured him he would send him a copy of his own book *God Passes By*—which he later did, and which was acknowledged with thanks.

Typical of the whole history of the Cause and the constant problems that beset it was a long article which appeared in the leading English-language newspaper on December 20, 1948, in which, in the most favourable terms, its teachings were set forth and the station of Shoghi Effendi as its World Head mentioned. On January 28, 1949, there appeared in the letter column of this paper a short and extraordinary statement, signed "Bahai U.N. Observer", which flatly refuted the article and asserted, "Mr. Rabbani is not the Guardian of the Bahai faith, nor its World Leader" and gave the New History Society in New York as a source of further information. As there was no such thing as a "Bahai U.N. Observer" this move was plainly inspired by the once-more hopeful band of old Covenant-breakers, who sought, at the outset of a new regime, to blacken Shoghi Effendi's reputation and divert attention from his station by referring to Aḥmad Sohrab's rootless group in America. At a later date, when in 1952 the Covenant-breakers in Bahjí brought their case in the local courts against Shoghi Effendi for the demolition of an old building near the Mansion of Bahá'u'lláh, Sohrab sought, unsuccessfully, to bring pressure on the Minister of Religious Affairs to discredit the Bahá'í claims. It was with attacks such as this, both open and covert, that the Guardian, on the threshold of a new phase in the development of the affairs of the Faith at its World Centre, once more had to contend.

It had long been the desire of Shoghi Effendi to obtain control of the Mansion at Mazra'ih, where Bahá'u'lláh had first lived when He quitted once-for-all the walls of the prison-city of 'Akká. This property was a Muslim religious endowment and had now fallen vacant. It was planned by the government to turn it into a rest home for officials. All efforts, through the departments concerned, to procure this property were unavailing until Shoghi Effendi appealed directly to Ben Gurion, explaining its significance to the Bahá'ís and his desire to have it visited by pilgrims as a place so closely associated with Bahá'u'lláh. The Prime Minister himself then intervened in the matter and it was leased to the Bahá'ís as an historic site. Shoghi Effendi proudly informed the Bahá'í world, on December 16, 1950, that its keys had been delivered to us, by the Israeli authorities, after the lapse of more than fifty years.

The affairs of the Bahá'í Community, in matters concerning its day-to-day dealings with the government in connection with the work at the World Centre, had been placed under the jurisdiction of the Ministry of Religious Affairs and was at first handled by the head of the Department that dealt with Muslim affairs. This Shoghi Effendi violently objected to as it implied the Faith was in some way identified with Islám. After much negotiation a letter was received from the Minister of Religious Affairs, dated December 13, 1953, addressed to "His Eminence, Shoghi Effendi Rabbani, World Head of the Bahá'í Faith" in which he said:

". . . I am pleased to inform you of my decision to establish in our Ministry a separate Department for the Bahá'í Faith. I hope that this department will be of assistance to you in matters concerning the Bahá'í Centre in our State.

In the name of the Ministry of Religious Affairs of the State of Israel, I wish to assure Your Eminence that full protection will be given to the Holy Places as well as to the World Centre of the Bahá'í Faith."

The victory was all the more welcome, following as it did the previously mentioned court case against Shoghi Effendi brought on a technicality by the Covenant-breakers in connection with the demolition of a house adjoining the Shrine and Mansion of Bahá'u'lláh in Bahjí. Never tired of seeking to publicly humiliate and discredit the Head of the Faith, be it 'Abdu'l-Bahá or the Guardian, they had had the temerity to summon Shoghi Effendi to appear in court as a witness. Once more, greatly concerned for the honour of the Cause at its World Centre, Shoghi Effendi appealed direct to the Prime Minister, sending as his representatives the President, Secretary-General and Member-at-Large of the International Bahá'í Council (whom he had summoned from Italy for this purpose) to Jerusalem on more than one visit to press the strategy he himself had devised. These representations were successful and on the grounds of its being a purely religious issue it was removed by Government from the jurisdiction of the civil courts. As soon as the plaintiffs found their plan to humiliate Shoghi Effendi had been forestalled, they were willing to settle the case by negotiation. That the authorities and the Bahá'í Community were equally pleased by this conclusion of the matter is shown in these letters written to the Guardian by members of the Prime Minister's staff—two men to whom the Faith owed much for their sympathetic efforts on its behalf at that time:

PRIME MINISTER'S OFFICE

Jerusalem, 19th May, 1952.

His Eminence Shoghi Rabbani,
World Head of the Bahá'í Faith,
Haifa.

Your Eminence,

I am instructed to acknowledge receipt of your letter of the 16th May addressed to the Prime Minister.

As you are no doubt aware, the dispute between yourself as the World Head of the Bahá'í Faith and members of the family of the founder of the Faith has found its solution and there is no need, therefore, to take any administrative action in order to solve the problem.

May I express to you our gratitude for your wise and benevolent attitude taken in the dispute which enabled us to impose a just and, we hope, a lasting solution on the dissident group?

The Prime Minister assures you of his personal esteem and sends you his best wishes.

Yours sincerely,
S. Eynath
Legal Adviser

The second letter was from Walter Eytan, Director-General of the Ministry for Foreign Affairs, and was written to Shoghi Effendi the following day. In it he says: ". . . Having done my best throughout to be of assistance to Your Eminence in the solution of these vexing problems, I heard with great satisfaction this morning that complete agreement had been reached. I sincerely trust that this puts an end to a period of anxiety for Your Eminence and the members of the Bahá'í Faith, and that you will now be able to proceed with your plans without further interference from any quarter."

It is significant to note that they address Shoghi Effendi as "His Eminence", a title which, though still far below what his position merited, was the one that had been introduced in the earliest days of his ministry, but never really used by any officials until the formation of the Jewish State.

The cordial nature of the relations established between the Guardian and the officials of the State of Israel encouraged Shoghi Effendi to ascertain if the President would care to visit the Bahá'í Shrine in Haifa; when word was received that he would accept such an invitation, Shoghi Effendi formally invited him to do so and arrangements were made for the morning of April 26, 1954, at which time, the Director of the President's Office wrote to Shoghi Effendi, the President would "be pleased to pay you an official visit". Accordingly the President and his wife arrived at the home of the Master, attended by two officials, partook of light refreshment and were presented by the Guardian with a Persian album, painted with miniatures and bound in silver, containing some photographs of the Shrines, as a memento of their visit. The Presidential party, with Shoghi Effendi and those who accompanied him, then proceeded to the gardens on Mt. Carmel. It was the first time in the history of the Cause that the Head of an independent nation had ever made an official visit of this kind and it constituted another milestone in the development of the World Centre of the Faith. The President and his companions showed the greatest respect to the Shrine of the Báb, removing their shoes as we did, before entering it, the men keeping their hats on out of reverence as Jews for a holy place; it was a very moving moment to see President Ben Zvi standing beside Shoghi Effendi, the former with his European hat, the latter with his simple black fez, before the threshold. After a few words of explanation from Shoghi Effendi we all withdrew and walked about the gardens for a few minutes before saying good-bye in front of the Oriental Pilgrim House where the President's car was awaiting him.

On April 29th the President wrote personally to the Guardian: "I should like to express my thanks for your kind hospitality and for the interesting time I spent with you visiting the beautiful Gardens and remarkable Shrine . . . I do appreciate the friendship which the Bahá'í Community has for Israel and it is my sincere hope that we may all live to see the strengthening of amity between all peoples on earth." On May 5th the Guardian replied to this letter in equally warm terms: ". . . It was a great pleasure to meet Your Excellency and Mrs. Ben Zvi, and be able to show you one of our places of Bahá'í pilgrimage in Israel . . . If it suits your convenience, Mrs. Rabbani and I, accompanied by Mr. Ioas, would like to call upon Your Excellency and Mrs. Ben Zvi in Jerusalem . . ." The time for this return call was set for the afternoon of May 26th and we had tea and a pleasant conversation with the President and his wife, in her own way as much a personality as her husband and equally nice. In the interim between these two visits Shoghi Effendi had sent to the President some Bahá'í books which he had promised him and these had been acknowledged with the thanks of the President and the assurance that he would read them with great interest. Ever meticulous in all matters, Shoghi Effendi wrote on June 3rd to the President: "I wish to thank you and Mrs. Ben Zvi for your kind hospitality. Mrs. Rabbani and I enjoyed our visit with you very much, and I feel sure that this opportunity we have had of visiting with you our Bahá'í Holy Places and calling upon you in the capital of Israel has served to reinforce the bonds of affection and esteem which unite the Bahá'ís to the people and Government of Israel. With kind regards to you and Mrs. Ben Zvi . . ." Thus ended another memorable chapter in the process of winning recognition for the Faith at its World Centre.

Although the major affairs of the World Centre had usually to be handled in Jerusalem with the highest officials, much of its work needed to be transacted with the help of the municipal officials in both 'Akká and Haifa—particularly the latter. It is an interesting fact that of the many dealings with Haifa municipal engineers which the Bahá'í Community had over the years the first was in the days of 'Abdu'l-Bahá Himself when a Dr. Ciffrin had submitted to Him his design for a monumental staircase and cypress avenue leading from the old Templar Colony at the foot of Mt. Carmel up to the Báb's Shrine. The Master had not only approved of this scheme but had granted land for its realization and headed the list of subscribers to the "Báb's Monumental Stairway", as the project was called, by contributing £100.

Aside from the struggle on Shoghi's Effendi's part, carried on shrewdly and persistently, to win concessions from municipal officials as well as recognition of the unique status of the Bahá'í Faith in both Haifa and 'Akká—the twin cities harbouring its World Centre—he maintained a friendly and co-operative relationship with the Mayor of Haifa in respect to many municipal undertakings, not the least of which was the support he gave the authorities—either the Municipality, or in the early days, the District Commissioner—when there was some special need for financial help in charitable work.

Nothing could better describe Shoghi Effendi's attitude and policy in such matters than the letter he wrote, on February 7, 1923, so early in his ministry, to Colonel Symes: "I have just heard of the Charity Ball which Mrs. Symes is organizing to aid the poor of Haifa. Realizing how their cause was consistently upheld by my beloved Grandfather, and it being my earnest endeavour to follow in his footsteps, I beg to enclose the sum of £20– as a contribution to the fund . . . I trust you have had a very enjoyable time in Egypt, and hoping to meet you and Mrs. Symes in the near future . . ." The same sentiment is expressed with equal feeling two years later in another letter to Colonel Symes: "The perusal of your circular letter of February 16th, 1925 with reference to the establishment of the Haifa Charitable Fund has served to remind me of the keen interest 'Abdu'l-Bahá took in charitable institutions. Animated by the same sentiment and desirous to walk in the footsteps of my beloved Grandfather, I hasten to enclose herewith the sum of £20– towards the relief of the sufferings of the poor in Haifa."

Whenever calamity overtook the people, Shoghi Effendi

responded warmly to the need. In April 1926 he wrote to the Commissioner of the Northern District: "Fully aware of the intense suffering caused by recent disturbances, and mindful of the loving care bestowed by 'Abdu'l-Bahá on the suffering and needy, I take great pleasure in enclosing the sum of £30– as my contribution towards the relief of the poor and shelterless . . . I shall be grateful if you will let me know from time to time if any such need arises, in whatever place and on behalf of whatever denomination." In 1927 we find him again responding to disaster by sending the Secretariat of the Government in Jerusalem £100 as his contribution to the Earthquake Relief Fund. Over the years, in large or in small amounts, he followed in the ways of the Master who had been called "the Father of the Poor".

That these contributions to various causes were warmly received is self-evident: the District Commissioner for the Northern District thanks Shoghi Effendi, in 1934, for his "most generous contribution towards the relief of distress in Tiberias" and also for his "message of sympathy which I will convey to District Commissioner of Tiberias." In 1950 we find the Chairman of the Haifa Municipal Commission, the Mayor, thanking Shoghi Effendi for the £500 "being your Eminence's generous contribution for the relief of the poor in Haifa, on the occasion of the 100th anniversary of the Martyrdom of the Báb." Almost invariably, when forwarding such contributions, the Guardian would add that they were to "be distributed equally among the needy members of all communities, irrespective of their race or religion."

The general policy of the Faith in matters of charity was made abundantly clear by a letter he wrote to the Mayor of Haifa, on May 7, 1929, in which he acknowledges receiving his circular related to the prevention of mendicancy in the city of Haifa and states: "Fortunately, this is a problem which does not affect the Bahá'í Community, as under our laws begging is strictly prohibited. I appreciate, however, the importance and timeliness of the measure you are considering and take pleasure in enclosing a cheque to your order for £50– in behalf of the Bahá'í Community in anticipation of any plan that the Municipality may devise for the alleviation of poverty and the help of the needy in Haifa. You may be assured that the Community will rigidly observe any regulations that may be put into effect."

In the years when the people of Palestine and, later, of Israel were undergoing great hardships, between 1940 and 1952 alone, the Guardian gave the Municipality of Haifa over ten thousand dollars for the poor of all denominations. In addition to such help given through government and municipal agencies he also responded to the appeals of many charities, gave individually to those he deemed worthy, and, even sometimes contributed money for some special purpose connected with the mosque in Haifa. Many times he gave contributions spontaneously, such as the £100 he donated to the Government Lunatic Asylum in 'Akká—the former Turkish barracks—when the room occupied by Bahá'u'lláh was turned over to the custody of the Bahá'ís, and the sum he presented towards the construction of the Institute of Physics which the Weizmann National Memorial was undertaking.

But this was not the only way in which he demonstrated to the local authorities his good will. Whatever demands were made of him he usually found he was in a position to respond to them most cordially. An example of this is an exchange of correspondence with Aba Khoushy, the Mayor of Haifa, which took place in 1952. A country-wide Symposium on Problems of Illumination was to take place at the Hebrew Technical College in Haifa and would coincide with the Jewish Feast of Hanukka, the Feast of Lights. His Worship in a letter to Shoghi Effendi informed him of this and wrote that: "I should be grateful if you too could share in our efforts to make this conference a success and would kindly issue instructions to have the beautiful Shrine of your Faith, on the Carmel slopes, illuminated festively during the week Dec. 12–Dec. 19, 1952, inclusively." As usual, whenever he was approached courteously, Shoghi Effendi responded warmly. On December 7th he wrote to the Mayor:

Your Worship:
Your letter of November 30th has been received by me on my return from Bahjí, and I wish to assure you that the Bahá'í Community will be happy to cooperate in making the city of Haifa luminous and beautiful, in connection with the Symposium to be held at the Hebrew Technical College on Problems of Illumination, especially so as this Symposium will be held during Hanukka.

I will give instructions that the period of illumination of our Shrine should be extended during these days [the Shrine was always flood-lit every night at sunset for a short time], and wish also to extend through Your Worship an invitation to the delegates and visitors attending the Symposium to enter the Shrine and gardens on one of the evenings when they will be touring our city, to enjoy the illumination. The necessary arrangements can be made to open the gates and Shrine for them, if we are informed in advance.

Yours sincerely,
Shoghi Rabbani
World Head of the Bahá'í Faith

Another significant example of the spirit in which Shoghi Effendi responded to worthy causes pressed upon his attention is the co-operation he gave the 'Akká District Commissioner when in 1943 he wrote to him that he could find no place to house a children's school and would he consider leasing eight rooms in the house of 'Abbúd (a large building and a place of Bahá'í pilgrimage) for this purpose? Shoghi Effendi permitted the school to use some of the rooms, but said he would not take any payment for them.

XI

THE RISE OF THE ADMINISTRATIVE ORDER

During the years when the Guardian was building up not only the material, tangible assets of the Faith at its World Centre but winning for it the recognition of both the government of the country in which that Centre was situated and the municipal authorities in whose city its chief institutions were to have their permanent headquarters, he was performing at the same time a similar function abroad. Years later he defined what this had been: a triple, worldwide effort to demonstrate the independent character of the Faith, to enlarge its limits and to swell the number of its supporters. In order, however, to accomplish this he had to have instruments and those instruments, so clearly provided for in the teachings, were the local and National Assemblies, the building blocks of its Administrative Order.

It is not surprising to find that Shoghi Effendi characterized the period of the Faith that was ushered in after 'Abdu'l-Bahá's ascension as the "Iron Age", "the Age of Transition", "the Formative Period". It was the Age in which the institutions of the Cause, whether national, local or international were being created, institutions which, the Guardian said, constitute the embryonic pattern that needs must evolve, during the Golden Age of the Bahá'í Dispensation, into a World Commonwealth. The principles governing the Administrative Order established in the *Will and Testament* were defined by him during the first years of his ministry in a flood of letters to the believers all over the world in which he made clear the functions of Assemblies, their fields of jurisdiction and—what was still more essential—the spirit that must animate them if they were to fulfil their purpose in the immediate future.

The administrative institutions may be likened to the veins and arteries of the body that carry in their network the vital flow of Bahá'u'lláh's teachings to all parts of the world; through their instrumentality a re-created society, "that Christ-promised Kingdom, that World Order whose generative impulse is none other than Bahá'u'lláh Himself, whose dominion is the entire planet, whose watchword is unity, whose animating power is the force of Justice, whose directive purpose is the reign of righteousness and truth, and whose supreme glory is the complete, the undisturbed and everlasting felicity of the whole of humankind", can be brought into being.

After defining the purely mechanical technique of how Assemblies should be elected and conduct their business, the Guardian's early admonitions to them often dealt with the subject of unity; if the "watchword" of future society was going to be "unity" it was obviously essential it should be assiduously cultivated amongst the Bahá'ís themselves. In 1923 he wrote to one of the local Assemblies: "Full harmony and understanding among the friends, outside and within the Spiritual Assembly; implicit confidence on the part of the non-members in every decision passed by their elected representatives; and the determination of these to disregard their likes and dislikes and seek naught but the general interests of the Movement—these constitute the only and sure foundation upon which any constructive work can be built in future and prove serviceable to the interests of the Cause." His letters to National Assemblies were no less emphatic: "An active, united, and harmonious National Spiritual Assembly, properly and conscientiously elected, vigorously functioning, alert and conscious of its many and pressing responsibilities, in close and continuous contact with the international centre in the Holy Land, and keenly watchful of every development throughout the length and breadth of its ever-expanding field of work—is surely in this day of urgent necessity and paramount importance, for it is the cornerstone on which the edifice of Divine Administration must ultimately rest."

No sooner had Shoghi Effendi got national bodies properly elected and functioning—in those countries where such a step was possible—than he set about putting these bodies on an unequivocal, clear legal basis. Through his encouragement one of the great milestones in Bahá'í history was set up in 1927, five years after he had begun to function as Guardian of the Faith. That milestone was no less than "the drafting and adoption of a Bahá'í National constitution, first framed and promulgated by the elected representatives of the American Bahá'í Community". He has described this as the initial step in "the unification of the Bahá'í World

Community and the consolidation of its Administrative Order".

This document became the "charter" for all National Assemblies, was translated into such major languages in use throughout the Bahá'í world as Persian, Arabic, French, German and Spanish, and its provisions—based on those guiding lines Shoghi Effendi himself had been providing in his interpretive writings on the teachings of the Faith and the, as he described it, "complete system of world administration implicit in the teachings of Bahá'u'lláh"—were summarized by him in the following words: "The text of this national constitution comprises a Declaration of Trust, whose articles set forth the character and objects of the national Bahá'í community, establish the functions, designate the central office, and describe the official seal, of the body of its elected representatives, as well as a set of by-laws which define the status, the mode of election, the powers and duties of both local and national Assemblies, describe the relation of the National Assembly to the International House of Justice as well as to local Assemblies and individual believers, outline the rights and obligations of the National Convention and its relation to the National Assembly, disclose the character of Bahá'í elections, and lay down the requirements of voting membership in all Bahá'í communities."

The drafting of the By-Laws of the Spiritual Assembly of the Bahá'ís of the City of New York, in 1931, was likewise another great step forward in the evolution of the Administrative Order and was followed, a year later, by the legal incorporation of that Assembly in the State of New York. Of these by-laws Shoghi Effendi wrote that they would "serve as a pattern for every Bahá'í local Assembly in America and a model for every local community throughout the Bahá'í world."

The formulation of this prototype for all national Bahá'í constitutions, as well as the framing of by-laws suitable for any local Spiritual Assembly, laid a firm basis on which both national and local Bahá'í Assemblies could obtain incorporation or registration, according to the law of the country in which they functioned, and thus hold legal title to such endowments of the Faith as land, national and local headquarters, historic sites, and in some cases Bahá'í Houses of Worship—steps to which Shoghi Effendi attached the utmost importance. During 1928 the Guardian began to urge the oriental National Assemblies to form their national constitutions, patterned on the American one, and in addition to seek recognition as religious courts empowered to administer the

Bahá'í laws on matters of personal status, such as marriage, divorce, inheritance and so on, which in many Islamic countries do not come within the jurisdiction of the usual civil courts.

All this primarily involved the battle of an independent Faith to obtain full recognition of its position in history and to be treated on an equal footing with other world religions. In the constant process of orienting the destinies of individual Bahá'í communities towards their common goal of becoming a completely unified international body, directed from a World Centre and labouring to achieve no less than the universal brotherhood of man, world peace and eventually a world commonwealth of nations, Shoghi Effendi seized upon the formation of the United Nations as a further means of hastening the attainment of this supreme objective.

As soon as it became apparent that the framework of this international body permitted non-governmental organizations to send their accredited representatives to various conferences convened under its auspices, Shoghi Effendi urged what was then the National Spiritual Assembly of the Bahá'ís of the United States and Canada to apply for this status, which was obtained by that body in 1947. At the time it made its application it submitted a Bahá'í Declaration of Human Obligations and Rights as well as a Bahá'í Statement on the Rights of Women. A Bahá'í United Nations Committee was appointed and a Bahá'í observer attended United Nations sessions. As this status was very limited in scope ways and means were found by which it could be enlarged. This was achieved during the winter of 1947–1948 through seven National Spiritual Assemblies' authorizing the American national body to act on their behalf as their representative under the title Bahá'í International Community, duly recognized as an international organization accredited to the United Nations, a status that both enhanced the prestige of the Faith and increased the privileges of the official Bahá'í representatives who regularly attended and took part in various United Nations conferences of a type open to those enjoying such status. As new National Spiritual Assemblies were formed these too joined in and reinforced the organization representing the Bahá'í world.

The importance Shoghi Effendi attached to this tie linking the Cause with the greatest international instrument ever forged in human history is reflected in his own words: "it marks an important step forward in the struggle of our beloved Faith to receive in the eyes of the world its just due, and be recognized as an independent World Religion. Indeed, this step should have a favourable reaction on the progress of the Cause everywhere, especially in those parts of the world where it is still persecuted, belittled, or scorned, particularly in the East." At the time of the intense wave of persecution that swept over the Bahá'í Community of Persia in 1955 the carefully established and fostered relationship with the United Nations bore fruit; in consequence of the detailed documentation of the injuries and atrocities the followers of Bahá'u'lláh in His native land had been made to suffer, which was submitted to the Secretary-General of the United Nations, a commission was appointed by him, headed by the High Commissioner for Refugees, and instructed to contact the Persian Government and obtain formal assurance from it that the rights of the Bahá'í minority would be safeguarded. So much importance did the Guardian attach to this relationship that one of the twenty-seven listed objectives of the Ten Year International Teaching and Consolidation Plan—the World Crusade—was the "Reinforcement of the ties binding the Bahá'í World Community to the United Nations."

The history of the Cause, Shoghi Effendi wrote, "if read aright, may be said to resolve itself into a series of pulsations, of alternating crises and triumphs, leading it ever nearer to its divinely appointed destiny." Although the passing of the Central Figure of the Faith— whether it was the Báb, Bahá'u'lláh or 'Abdu'l-Bahá—had inevitably precipitated a crisis, the majority of such shocks which impelled it forward were the result of the persecutions it suffered, usually, though not exclusively, at the hands of its inveterate enemies, the Muslim ecclesiastics. During the thirty-six years of Shoghi Effendi's ministry there were repeated and violent outbreaks, locally and on a national scale, of a most brutal and bloodthirsty nature, against the followers of the Faith in Persia; its adherents in Turkey were suppressed, persecuted and falsely accused; its followers in Egypt were subjected to attacks upon their persons, their properties, their cemeteries and their legal rights; its adherents in Russia had their Assemblies dissolved, their Temple confiscated and were themselves, for the most part either deported or exiled; the Bahá'í Community in Germany was officially dissolved and its activities forbidden in June 1937, its national archives were confiscated, some of its members interrogated and even placed under arrest.

Such events caused the Guardian keen distress, took up a great deal of his time and added to the burdens of an already overburdened heart and mind. The major problem, however, was always Persia, where a "long-abused, down-trodden, sorely tried community" perpetually struggled for its very existence in the face of continual persecution. This "dearly-beloved" Community—as he so lovingly and repeatedly referred to it—preoccupied him from the earliest to the latest days of his ministry. A steady flow of communications from him poured out to its members and its elected national body, and in his communication to the Bahá'ís of the West it was the frequent subject of his solicitude, his appeals for assistance in defending it and his explanations of why this community—which he said had led the Heroic Age of the Faith—was so bitterly set upon by the people of its native land.

There was a time, as indicated in his letters, when Shoghi Effendi hoped the founder of the new Pahlaví dynasty—who was introducing many much needed reforms—would speedily usher in a new phase in the development of Bahá'u'lláh's Faith in that country. In 1929 Shoghi Effendi had written that the believers there were "tasting the first fruits of their long-dreamed emancipation". It was in view of this process of reform now taking place that he had advised the National Assembly to press for permission to print books and establish a Bahá'í Publishing Trust. This having been refused we find him cabling America in January 1932: "Urge transmit promptly through Teheran Assembly two written communications Persian Government and Shah expressing behalf American believers lively appreciation recent beneficial internal reforms, emphasizing spiritual ties binding two countries and earnestly pleading removal ban entry Bahá'í literature . . ." Shoghi Effendi's hopes, however, were short-lived; the reforms were not big enough to include a bitterly hated community and this request too was refused.

In December 1934 Shoghi Effendi wired the Persian National Assembly: "Has Tarbiyat School been permanently closed enquire and wire". The background of this question is reflected in the answer of that Assembly to the Guardian: "Pursuant with your request on day Báb's Martyrdom both Tarbiyat Schools Teheran were closed therefore Ministry Education obliged close both schools and asked why we did not dissimulate . . ." This case might be cited as a classic example of the struggle of the Persian Bahá'ís—constantly spurred on and guided by Shoghi Effendi—to obtain at least a reasonable measure of liberty in following their own religion, which numerically was, after Islám, the largest in the country. The Tarbiyat boys and girls School, owned and managed entirely by the Bahá'ís, had been in existence for thirty-six years. Founded in 1898, in the days of 'Abdu'l-Bahá, it had been a project dear to His heart; it had always had an excellent reputation, and although its pupils were mainly Bahá'í, children of all denominations attended it. The School had always closed on the nine Bahá'í Holy Days but now, on the flimsy pretext that the Bahá'ís belonged to a denomination not officially recognized in Persia, the Ministry of Education had suddenly required the School to remain open on these days. This meant a retreat instead of an advance in the battle for emancipation the Cause was struggling so desperately to win and Shoghi Effendi flatly refused, ordering the Assembly to close the School on the anniversary of the Báb's Martyrdom. As he was neither willing to advise the believers to dissimulate their Faith, nor to keep the School open on Bahá'í Holy Days, and the government refused to change its orders, the Tarbiyat School, one of the best in Persia, was closed and remains closed to the present day.

In announcing this bad news, the day after he received his answer from Ṭihrán, to the Bahá'ís in that land where they enjoyed the greatest degree of freedom throughout the entire world the anger of the Guardian is reflected in every word as he pours out the list of indignities and sufferings to which the Bahá'ís of Persia are being subjected: "Information just received indicates deliberate efforts undermine all Bahá'í institutions in Persia. Schools in Kashan, Qazvin, Sultanabad closed. In several leading centres including Qazvin Kirmanshah orders issued suspend teaching activities, prohibit gatherings, close Bahá'í Hall, deny right burial in Bahá'í cemeteries. Bahá'ís of Teheran compelled under penalty imprisonment register themselves Moslems in identity papers. Elated clergy inciting population. National Teheran Assembly's petitions to Shah undelivered rejected. Impress Persian Minister gravity intolerable situation".

In face of these wholly unwarranted blows received at a time when it could logically be expected that the more liberal policy affecting the entire country would be stretched to include the members of a Faith that since the days of Darius and his successors constituted that nation's only serious claim to fame—at such a time the Persian Bahá'ís were able to hold a convention whose delegates were sufficiently representative of the Bahá'í Community within that country to elect a National Assembly that Shoghi Effendi officially lists in his statistical pamphlets as having been formed in 1934.

The situation of the Bahá'ís in the East and particularly Persia is never really quiet, is always precariously balanced, ever ready to flare up into a violent and all-too-frequently bloody outbreak of persecution. Repeatedly there were isolated cases of Bahá'ís being killed—some of whom the Guardian mentioned as martyrs; constantly there was a temperature of persecution, sometimes hotter here and sometimes hotter there, but always present. To all the vicissitudes afflicting the Persian friends the Guardian responded with loving messages, with sums of money for relief, with instructions, usually to the American National Assembly, to intervene on their behalf and solicit justice in their cause.

The worst crisis, however, which the Persian Bahá'í Community experienced in the thirty-six years of the Guardian's ministry, arose in 1955, when, as he cabled, a sudden deterioration took place in the affairs of this largest community in the Bahá'í world. In a long cable, dated August 23rd, he reported to the Hands and National Assemblies what had been taking place: Following the seizure by the authorities of the National Headquarters of the Persian believers in Ṭihrán and the destruction of its large ornamental dome (a destruction during which one of the country's leading divines and a general of its army, themselves took up pickaxes and went to work), local Bahá'í administrative headquarters all over Persia were seized and occupied, the Parliament of the country outlawed the Faith, a virulent press and radio campaign was started, distorting its history, calumniating its Founders, misrepresenting its teachings, and obscuring its aims and purposes—following all this a series of atrocities was perpetrated against the members of this sorely tried community throughout the entire country. In his summary of the terrible damage done and the "barbarous acts" committed, he cited such events as: the desecration of the House of the Báb in Shíráz, the foremost Shrine of the Faith in Persia, which had been severely damaged; the occupation of the ancestral home of Bahá'u'lláh; the pillaging of shops and farms owned by the believers and the looting of their homes, destruction of their livestock, burning of their crops and digging up and desecration of the Bahá'í dead in their cemeteries; adults were beaten; young women abducted and forced into marriage with Muslims; children were mocked, reviled and expelled from schools as well as being beaten; tradesmen boycotted Bahá'ís and refused to sell them food; a girl of fifteen was raped; an eleven month old baby was trampled underfoot; pressure was brought on believers to recant their Faith. More recently, he went on to say, a mob two thousand strong had hacked to pieces with spades and axes a family of seven—the oldest eighty and the youngest nineteen—to the sound of music and drums.

The Bahá'ís, at the instruction of their Guardian, had already, through the intermediary of telegrams and letters to the authorities in Persia from over one thousand groups and Assemblies throughout the world, protested against such unjust and lawless acts committed against their law-abiding brethren. In addition all National Assemblies had addressed letters to the Sháh, the Government and the Parliament protesting this unwarranted persecution of a harmless community on purely religious grounds. As all this brought forth no acknowledgement whatsoever from official quarters the Guardian instructed the International Bahá'í Community, accredited as a Non-Governmental Organization to the United Nations, to take the question to that body in Geneva, he himself nominating those whom he wished to act as representatives of the Community on this important occasion. Copies of the Bahá'í appeal were delivered to representatives of the member nations of the Social and Economic Council, the Director of the Human Rights Division, as well as to certain specialized agencies of Non-Governmental Organizations enjoying consultative status. The President of the United States was likewise appealed to by the American National Assembly and by all groups and local Assemblies in the country to intervene on behalf of their oppressed sister community in Persia.

This was the first time in its history that an attacked Faith was able to fight back with weapons that possessed some strength to defend it. The significance of this was clearly brought out by Shoghi Effendi. Whatever the outcome of these "heart-rending" events might be, one fact had clearly emerged: God's infant Faith, which had during the twenty-five years following the ascension of 'Abdu'l-Bahá provided itself with the machinery of its divinely appointed Administrative Order, and subsequently utilized its newly-born administrative agencies to systematically propagate that Faith through a series of national plans that had culminated in the World Crusade, was now, in the wake of this ordeal convulsing the overwhelming majority of its followers, emerging from obscurity. The world-wide reverberations of these events would be hailed by posterity as the "mighty blast of God's trumpet" which, through the instrumentality of the "oldest, most redoubtable, most vicious, most fanatical adversaries" of the Cause must awaken governments and heads of governments, in both East and West, to the existence and the implications of this Faith. So stormy were the circumstances surrounding these events in Persia and so impressive their repercussions abroad that the Guardian stated they were bound to pave the way for the emancipation of the Faith from the fetters of orthodoxy in Islamic countries as well as for the ultimate recognition in His own homeland of the independent character of the Revelation of Bahá'u'lláh.

In view of the great sufferings and pitiful condition of the Persian believers Shoghi Effendi inaugurated an "Aid the Persecuted" fund and opened it by himself contributing the equivalent of eighteen thousand dollars for "this noble purpose". Not content with this evidence of Bahá'í solidarity he called for the construction in Kampala, in the heart of Africa, of the "Mother Temple" of that continent as a "supreme consolation" to the "oppressed masses" of our "valiant brethren" in the cradle of the Faith. He struck back at the forces of darkness swarming over the oldest bastion of that Faith in the world, with the greatest weapons at his disposal—the forces of creative progress, enlightenment and faith.

Turning to the question of the liquidation of the Faith in Russia we must remember that one of the earliest Bahá'í communities in the world had existed there, in the Caucasus and Turkistán, from the end of the last century, where many Persians had found a welcome refuge from the persecutions to which they were so constantly subjected in their native land. They had established themselves in a number of towns, particularly in 'Ishqábád, where they had erected the first Temple of the entire Bahá'í world and opened schools for the Bahá'í children which remained in existence for over thirty years. Their affairs were well organized. They had, in 1928, a number of Spiritual Assemblies (including one in Moscow) and two central Assemblies had, pending the holding of proper, representative national elections, administered their affairs, appearing on lists published in the United States as the National Assemblies of the Caucasus and of Turkistán. In a letter addressed in September 1927 to the Local Spiritual Assembly of 'Ishqábád Shoghi Effendi instructed them to gradually prepare for delegates from all Assemblies in Turkistán to meet in 'Ishqábád and hold the election of their National Assembly. On June 22, 1928, Shoghi Effendi received a cable from the 'Ishqábád Assembly as follows: "In accordance general agreement 1917 Soviet Government has nationalized all Temples but under special conditions has provided free

MOUNTAIN HAZARDS
Shoghi Effendi surveys a glacial crevice in the Swiss Alps

SHOGHI EFFENDI WALKING IN THE SWISS ALPS
The solitude of the mountains and the challenge of mountaineering became a healing for the young Guardian

ON TOP OF THE WORLD

His bicycle – the poor man's car – became a favourite of Shoghi Effendi. He sometimes climbed the highest passes in Switzerland, pushing it up and riding down

BICYCLING OVER SNOWY PASSES

In the high Alps of Switzerland the young Guardian sought refuge in the wilderness from his crushing spiritual burdens

rental to respective religious communities regarding Mashriqu'l-Adhkár government has provided same conditions agreement to Assembly supplicate guidance by telegram". The Guardian took immediate action, cabling the Moscow Assembly to "Intercede energetically authorities prevent expropriation Mashriqu'l-Adhkár. Enquire particulars 'Ishqábád . . ." and to 'Ishqábád to "refer Moscow Assembly address petition authorities behalf all Bahá'ís Russia. Act firmly assure you prayers".

In recalling the events which transpired in Russia a sharp distinction must be made—one which the Guardian himself recognized—between the hardships to which the Russian believers were subjected and the persecutions the Bahá'ís underwent in Persia. In Persia the believers were, and still are, singled out as victims of every form of injustice because they are the followers of Bahá'u'lláh; in Russia the situation was entirely different. The Bahá'ís were not discriminated against because they were Bahá'ís but suffered from a policy which the government pursued against all religious communities.

In all persecutions how much is exacerbated by the unwisdom of the persecuted themselves, interacting on the unwisdom of subordinates carrying out the instructions of superiors—who may or may not be ill disposed—is a mystery we are not likely ever to solve in this world. It does not seem unreasonable to suppose, however, that at least some of our misfortunes we amplify by our own acts.

What had transpired in Russia, Shoghi Effendi wrote in a long letter to the Bahá'ís of the West on January 1, 1929, was that the Russian Bahá'ís had at last been brought under the "rigid application of the principles already enunciated by the state authorities and universally enforced with regard to all other religious communities"; the Bahá'ís "as befits their position as loyal and law-abiding citizens" had obeyed the "measures which the State, in the free exercise of its legitimate rights, has chosen to enforce". The measures which the authorities had taken "faithful to their policy of expropriating in the interests of the State all edifices and monuments of a religious character" had led them to expropriate and assume the ownership and control over "that most cherished and universally prized Bahá'í possession, the Mashriqu'l-Adhkár of 'Ishqábád." In addition to this "state orders, orally and in writing," had "been officially communicated to the Bahá'í Assemblies and individual believers, suspending all meetings . . . suppressing the committees of all Bahá'í local and national Spiritual Assemblies, prohibiting the raising of funds . . . requiring the right of full and frequent inspection of the deliberations . . . of the Bahá'í Assemblies . . . imposing a strict censorship on all correspondence to and from Bahá'í Assemblies . . . suspending all Bahá'í periodicals . . . and requiring the deportation of leading personalities in the Cause whether as public teachers and speakers or officers of Bahá'í Assemblies. To all these", Shoghi Effendi stated, "the followers of the Faith of Bahá'u'lláh have with feelings of burning agony and heroic fortitude unanimously and unreservedly submitted, ever mindful of the guiding principles of Bahá'í conduct that in connection with their administrative activities, no matter how grievously interference with them might affect the course of the extension of the Movement, and the suspension of which does not constitute in itself a departure from the principle of loyalty to their Faith, the considered judgment and authoritative decrees issued by their responsible rulers must, if they be faithful to Bahá'u'lláh's and 'Abdu'l-Bahá's express injunctions, be thoroughly respected and loyally obeyed." He went on to say that after the Bahá'ís in Turkistán and the Caucasus had unsuccessfully exhausted every legitimate means for the alleviation of these restrictions imposed upon them, they had resolved to "conscientiously carry out the considered judgment of their recognized government" and "with a hope that no earthly power can dim . . . committed the interests of their Cause to the keeping of that vigilant, that all-powerful Divine Deliverer . . ."

Shoghi Effendi assured the Bahá'ís in this message that if he deemed it expedient to call upon the Bahá'í world to intervene at a later stage he would do so. In April 1930 he felt the time had come for this; the precious Temple, which the Bahá'ís had succeeded in renting from the authorities after its confiscation, was now placed in danger of passing once-for-all from their hands through a series of further and harsher measures imposed upon the friends. He therefore cabled the American National Assembly ". . . prompt action required. Stress international character Temple . . ." In his previous long letter he had already outlined the approach that should be made, when and if the time came for the believers abroad to raise their voices in protest and explanation: national as well as local Assemblies, East and West, in a gesture of Bahá'í solidarity, would call the attention of the Russian officials not only to their refutation of any implication of a political design or ulterior motive which might have been falsely imputed to their brethren in that land, but to the "humanitarian and spiritual nature of the work in which Bahá'ís in every land and of every race are unitedly engaged" and to the international character of that Edifice which had the distinction of being Bahá'u'lláh's first Universal House of Worship, whose design 'Abdu'l-Bahá had Himself conceived and which had been constructed under His direction and supported by the collective contributions of believers throughout the world.

But when the die was finally cast Shoghi Effendi cabled the 'Ishqábád Assembly to "abide by decision State Authorities". A case such as this, involving the first of the two Bahá'í Temples erected under the aegis of 'Abdu'l-Bahá, cannot but form a guiding pattern for Bahá'í Assemblies to follow throughout all time and a well of information to the individual believer on his duty towards his government, whatever the nature of that government may be.

Two other countries, Turkey and Egypt, formed with Russia, Persia and Germany the scene of serious repressive and restrictive measures imposed on the Faith during the lifetime of the Guardian. In Turkey, which ever since the downfall of the Caliphate had been the subject, as Shoghi Effendi wrote, of "an uncompromising policy aiming at the secularization of the State and the disestablishment of Islám", great civil reforms had taken place, reforms with which incidentally the Bahá'ís were wholly in sympathy. The troubles which arose there were therefore not based on religious prejudice but were rather brought about by the fact that the new regime had in the past discovered that so-called religious groups in Turkey had provided cover for political agitation and when its agents found the Bahá'í Community was organized and was pursuing its activities openly, teaching and spreading the Faith, they became suspicious and alarmed, searched many of the believers' homes, seized any literature they found, severely cross-examined some of them and put a good number in prison. The case brought a great deal of publicity to the Faith, to some extent abroad, but mostly in the Turkish press, which reacted in favour of the Bahá'ís and ensured for them, when it came before the Criminal Tribunal on December 13, 1928, a full and impartial hearing. It marked a new departure in the unfoldment of the Cause: "never before in Bahá'í history", Shoghi Effendi wrote, "have the followers of Bahá'u'lláh been called upon by the officials of a state . . . to unfold the history and principles of their Faith . . ."

It is interesting to note that in the papers seized by the authorities from the Assembly of Constantinople (the city now known as Istanbul), one of Queen Marie's tributes to the Faith was found and its implications were not lost upon the examining judges. The Chairman of the Constantinople Bahá'í Spiritual Assembly, in giving his testimony before the Court exposed in a most brilliant manner the tenets of the Faith and included this pointed quotation from Bahá'u'lláh's own words: *"Before Justice, tell the Truth and fear nothing."* The conclusion of this entire episode was that the Bahá'ís had to pay a fine for having infringed the law that all associations should be registered with the government and due authorization to hold public meetings be obtained, but its results were of great significance to the Faith, not only locally but abroad. The verdict of the Court was summarized by Shoghi Effendi in a general letter to the Bahá'ís of the West, written on February 12, 1929: "As to the verdict . . . it is stated clearly that although the followers of Bahá'u'lláh, in their innocent conception of the spiritual character of their Faith, found it unnecessary to apply for leave for the conduct of their administrative activities and have thus been made liable to the payment of a fine, yet they have, to the satisfaction of the legal representatives of the State, not only established the inculpability of the Cause of Bahá'u'lláh, but have also worthily acquitted themselves of the task of vindicating its independence, its Divine origin, and its suitability to the circumstances and requirements of the present age."

Although this was the first major episode involving the Bahá'ís with the new State that had evolved in Turkey after the downfall of the Caliphate, it was not to be the last. The secular powers were constantly on their guard against reactionary forces in the State and, as the official memory was short, in 1933 there was a recrudescence of the same suspicions and accusations that had brought about the case in 1928. On January 27th we find Shoghi Effendi cabling the American National Assembly: "Bahá'ís Constantinople and Adana numbering about forty imprisoned charged subversive motives. Urge induce Turkish Minister Washington make immediate representations his government release law abiding followers non-political Faith. Advise also National Assembly cable authorities Angora and approach State Department". At the same time he wired the Persian National Assembly: "Urge immediate representations Turkish Ambassador behalf imprisoned Bahá'ís Stamboul and Adana charged political motives". The next day he wired a prominent Turk:

His Excellency Ismat Pasha
Ankara

As Head of Bahá'í Faith learned with amazement and grief imprisonment followers of Bahá'u'lláh in Stamboul and Adana. Respectfully appeal Your Excellency's intervention on behalf followers of a Faith pledged loyalty to your Government for whose epochal reforms its adherents world over cherish abiding admiration.

The Bahá'ís, familiar with the whole situation through the detailed letters the Guardian had written at the time of the previous case, immediately took action and their representations to the Turkish authorities, as well, no doubt, as moves made in Turkey to cite the verdict the Criminal Court had given in the former case, secured, after many months of effort, the release and acquittal of the believers. On March 5th the Guardian informed the American Assembly: "Istanbul friends acquitted 53 still imprisoned Adana urge renew energetically representations immediate release" and on April 4th he cabled them: "Adana friends released. Advise convey appreciation Turkish Ambassador".

In spite of a regular recrudescence of suspicion on the part of the Turkish authorities the Guardian was able to lay, during his own lifetime, sufficiently strong foundations in the Bahá'í community of that country for it to elect after his passing, in fulfilment of one of his goals of the Ten Year Plan, its own independent National Spiritual Assembly.

In Egypt, one of the earliest countries to receive, during His own days, the Light of Bahá'u'lláh's Revelation, events transpired, three years before the first court case of the believers in Turkey took place, to which the Guardian attached supreme significance. Beginning by a fierce attack on a small band of Bahá'ís in an obscure village of Upper Egypt it ended in being the "first step", Shoghi Effendi said, in "the eventual universal acceptance of the Bahá'í Faith, as one of the independent recognized religious systems of the world". The laws of personal status in almost all Islamic countries are administered by religious courts; when the Bahá'ís of that village formed their Spiritual Assembly, the headman, inflamed by religious fanaticism, began to stir up feeling against three married men who had become Bahá'ís; through legal channels a demand was made that their Muḥammadan wives divorce them on the grounds that they were now married to heretics. The case went to the Appelate religious courts of Beba, which delivered its Judgement on May 10, 1925, in which it strongly condemned the heretics for violating the laws and ordinances of Islám and annulled the marriages. This in itself was a significant move but what the Guardian attached the most importance to was that "It even went so far as to make the positive, the startling and indeed the historic assertion that the Faith embraced by these heretics is to be regarded as a distinct religion, wholly independent of the religious systems that have preceded it". In his résumé of that verdict Shoghi Effendi quoted the actual words of the Judgement, of such immense historic importance to the Bahá'ís:

> "The Bahá'í Faith is a new religion, entirely independent, with beliefs, principles and laws of its own, which differ from, and are utterly in conflict with, the beliefs, principles and laws of Islám. No Bahá'í, therefore, can be regarded a Muslim or vice-versa, even as no Buddhist, Brahmin, or Christian can be regarded a Muslim or vice-versa."

Even if this verdict had remained an isolated phenomenon in an obscure local court of Egypt it would have been an invaluable weapon in the hands of the believers all over the world who were seeking to assert just that independence so clearly enunciated in this Judgement. But it did not rest there; it was subsequently sanctioned and upheld by the highest ecclesiastical authorities in Cairo, and printed and circulated by the Muslims themselves.

The Guardian, who was ever ready to seize upon the most insignificant and flimsy tools—from human beings to pieces of paper—and wield them as weapons in his battle to secure the recognition and emancipation of the Faith, grasped this sharp new sword placed in his hands by the enemies of the Faith themselves and went on striking with it until the end of his life. It was, he stated, the first Charter of the emancipation of the Cause from the fetters of Islám. In the East the Bahá'ís used it, under his astute guidance, as a lever to win for them a reluctant admission that the Faith was not a heresy inside Islám and in the West to assert its disavowal of that same accusation. It was even cited, at the time Shoghi Effendi made strong representations to the Israeli Minister for Religious Affairs, as a reason for his insistence that the affairs of the Bahá'í Community should not be handled by the same departmental head who was responsible for the Muslim Community in Israel, pointing out that this created the impression we were a branch of Islám, and stating he preferred to have Bahá'í matters placed under the jurisdiction of the Christian Department as in this way there could be no ambiguity as regards the independent status of the Bahá'í Faith. It was as a result of such arguments as these that the Ministry for Religious Affairs set up a Bahá'í Department with a head of its own.

With the powerful lever of the Beba Court's Judgement the National Spiritual Assembly of the Bahá'ís of Egypt fought, over a period of years, to obtain for its Community at least a modicum of recognition of its independent religious status. To facilitate this the Assembly published a compilation of the Bahá'í laws related to matters of personal status and with the force of this document behind it, and using repeated incidents provoked by fanatical Muslims against the Bahá'ís, succeeded in obtaining from the Egyptian Government plots of land, officially granted to it in those cities where there was a relatively large group of believers, to be used as exclusively Bahá'í burial grounds.

This compilation of the laws regarding personal status was translated into Persian as well as English and used as a guide in the conduct of Bahá'í affairs in those countries which did not have civil laws covering such matters. Although certain concessions were won from the authorities in Muslim countries such as Egypt, Persia, Palestine and in India as a result of this, the fact remained that the legal situation of the Bahá'ís, particularly in Egypt and Persia, was highly ambiguous and they often found themselves with no rights at all in certain respects, living in a kind of legal no man's land. This was particularly true of their marriages and divorces which were registered with their Assemblies, took place according to Bahá'í law, but were viewed as non-existent in the eyes of the government of their country. The fact that large communities of believers accepted this hardship proudly, refusing to be humiliated in the eyes of their derisive fellow-countrymen, and continue to this day the struggle for recognition in such fundamental matters, is the highest possible tribute to the spirit of faith the teachings of Bahá'u'lláh have engendered in their hearts, and to the loyalty with which they carried out the instructions of their beloved Guardian not to mind "any wave of unpopularity, of distrust or criticism, which a strict adherence to their standards might provoke."

In his recapitulation of those events which must ultimately lead to the recognition and emancipation of the Faith Shoghi Effendi, in

God Passes By, wrote these memorable words: "To all administrative regulations which the civil authorities have issued from time to time . . . the Bahá'í community, faithful to its sacred obligations towards its government, and conscious of its civic duties, has yielded, and will continue to yield implicit obedience . . . To such orders, however, as are tantamount to a recantation of their faith by its members, or constitute an act of disloyalty to its spiritual, its basic and God-given principles and precepts, it will stubbornly refuse to bow, preferring imprisonment, deportation and all manner of persecution, including death—as already suffered by the twenty thousand martyrs that have laid down their lives in the path of its Founders—rather than follow the dictates of a temporal authority requiring it to renounce its allegiance to its cause."

In Shoghi Effendi's administration of the affairs of the Faith there was a quality of rigidity in essentials and fluidity in non-essentials that must always characterize a truly great leader. Whereas in matters that are fundamental there can be no compromise, there can and should be, in administering the affairs of a world-wide community, recognition of the fact that people are in different stages of evolution. An example of the wisdom and skill of Shoghi Effendi is the way he treated different communities differently, never permitting any community—be it in one of the world's great and most sophisticated metropolises or in a village of illiterate peasants—to disregard the fundamental teachings of Bahá'u'lláh, but recognizing at the same time the fact that one does not require of a five-year-old child what one does of an adolescent or demand the same wisdom, obedience and experience in a young man of twenty-one that one expects from a person who has passed through three score years and ten in the school of life.

No better example of this differentiation in the stages of development that characterize different Bahá'í communities at the present time could be found than in the last letter Shoghi Effendi addressed to one of the great African Regional Assemblies. Dated August 8, 1957 (less than three months before he died), and written at the instruction of the Guardian himself, his secretary pointed out the very essence of his thoughts on such a supremely important subject at this stage in Bahá'í history: "We cannot expect people who are illiterate (which is no reflection on their mental abilities or capacities) to have studied the Teachings, especially when so little literature is available in their own language in the first place, and grasp all their ramifications, the way an African, say in London, is

THE MOUNTAINEER
Shoghi Effendi, from his years of mountain climbing, was a steady and tireless walker; above, in the Holy Land; below in Switzerland

A PHOTOGRAPH BY SHOGHI EFFENDI

Shoghi Effendi had a particular fondness for waterfalls and for taking artistic

VICTORIA FALLS, RHODESIA, 1929
Shoghi Effendi's masterly photograph of one of the world's greatest waterfalls, Zimbabwe, Africa

A FERRY ON THE NILE

Getting the ferry boat through a papyrus swamp on the Nile River, 1929.
Photograph by Shoghi Effendi

expected to. The spirit of the person is the important thing, the recognition of Bahá'u'lláh and His position in the world in this day . . . The purpose of the new National Assemblies in Africa, and the purpose of any administrative body, is to carry the Message to the people and enlist the sincere under the banner of this Faith . . . Therefore, those responsible for accepting new enrollments must just be sure of one thing—that the heart of the applicant has been touched with the spirit of the Faith. Everything else can be built on this foundation gradually."

What Shoghi Effendi made us understand is that the great tree of the World Order of Bahá'u'lláh when first planted is a tiny seed— belief in Him. Gradually it will grow, like any living thing, bigger and bigger and become more and more mature. Shoghi Effendi conceived it his major task, pursuant to 'Abdu'l-Bahá's instructions in His Will, to promulgate the Faith throughout the entire planet and enlist under its banner all the peoples of the world; he realized the raw material must first be assembled from which could be shaped the future society of that world; although so many things were required to shape that future society and were admittedly essential prerequisites to its creation, the supreme fact remained that the masses must be first brought under the shadow of Bahá'u'lláh before His World Order could emerge in all its glory.

In North America, the Cradle of the Administrative Order of the Faith, the Guardian spent sixteen years in laying a firm foundation and creating a pattern for all Bahá'í administrative institutions. In our modern terminology he built a launching pad from which he could send off his rockets—the great teaching Plans that occupied so much of his time during the last two decades of his life. That "the administration of the Cause is to be conceived as an instrument and not a substitute for the Faith of Bahá'u'lláh, that it should be regarded as a channel through which His promised blessings may flow, that it should guard against such rigidity as would clog and fetter the liberating forces released by His Revelation . . ." Shoghi Effendi made absolutely clear.

Just as in the universe there are many galaxies in different stages of evolution, so in the global universe of God's Cause different parts of the Bahá'í world were in different states of development. The communities of the Middle East were much farther advanced in applying the Bahá'í laws and ordinances in the lives of the believers that composed them, but they were neither emancipated, recognized nor free. The communities in the West, in the Americas,

Europe and Australasia were free, but, because of their cultural past, and the fact that in their countries laws of personal status were administered by civil and not religious courts, were far behind the East in applying many of the laws of their Faith as well as in observing its ordinances. The new Bahá'ís in many of the world's more backward countries were free in the sense of not being, like their brethren in the East, the victims of fanatical governments whose state religion was Islám, but were not always able to apply the Bahá'í laws because of the tribal societies in which many of them lived, and were also handicapped, at least temporarily, by the fact that the historical backgrounds from which they had sprung were so different in many respects from those of the peoples of Jewish, Christian and Muḥammadan antecedents, whose common background was that from which the Bahá'í Faith itself had come. Because of these factors Shoghi Effendi, like the conductor of a great orchestra, made sure that each community within the Bahá'í world was playing its own notes in the symphony of the whole. Though the parts were different each one had to follow the notes he had been given. Unless we grasp this picture of what our Bahá'í world is like at this present stage of its development, we will never be able to properly understand just what Shoghi Effendi did create, did accomplish, during his ministry and how thrilling his achievements are.

These different examples indicate that although mankind is one and its World Order will be one, the enforcement of the laws, ordinances, and administrative procedures of the Cause must perforce progress at different rates of speed in different places. Shoghi Effendi spent many years erecting, on the foundation already created by the Master, an organized system in which a Bahá'í was clearly differentiated from a non-Bahá'í—through his beliefs, his privileges and his responsibilities—before he could take the step of devising a way to ensure that inside the Bahá'í communities the believers made reasonable effort to follow the Bahá'í teachings and that if they too flagrantly disregarded them there was a means of punishment—a sanction—at hand to ensure they did not place in jeopardy the good name and independent character of the Faith and as a means of protecting the reputation of the community. This sanction was the removal of the administrative rights of a believer; it meant that he or she could no longer vote in Bahá'í elections, be elected to or appointed on Bahá'í Assemblies and committees, receive a Bahá'í marriage or divorce and attend those meetings where the Bahá'ís as a community were gathered. In the East, where many laws of personal status were administered by Assemblies, it involved a number of the provisions of the Aqdas; in the West, where a different situation existed, it involved obedience to those laws the Guardian considered the Bahá'ís must now follow, such as obtaining the consent of both parents to marriage, having a Bahá'í marriage ceremony, and following the Bahá'í divorce laws. This sanction was also invoked in cases where Bahá'ís, completely disregarding the teachings of their Faith, entered into political matters, or in cases of what he carefully termed "flagrant immorality" which brought the whole community into disrepute, or for other serious breaches of what he called those "directing and regulating principles of Bahá'í belief" which "the upholders of the Cause . . . feel bound, as their Administrative Order expands and consolidates itself, to assert and vigilantly apply." Shoghi Effendi made it clear that the removal of voting rights must never be used lightly and its use at all should be avoided as much as possible.

A procedure as fundamental as this was one which Shoghi Effendi universally applied to Bahá'ís everywhere in the world, no matter what type of society they were living in, and was part of his gradual implementation of the laws and principles ordained by Bahá'u'lláh "which constituted", he stated, "the warp and woof of the institutions upon which the structure of His World Order must ultimately rest".

This direction of a Faith from its World Centre, which necessitated rigidity and universality in fundamental matters and permitted and even encouraged fluidity in secondary matters, forms a fascinating subject for observation. Shoghi Effendi's ministry was a constant breaking of the various shackles binding the Bahá'ís to the past, to the societies in which they lived, and a building up of their knowledge of the Faith and of its administrative institutions. Like a skilled physician he gave general health rules to all and specific remedies in specific cases.

A typical example of the wonderful balance Shoghi Effendi expressed in all his views is that reflected in his attitude towards the subject of the Funds of the Faith. Provisions for the support of the Cause of God had been made by Bahá'u'lláh Himself and mentioned by 'Abdu'l-Bahá on many occasions; but it was not until 1923 that Shoghi Effendi began to lay the foundations of systematic financial support of the work.

On one hand it was apparent that under no circumstances could the world redeeming Order of Bahá'u'lláh be established without great financial expenditures and on the other there were two principles that Shoghi Effendi felt compelled to call to the attention of the Bahá'ís which, if not correctly understood and exposed in their proper light, could militate against the much-needed flow of contributions into the various Funds of the Faith. The first was that as the Bahá'ís had received the bounty of knowing of and accepting Bahá'u'lláh in this great new day, they were the ones to freely give back to their fellow men the benefits that this had brought them. Shoghi Effendi made this very clear as early as 1929: "we should, I feel, regard it as an axiom and guiding principle of Bahá'í administration that in the conduct of every specific Bahá'í activity . . . only those who have already identified themselves with the Faith and are regarded as its avowed and unreserved supporters should be invited to join and collaborate." Bahá'ís could only accept money from non-Bahá'ís for purely humanitarian purposes, such as charity to be expended for peoples of all racial and religious backgrounds and not just for Bahá'ís.

The second, and what he termed "the cardinal principle" in a message to the American National Assembly in 1926, was "that all contributions to the Fund are to be purely and strictly voluntary in character. It should be made clear and evident to everyone that any form of compulsion, however slight and indirect, strikes at the very root of the principle underlying the formation of the Fund ever since its inception." This instruction was the logical concomitant of the attitude of the Bahá'í religion that the Message of the Manifestation of God in this day is His free gift to the peoples of the world; that all men have been called by Him to enter the Divine Fold and that in doing so not money but faith is required of them. Unlike so many churches there were no entrance fees, no obligatory dues to be paid, no seats in the Temples to be purchased, no forced contributions. The poor could find a refuge and the rich be welcomed on equal terms.

Shoghi Effendi made it clear that one of the duties and privileges of being a follower of Bahá'u'lláh was to support His work in this world. He also made it clear that it was the principle involved in giving that was more important than the sum involved; the penny of a poor man, which might for him and his family represent a real sacrifice, was as precious, as much needed and just as respectable a contribution as the hundreds or thousands of dollars a more well-to-do Bahá'í might be able to give. Over and over again he stressed these two things: universality in giving, the participation of all as a symbol of our common love for and solidarity in our Faith, and sacrifice in giving. At the time when the great Mother Temple of the West was in urgent need of contributions to raise its structure the Guardian wrote: "It cannot be denied that the emanations of spiritual power and inspiration destined to radiate from the central Edifice of the Mashriqu'l-Adhkár will to a very large extent depend upon the range and variety of contributing believers, as well as upon the nature and degree of self-abnegation which their unsolicited offerings will entail." It is hard for a wealthy person to sacrifice because he has so much; but for a poor person to sacrifice is easier because he has so little. Money given to the Cause at a sacrifice on the part of any giver carries a particular blessing with it.

Shoghi Effendi himself repeatedly supported various undertakings in different countries. Shortly after the Master's passing he began to contribute to the American Temple; in 1957 he announced he himself would defray one-third of the cost of erecting the three new Bahá'í Temples to be constructed during the World Crusade; he supported much of the translation and printing of Bahá'í books, contributed to Bahá'í cemeteries and the purchase of various Bahá'í headquarters, and innumerable other activities. In doing this he set an example to all believers and all Bahá'í institutions of giving, of participating with others in the joy of bringing to fruition plans of the Cause of God. His complete frankness in such matters, his avowal on some occasions that he did not have the money needed to do a certain thing he wanted to do for the Cause, the touching words with which he sent a small sum for the American Temple: "I beg to enclose my humble contribution of 19 pounds, as my share of the numerous donations that have reached the Temple Treasury in the past year", all provide not only an example but a very real encouragement to believers rich or poor to follow in his footsteps, happy they have such footsteps to tread in.

In his constant encouragement of the Bahá'ís to arise and spread their Faith among the spiritually hungry multitudes of their fellow men the Guardian frequently recalled to them the injunction of Bahá'u'lláh Himself: *"Centre your energies in the propagation of the Faith of God. Whoso is worthy of so high a calling, let him arise and promote it. Whoso is unable, it is his duty to appoint him who will, in his stead, proclaim this Revelation . . ."* and said that those who were not able to go forth and establish themselves in those places where Bahá'ís were so urgently needed, should, mindful of these words of Bahá'u'lláh, "determine . . . to appoint a deputy who, on that believer's behalf, will arise and carry out so noble an enterprise." On more than one occasion he himself, through a National Assembly, deputized a number of Bahá'ís to fulfil specific goals.

XII

FUNDAMENTAL TRUTHS AND GUIDELINES

A proper understanding of the evolution of the Cause of God cannot be achieved unless certain fundamental truths enshrined in it are made clear. 'Abdu'l-Bahá stated one of these when He wrote: *"From the beginning of time until the present day, the light of Divine Revelation hath risen in the East and shed its radiance upon the West. The illumination thus shed hath, however, acquired in the West an extraordinary brilliancy."* This was the statement of a general principle common to the phenomenon of religion on this planet, but in this Bahá'í Dispensation the clear and specific working of this principle has been laid bare to our eyes over a period of more than one hundred and forty years.

The combination of the love of the Father for the first-born, for the first nation in the West to respond to His Message, and the vitality of the New World itself, seems, in a mysterious and beautiful way, to have invested the Bahá'ís of North America with a station and powers unparalleled in history; Shoghi Effendi said they had been given "spiritual primacy" by 'Abdu'l-Bahá, and were "the appointed, the chief trustees" of that "divinely conceived, world-encompassing" Divine Plan which conferred on them a world mission which was the "sacred birthright of the American followers of Bahá'u'lláh". In his observation of the fulfilment of the truths enshrined in the Teachings, Shoghi Effendi pointed out that there had been forces at work "which, through a remarkable swing of the pendulum, have caused the administrative centre of the Faith to gravitate away from its cradle, to the shores of the American Continent." "To their Persian brethren, who in the Heroic Age of the Faith had won the crown of Martyrdom, the American believers, forerunners of its Golden Age, were now worthily succeeding"; they had become the "spiritual descendants of the heroes of God's Cause". It was their destiny—the destiny of this "much loved", "high minded and valiant", "God-chosen" community—to "be acclaimed as the creator and champion-builder of the World Order of Bahá'u'lláh".

In one of his earliest letters as Guardian, addressed to the New York Spiritual Assembly in 1923, Shoghi Effendi states in a few words his attitude towards America, an attitude that never altered until the end of his life: "Conscious of the clear and emphatic predictions of our beloved Master as to the predominant part the West is destined to play during the early stages in the universal triumph of the Movement, I have, ever since His departure, turned my eyes in hopeful expectation to the distant shores of that continent . . ."

A mutually trusting and tender relationship grew up between the young Guardian and those he called "the children of 'Abdu'l-Bahá" from the very first moment they heard he had been named the Master's successor.

We must always bear in mind that it was this early partnership with America, inherent in the destiny of the Faith, that led to the establishment and growth of the Administrative Order all over the world. The matrix of that Order was perfected in America, though in an embryonic form it had existed already in the days of 'Abdu'l-Bahá. Shoghi Effendi began to actively guide America, finding her eager and responsive, from the very outset of his ministry. To the 1923 Convention he cabled: "That this year's Convention may . . . inaugurate an unexampled campaign of teaching is indeed my ardent prayer. Let this be Riḍván's Message: unite, deepen, arise." The captain had placed his hand on the helm. Through every storm, in calm waters, in years of trial and vicissitude, through war and peace, in youth, in middle age, at the end of his life, Shoghi Effendi never ceased to guide, turn to, love, admonish and hearten this "preeminent community of the Bahá'í world".

With few exceptions, for thirty-six years, the pattern in administrative matters, the great directives concerning teaching, the world-shaping concepts and plans conveyed in the general letters of the Guardian were addressed to, published by, or relayed through, this community. This does not mean the Guardian ignored Persia and other Bahá'í communities; far from it. He had an independent, intensely personal and loving relationship to each and every one of them, formed, with the older communities, at the same time as that with America, which neither flagged nor suffered neglect throughout the years, but rather grew in scope and intensity with the passage of time. He was always everyone's Guardian.

A born administrator, with a brain and temperament that was invariably orderly and tidy, Shoghi Effendi set about organizing the affairs of the Faith in a highly systematic manner. During the first two or three years he kept lists of his letters, before his correspondence, his problems, his fatigue and lack of proper helpers made it impossible for him to handle his mail in this manner. From these lists we gather he wrote to the following places: America, Britain, France, Germany, Japan, Mesopotamia, Caucasus, Persia, Turkistán, Turkey, Australia, Switzerland, India, Syria, Italy, Burma, Canada, Pacific Islands, Egypt, Palestine, Sweden and Europe. He also wrote to many individual centres in America, Europe, North Africa, the Middle and Far East. He lists sixty-seven of these in the 1922–23 period, eighty-eight during the period 1923–24, and ninety-six in the 1924–25 period.

The vast majority of Bahá'ís still resided in Persia and neighbouring territories; there was a small but equally loyal and devoted community in North America, even smaller ones in Europe, Africa, the Indian sub-continent and the Pacific region. Most of these believers were anything but clear in their minds as to just what the Faith represented, had no idea of what form it was about to take, pursuant to the Master's instructions in His Will, and still less any real understanding of its Administrative Order. Although there were bodies called Spiritual Assemblies, they were often called by other names too, and their functioning and membership were frequently vague and bore small resemblance to what we now understand a Spiritual Assembly to be.

This dispersed, heterogeneous, unorganized but loyal mass of believers throughout the world had other handicaps to overcome. The Persian friends, though fully aware of the completely independent character of their Faith—an independence they had unstintingly sacrificed their lives to assert—nevertheless had not yet succeeded in cutting themselves off completely from certain national customs and evils at complete variance with the teachings of its Founder. There was still a twilight-land of over-lapping with the customs of Islám and the many abuses to which its gradual decline had given rise over the centuries. The principle of monogamy was neither strictly practised nor properly understood; the drinking of alcohol was still widespread; the categoric ban of Bahá'u'lláh on the use of narcotics had not been fully grasped in a land which was riddled through and through with the pernicious use of opium and other drugs. In the West, particularly in America where the largest group of its occidental followers was to be found, the Bahá'ís, however attached they might be to this new Faith they had accepted, were still entangled with church affiliations and membership in various societies, which only served to dissipate their extremely limited resources, squander their capacity for concerted and concentrated activity for the Cause of God, and weaken any claims they might make as to its independent character. Neither in the East nor in the West were the Bahá'ís clear in their minds as to the degree they should shun all political affiliations and activities. Shoghi Effendi attacked this somewhat nebulous condition of the Bahá'í world in two ways. The first was to create a universal, consistent and coherent method of carrying on Bahá'í community life and organizing its affairs, based on the Teachings and the Master's elaboration of them, and the second was to educate the believers in an understanding of the objectives and implications of their religion and the truths enshrined in it.

Shoghi Effendi's genius for organization became increasingly manifest and a uniform system of national and local Assemblies was quickly and carefully built up by him throughout the world.

Some communities already had, in response to 'Abdu'l-Bahá's encouragement, established committees. Correspondence in 1922 and 1923 between Shoghi Effendi and the American National Assembly shows that there were in existence such National Committees as Teaching, Publishing and Reviewing, Children's Education, Library, Star of the West, Race Amity, and National Archives. In going over the Guardian's early acts and communications it is both astonishing and fascinating to see how everything that was there at the end of his ministry was there at the beginning too. As the years went by he amplified his thoughts and elaborated his themes, himself matured, and the Cause matured with him, but it was all quite complete in embryo when he first started directing the affairs of the Faith.

The education of the Bahá'ís in the principles underlying Bahá'u'lláh's social system became, for many years, the paramount concern of the Guardian. They were used to believing in the Teachings, to trying to spread them amongst their fellow men, to at least a modicum of community life through feasts, meetings and commemoration of their Holy Days. They were not used to working in an organized manner as members of an organization in the truest sense of that word. They were also not used to keeping the system of communication within the Faith open. Shoghi Effendi realized from the outset that the work that lay before him required that he, in particular, should have a thorough knowledge of what was going on in the Bahá'í communities throughout the world and of the state of their activities and their response to the up-building of the administrative system of the Cause. This required a close correspondence with not only all the national bodies, but with all the local Assemblies; the national bodies were weak or practically non-existent, the local Assemblies usually even weaker. He felt it essential to be in contact with them all, East and West. His plan was not only to collect information at the World Centre but to stimulate and encourage the oppressed oriental communities through relaying to them glad-tidings from their sister communities in the West.

In their hearts the Bahá'ís, a sincere and loving group of people gathered about Bahá'u'lláh in belief and confidence, were deeply aware of their international bond of unity in faith. But this was not sufficient. The time had come for a dynamic, working, every-day consciousness of this to take place. In addition to creating a uniform system of Bahá'í elections and a flow of reports and correspondence to him and from him, Shoghi Effendi took steps to greatly reinforce and reinvigorate certain Bahá'í publications already in existence when he became Guardian and which had been encouraged and supported by 'Abdu'l-Bahá Himself. The *Star of the West*, published in America, was the oldest and most famous of these. In addition there were the *Sun of Truth* published in Germany, *The Dawn* published in Burma, *The Bahá'í News of India* published there, and the *Khorshid-i-Khavar* published in 'Ishqábád. To all these Shoghi Effendi gave his enthusiastic support.

In addition to this Shoghi Effendi inaugurated a "circular letter which the Haifa Bahá'í Spiritual Assembly forwards every nineteen days to all Bahá'í Centres throughout the East." This was in Persian. It had an English counterpart. "The Spiritual Assembly which has been established in Haifa", he wrote to the Swiss Bahá'ís in February 1923, "will from now on send you regularly the news of the Holy Land . . ." Measures such as these had the effect of a giant spoon by which he vigorously stirred the entire community of the faithful all over the world, blending, stimulating, challenging its component parts to greater action, co-operation and understanding.

But what, we should pause and ask, was this Administration the Guardian was so tirelessly working to establish? As it evolved it would, he said, "at once incarnate, safeguard and foster" the spirit of this invincible Faith. It was unique in history, divinely conceived, and different from any system which had existed in the religions of the past. Fundamentally it was the vehicle of a future World Order and World Civilization which would constitute no less than a World Commonwealth of all the nations on this planet. Though its entire structure of elected bodies was based on principles of universal suffrage and election by secret ballot, its ultimate workings were conceived of in a different light, for, unlike the paramount principle of democracy by which the elected are constantly responsible to the electors, Bahá'í bodies are responsible at all times to the Founder of their Faith and His teachings. Whereas in democracy the ruling factor at the top can go no higher than their own councils and their decisions are subject to the scrutiny and approval of those they represent, this ruling factor in the Cause of God is at once the servant of all the servants of God—in other words the body of the faithful—but responsible to a higher factor, divinely guided and inspired, the Guardian or sole interpreter, and the Universal House of Justice, the supreme, elected body, or sole legislator. It will be seen that in this system the people, divorced from the corrupt influences of nomination, political canvassing and the violence of those whims and dissatisfactions so easily engendered in the masses by the working of the democratic principle alone, are free to choose those they deem best qualified to direct their affairs and safeguard their rights on the one hand, and to protect and serve the interests of the Cause of God on the other.

The elected Bahá'í bodies might be likened to a great network of irrigation pipes, selected and put together by the people for their own benefit. But life-giving waters from on high flow through this system, independent of the people, independent of any will of the pipes, and this water is the divinely guided and inspired counsels of the Guardian and the Supreme Body of the Cause, which they receive, in this Bahá'í Dispensation, from no less a source than the Twin Manifestations of God. The system of Bahá'u'lláh, Shoghi Effendi wrote, "cannot ever degenerate into any form of despotism, of oligarchy, or of demagogy which must sooner or later corrupt the machinery of all man-made and essentially defective political institutions." Already, in 1934, Shoghi Effendi was able to write of the workings of this system, which was so rapidly growing and spreading its roots steadily throughout the Bahá'í world, that it had evinced a power which a "disillusioned and sadly shaken society" could ill afford to ignore. The vitality of its institutions, the obstacles overcome by its administrators, the enthusiasm of its itinerant teachers, the heights of self-sacrifice attained by its champion-builders, the vision, hope, joy, inward peace, integrity, discipline and unity that were manifested by its stalwart defenders, the manner in which diversified peoples were cleansed of their prejudices and fused into the structure of this system—all testified, Shoghi Effendi wrote, to the power of this ever-expanding Order of Bahá'u'lláh.

Shoghi Effendi had the qualities of true statesmanship. Unlike many of the Bahá'ís, who, alas, are prone like Icarus to take off on wings of wax, full of hope and faith alone, Shoghi Effendi forged his flying machine of airworthy materials, building it carefully, piece by piece. Within the first few years of his ministry he had created uniformity in essential matters of Bahá'í Administration. He had established his bed-rock of local Assemblies and a national body, wherever the national communities were strong enough to support such an institution.

One of the most wonderful things about Shoghi Effendi was that he pushed the horizons of our minds ever further away. His vision of the Cause was seen from the Everest of his all-embracing understanding of its implications. In thirty-six years nothing ever grew smaller, everything grew bigger and bigger. There was infinite room not only to breathe but to dream. Bahá'u'lláh was the Inaugurator of a five-hundred-thousand-year cycle. He was the culmination of a six-thousand-year cycle of prophecy beginning with Adam. Withal, His Revelation was but part of an infinite chain of Divine Guidance. The Guardian summed up this concept in his masterly statement submitted to the United Nations Special Palestine Committee: "The fundamental principle enunciated by Bahá'u'lláh . . . is that religious truth is not absolute but relative, that Divine Revelation is a continuous and progressive process, that all the great religions of the world are divine in origin, that their basic principles are in complete harmony, that their aims and purposes are one and the same, that their teachings are but facets of one truth, that their functions are complementary, that they differ only in the non-essential aspects of their doctrines, and that their missions represent successive stages in the spiritual evolution of human society. The aim of Bahá'u'lláh . . . is not to destroy but to fulfil the Revelations of the past . . . His purpose . . . is to restate the basic truths which these teachings enshrine in a manner that would conform to the needs . . . of the age in which we live . . . Nor does Bahá'u'lláh claim finality for His own Revelation, but rather stipulates that a fuller measure of truth . . . must needs be disclosed at future stages in the constant and limitless evolution of mankind."

In that same statement he places the Administrative Order, in words of crystal clearness, in its proper relationship to this Revelation: "The Administrative Order of the Faith of Bahá'u'lláh, which is destined to evolve into the Bahá'í World Commonwealth . . . unlike the systems evolved after the death of the Founders of the various religions, is divine in origin . . . The Faith which this Order serves, safeguards and promotes, is, it should be noted in this connection, essentially supernatural, supranational, entirely non-political, non-partisan, and diametrically opposed to any policy or school of thought that seeks to exalt any particular race, class or nation. It is free from any form of ecclesiasticism, has neither priesthood nor rituals, and is supported exclusively by voluntary contributions made by its avowed adherents."

What this concept would lead to was expressed on another occasion in one of the Guardian's communications to the Bahá'ís of the West: "A world federal system, ruling the whole earth . . . blending and embodying the ideals of both the East and the West, liberated from the curse of war . . . a system in which Force is made the servant of Justice, whose life is sustained by its universal recognition of one God and by its allegiance to one common Revelation—such is the goal towards which humanity, impelled by the unifying forces of life, is moving."

All this being so, something was very much the matter with the world. What it was Shoghi Effendi also made clear to us in *The Promised Day Is Come*: "For a whole century God has respited mankind, that it might acknowledge the Founder of such a Revelation, espouse His Cause, proclaim His greatness and establish His Order. In a hundred volumes . . . the Bearer of such a Message has proclaimed, as no Prophet before Him has done, the Mission with which God had entrusted Him . . . How—we may well ask ourselves—has the world, the object of such Divine solicitude, repaid Him Who sacrificed His all for its sake?" Bahá'u'lláh's Message met, Shoghi Effendi wrote, with unmitigated indifference from the élite, unrelenting hatred from the ecclesiastics, scorn from the people of Persia, utter contempt from most of the rulers addressed by Him, the envy and malice of those in foreign lands, all of which were evidences of the treatment such a Message received from "a generation sunk in self-content, careless of its God, and oblivious of the omens, warnings and admonitions revealed by His Messengers." Man was therefore to taste what his own hands had wrought. He had refused to take the direct road leading him to his great destiny, through acceptance of the Promised One for this Day, and had chosen the long road, bitter, blood-stained, dark, literally leading him through hell, before he once again could near the goal originally placed at his finger tips for him to seize.

From the very beginning of his ministry, steeped as he was in the Teachings, Shoghi Effendi foresaw the course events seemed inevitably to be taking. As early as January 1923, he painted the picture of the future in a letter to an American local Assembly: "Individuals and nations", he wrote, "are being swept by a whirlwind of insincerity and selfishness, which if not resisted may imperil, nay destroy civilization itself. It is our task and privilege to capture gradually and persistently the attention of the world by the sincerity of our motives, by the breadth of our outlook and the devotion and tenacity with which we pursue our work of service to mankind." He was not only clear as to the situation and the remedy, but sufficiently shrewd to doubt the possibility, after eighty years of neglect on the part of humanity, of averting universal catastrophe. "The world", he wrote in February 1923, was "apparently drifting further and further from the spirit of the Divine Teachings . . ." Many times, in both his writings and his words to visiting pilgrims, Shoghi Effendi reminded the Bahá'ís of the formidable warning of Bahá'u'lláh: *"The civilization, so often vaunted by the learned exponents of arts and sciences, will, if allowed to overleap the bounds of moderation, bring great evil upon men. Thus warneth you He Who is the All-Knowing. If carried to excess, civilization will prove as prolific a source of evil as it had been of goodness when kept within the restraints of moderation . . . The day is approaching when its flame will devour the cities."*

From the outset Shoghi Effendi realized that there was a great cancer eating away at the vitals of men, a materialism reaching a state of development in the West unrivalled by the decadence it had invariably produced in past civilizations when their decline set in. As very many people do not know what materialism means it can do no harm to quote Webster who defines certain of its aspects as "the tendency to give undue importance to material interests; devotion to the material nature and its wants" and says another definition is the theory that human phenomena should be viewed and interpreted in terms of physical and material causes rather than spiritual and ethical causes. Shoghi Effendi's attitude towards this subject, the evils that produce it and the evils it in turn gives rise to, is reflected in innumerable passages of his writings, beginning in 1923 and going on to 1957. In 1923 he refers to "the confusion and the gross materialism in which mankind is now sunk . . ." A few years later he writes of "the apathy, the gross materialism and superficiality of society today". In 1927 he wrote to the American National Assembly: ". . . in the heart of society itself, where the ominous signs of increasing extravagance and profligacy are but lending fresh impetus to the forces of revolt and reaction that are growing more distinct every day . . ." In 1933, in a general letter to the American Bahá'ís, he speaks of the "follies and furies, the shifts, shams and compromises that characterize the present age". In 1934, in a general letter to the Bahá'ís throughout the West, he speaks of "the signs of an impending catastrophe, strongly reminiscent of the Fall of the Roman Empire in the West, which threatens to engulf the whole structure of present-day civilization . . ." In that same communication he says: "How disquieting the lawlessness, the corruption, the unbelief that are eating into the vitals of a tottering civilization!" In his general letter to the Bahá'ís of the West, in 1936, he says: "in whichever direction we turn our gaze . . . we cannot fail to be struck by the evidences of moral decadence which, in their individual lives no less than in their collective capacity, men and women around us exhibit . . ." In 1938 he warned of "the challenge of these times, so fraught with peril, so full of corruption . . ." and speaks of the root-evil of all: ". . . as the chill of irreligion creeps relentlessly over the limbs of mankind . . ." and of "A world, dimmed by the steadily dying-out light of religion", a world in which nationalism was blind and triumphant, in which racial and religious persecution was pitiless, a world in which false theories and doctrines threatened to supplant the worship of God, a world, in sum, "enervated by a rampant and brutal materialism; disintegrating through the corrosive influence of moral and spiritual decadence".

In 1941 Shoghi Effendi castigated the prevalent trends of society in no uncertain terms: "the spread of lawlessness, of drunkenness, of gambling, and of crime; the inordinate love of pleasure, of riches, and other earthly vanities; the laxity in morals, revealing itself in the irresponsible attitude towards marriage, in the weakening of parental control, in the rising tide of divorce, in the deteriora-

AFRICAN VIEWS

Above, Shoghi Effendi's photograph of the giant baobab tree which grew near Victoria Falls; below, the Guardian standing at the grave of Cecil Rhodes

A PHOTOGRAPH BY THE GUARDIAN

A typical beautiful African mud village, taken by Shoghi Effendi when he crossed Africa from Cape Town to Cairo in 1929

SAFARI

The car in which Shoghi Effendi travelled as a passenger with an English hunter across part of East Africa, 1929

THE GUARDIAN STUDIES HIS GARDENS
Top: Shoghi Effendi views the Báb's Shrine from the top of Mt. Carmel.
Bottom: He surveys the newly developed area in Bahjí

tion in the standard of literature and of the press, and in the advocacy of theories that are the very negation of purity, of morality and chastity—these evidences of moral decadence, invading both the East and the West, permeating every stratum of society, and instilling their poison in its members of both sexes, young and old alike, blacken still further the scroll upon which are inscribed the manifold transgressions of an unrepentant humanity." In 1948 he again stigmatizes modern society as being: "politically convulsed, economically disrupted, socially subverted, morally decadent and spiritually moribund . . ." By such oft-repeated words as these the Guardian sought to protect the Bahá'í communities and alert them to the dangers by which they were surrounded.

However, it was towards the end of his life that Shoghi Effendi dwelt more openly and frequently on this subject, pointing out that although Europe was the cradle of a "godless", a "highly-vaunted yet lamentably defective civilization", the foremost protagonist of that civilization was now the United States and that in that country, at the present time, its manifestations had led to a degree of unbridled materialism which now presented a danger to the entire world. In 1954, in a letter to the Bahá'ís of the United States couched in terms he had never used before, he recapitulated the extraordinary privileges this community had enjoyed, the extraordinary victories it had won, but said it stood at a most critical juncture in its history, not only its own history but its nation's history—a nation he had described as "the shell that enshrines so precious a member of the world community of the followers" of Bahá'u'lláh. In this letter he pointed out that the country of which the American Bahá'ís formed a part "is passing through a crisis which, in its spiritual, moral, social and political aspects, is of extreme seriousness—a seriousness which to a superficial observer is liable to be dangerously underestimated.

"The steady and alarming deterioration in the standard of morality as exemplified by the appalling increase of crime, by political corruption in ever-widening and ever higher circles, by the loosening of the sacred ties of marriage, by the inordinate craving for pleasure and diversion, and by the marked and progressive slackening of parental control, is no doubt the most arresting and distressing aspect of the decline that has set in, and can be clearly perceived, in the fortunes of the entire nation.

"Parallel with this, and pervading all departments of life—an evil which the nation, and indeed all those within the capitalist system, though to a lesser degree, share with that state and its satellites regarded as the sworn enemies of that system—is the crass materialism, which lays excessive and ever-increasing emphasis on material well-being, forgetful of those things of the spirit on which alone a sure and stable foundation can be laid for human society. It is this same cancerous materialism, born originally in Europe, carried to excess in the North American continent, contaminating the Asiatic peoples and nations, spreading its ominous tentacles to the borders of Africa, and now invading its very heart, which Bahá'u'lláh in unequivocal and emphatic language denounced in His Writings, comparing it to a devouring flame and regarding it as the chief factor in precipitating the dire ordeals and world-shaking crises that must necessarily involve the burning of cities and the spread of terror and consternation in the hearts of men."

Shoghi Effendi reminded us that 'Abdu'l-Bahá, during His visit to both Europe and America, had, from platform and pulpit raised His voice "with pathetic persistence" against this "all-pervasive, pernicious materialism" and pointed out that as "this ominous laxity in morals, this progressive stress laid on man's material pursuits and well-being" continued, the political horizon was also darkening "as witnessed by the widening of the gulf separating the protagonists of two antagonistic schools of thought which, however divergent in their ideologies, are to be commonly condemned by the upholders of the standard of the Faith of Bahá'u'lláh for their materialistic philosophies and their neglect of those spiritual values and eternal verities on which alone a stable and flourishing civilization can be ultimately established."

The Guardian constantly called to our attention that the objectives, standards and practices of the present-day world were, for the most part, in opposition to or a corrupt form of what the Bahá'ís believe and seek to establish. The guidance he gave us in such matters was not confined to issues as blatant and burning as those cited in the above quotations. He educated us as well—if we accept to be educated by him—in matters of good taste, sound judgement and good breeding. So often he would say: this is a religion of the golden mean, the middle of the way, neither this extreme nor that. What he meant by this was not compromise but the very essence of the thought conveyed in these words of Bahá'u'lláh Himself: "*overstep not the bounds of moderation; whoso cleaveth to justice can, under no circumstances, transgress the limits of moderation.*" We live in perhaps the most immoderate society the world has ever seen, shaking itself to pieces because it has turned its back on God and refused His Messenger.

Shoghi Effendi did not see this society with the eyes that we see it. Had he done so he would not have been our guide and our shield. Whereas the Manifestation of God appears from celestial realms and brings a new age with Him, the Guardian's station and function was entirely different. He was very much a man of the Twentieth Century. Far from being alien to the world in which he lived one might say he represented the best of it in his clear and logical mind, his unembarrassed, uninhibited appraisal of it. His understanding of the weaknesses of others, however, produced in him no compromise, no acceptance of wrong trends as evils to be condoned because they were universal. Too much stress cannot be laid on this point. We are prone to think that because a thing is general it is the right thing; because our leaders and scholars hold a view, it is the right view; because experts assure us that this, that or the other thing is proper and enduring they speak with the voice of authority. No such complacence afflicted Shoghi Effendi. He saw everything in the world today—in the realm of politics, morality, art, music, literature, medicine, social science—against the framework of Bahá'u'lláh's teachings. Did it fit into the guiding lines laid down by Bahá'u'lláh? It was a sound trend. Did it not? It was on a wrong and dangerous track.

Shoghi Effendi gave us, over the years, what I like to call "guiding lines", clarification of great principles, doctrines and thoughts in our religion. Only a few can be arbitrarily selected for a work of this scope, but they are ones which to me have a special significance in shaping our Bahá'í outlook in the world we live in today. One of the most fallacious modern doctrines, diametrically opposed to the teachings of all religions, is that man is not responsible for his acts but is excused his wrongdoing because it is brought about by conditioning factors. This is a contention with which Shoghi Effendi had no patience, for it was not in accordance with the words of Bahá'u'lláh: *"That which traineth the world is justice, for it is upheld by two pillars, reward and punishment. These two pillars are the source of life to the world."* Individuals, nations, Bahá'í communities, the human race, are all accountable for their acts. Though there are many factors involved in all our decisions, the essence of Bahá'í belief is that God gives us the chance, the help, and the strength, to make the right one and that for it we will be rewarded and failing it we will be punished. This concept is almost the opposite of the teachings of modern psychology.

The Guardian's relationship with the entire Bahá'í world, as well as individuals, officials, and non-Bahá'ís, was based on this principle. He was immensely patient, but in the end punishment was swift and just; his rewards were swift too, and to me seemed always greater than deserved by those who received them.

The highest standards of literature and language are reflected, whether in Persian, Arabic or English, in the writings of the Báb, Bahá'u'lláh, 'Abdu'l-Bahá, and Shoghi Effendi. No debased coin of words was used by any of them. I remember once when a pilgrim, sincerely and modestly remonstrated with the Guardian about the difficulty ordinary people in America had in understanding his writings and suggested he make them a little bit easier. The Guardian pointed out, firmly, that this was not the answer; the answer was for people to raise their standard of English, adding, in his beautiful voice with its beautiful pronunciation—and a slight twinkle in his eye—that he himself wrote in English. The implication that a great deal of the writing on the other side of the Atlantic did not always fall in this category was quite clear! He urged Bahá'í magazines to use an "elevated and impressive style" and certainly set the example himself at all times.

When I was first married I was a little apprehensive of what the Guardian's attitude might be towards modern art. Loving the great periods of art in our own and other cultures I wondered what I would do if I found he admired modern trends in painting, sculpture and architecture. I need have had no fears. Occasionally we were able to visit famous European museums and art galleries together. I soon discovered, to my great relief, that his love of symmetry and beauty, of a mature style and a noble expression of real values, was deep and true. The blind search for a new style, however sincere and logical it may be, which has followed upon the general crumbling of the old order of things in the world, Shoghi Effendi never mistook for the evidence of a new, evolved expression of art, least of all a Bahá'í expression of anything. He knew history too well to mistake the lowest point of decay, the reflection of a decadent and moribund society, for the birth of a new style inspired by Bahá'u'lláh's World Order! He knew the fruit is the end product of the growth of the tree and not the first; he knew that a world system, drawing strength from world peace and unification, must come first and then be followed by the flowering, in the Golden Age, of a new, mature expression of art. Lest there be any doubt of this, look at the superstructure of the Shrine of the Báb and the International Archives building which he built; look at the four designs of the Temples for Mt. Carmel, Ṭihrán, Sydney, and Kampala he himself chose. They were admittedly conservative, based on past experience; but they were also based on styles that had withstood the test of time and would continue to do so until a new and organically evolved style could be produced as the world evolved under the influence of Bahá'u'lláh's teachings. In letters he wrote in 1956 to two different National Assemblies about two different Temples, his secretary states his views as follows: "He feels that, as this is the Mother Temple . . . it has a very great importance; and must under all circumstances be dignified, and not represent an extremist point of view in architecture. No one knows how the styles of the present day may be judged two or three generations from now; but the Bahá'ís cannot afford to build a second Temple if the one they build at the present time should seem too extreme and unsuitable at a future date." "He was sorry to have to disappoint Mr. F―― . . . However, there was no possible question of accepting something as extreme as this. The Guardian feels very strongly that, regardless of what the opinion of the latest school of architecture may be on the subject, the styles represented at present all over the world in architecture are not only very ugly, but completely lack the dignity and grace which must be at least partially present in a Bahá'í House of Worship. One must always bear in mind that the vast majority of human beings are not either very modern or very extreme in their tastes, and that what the advanced school may think is marvellous is often very distasteful indeed to just plain, simple people."

The same thoughts that moved the Guardian as regards literature and art applied to his feelings about music, of which he had a great love.

What one gleans from the above is that the Guardian desired to safeguard the Cause, to maintain for it and its precious institutions a standard of dignity and beauty that would protect its Holy Name, the sacred nature of its institutions, its international character, its newness and promise, from the whims and caprices of an age in transition and from the undue influence of a corrupt, wholly western civilization.

How many Bahá'ís appreciate the fact that just as chastity, honesty and truthfulness are required of them, courtesy, dignity and reverence are qualities upheld in the teachings of Bahá'u'lláh?

One of Shoghi Effendi's early cables to America stresses this point: "Dignity of Cause requires restraint use Master's voice record." The sense of the holiness of things is one of the greatest benedictions for man. Many times the Guardian brought this to our attention in instructions such as these: "ensure no one photographs Báb's portrait during display." To gaze upon the reproduction of the face of the Manifestation of God, were it the Báb or Bahá'u'lláh, was a unique privilege, to be approached as such, not just as one more reproduction to be passed about from hand to hand.

The sharp distinction between the coalescence of Bahá'u'lláh's followers in a unified, spiritually-motivated world system and the disintegration, side-taking and hatred decimating the races, religions and political parties of the world, was constantly pointed out by the Guardian and the dangers involved if the Bahá'ís did not hold themselves strictly aloof from these dissensions repeatedly emphasized. In September 1938, as humanity drifted towards the precipice of a second world war, Shoghi Effendi cabled a stern warning and unambiguous instruction to the believers on this policy of strict neutrality: "Loyalty World Order Bahá'u'lláh security its basic institutions both imperatively demand all its avowed supporters particularly its champion-builders American continent in these days when sinister uncontrollable forces are deepening cleavage sundering peoples nations creeds classes resolve despite pressure fast crystallizing public opinion abstain individually collectively in word action informally as well in all official utterances publications from assigning blame taking sides however indirectly in recurring political crises now agitating ultimately engulfing human society. Grave apprehension lest cumulative effect such compromises disintegrate fabric clog channel grace that sustains system God's essentially supranational supernatural order so laboriously evolved so recently established."

The patriotism of Bahá'ís is not manifest in an allegiance to national prejudices and political systems but rather in two ways: to serve one's country by fostering its highest spiritual interests and by implicit obedience to government, whatever that government may be. The Guardian pointed out, in 1932, that the extension of Bahá'í activities throughout the world and "the variety of the communities which labor under divers forms of government, so essentially different in their standards, policies and methods, make it absolutely essential for all . . . members of any one of these communities to avoid any action that might, by arousing the suspicion or exciting the antagonism of any one government, involve their brethren in fresh persecutions . . ." and went on to say: "How else, might I ask, could such a far-flung Faith, which transcends political and social boundaries, which includes within its pale so great a variety of races and nations, which will have to rely increasingly as it forges ahead, on the good-will and support of the diversified and contending governments of the earth—how else could such a Faith succeed in preserving its unity, in safeguarding its interests, and in ensuring the steady and peaceful development of its institutions?" On another occasion Shoghi Effendi wrote: "Let them proclaim that in whatever country they reside, and however advanced their institutions, or profound their desire to enforce the laws, and apply the principles enunciated by Bahá'u'lláh, they will, unhesitatingly, subordinate the operation of such laws and the application of such principles to the requirements of their respective governments. Theirs is not the purpose, while endeavouring to conduct and perfect the administrative affairs of their Faith, to violate, under any circumstances, the provisions of their country's constitution, much less to allow the machinery of their Administration to supersede the government of their respective countries." A telegram of the Guardian, sent in 1930 to one of the Near Eastern Assemblies, points very clearly to the correct Bahá'í attitude: "unless government objects formation Assembly essential". The Bahá'ís, as Shoghi Effendi said so aptly, belong to no political party but to "God's party". They are the agents of His Divine Polity.

The freedom of a sovereign state to pursue its own policies—however detrimental they might be to Bahá'í interests—was upheld by Shoghi Effendi in 1929 when the Soviet Government expropriated the first Bahá'í Temple of the world. In spite of the sorrow this action caused the Guardian he wrote that because of the articles of its own constitution the authorities had acted "within their recognized and legitimate rights". When every appeal had failed of its purpose, he instructed the Bahá'ís in that country to obey the decrees of their Government, trusting that in time, as he wrote, God would "lift the veil that now obscures the vision of their rulers, and reveal the nobility of aim, the innocence of purpose, the rectitude of conduct, and the humanitarian ideals that characterize the as yet small yet potentially powerful Bahá'í communities in every land and under any government."

It must not be thought that as this Faith grew in strength and passed from victory to victory there was a change in this fundamental policy enunciated by Shoghi Effendi only eight years after he became Guardian. Far from it. In 1955 he cabled a message to all National Assemblies, at a time when the number of countries enrolled under the banner of the Faith had almost doubled during two years, appealing to the believers who were engaged in the mightiest Crusade ever launched since the inception of the Faith "whether residing homelands overseas however repressive regimes under which they labour ponder anew full implications essential requirements their stewardship Cause Bahá'u'lláh . . . rise higher levels consecration vigilantly combat all forms misrepresentations eradicate suspicions dispel misgivings silence criticisms through still more compelling demonstration loyalty their respective governments win maintain strengthen confidence civil authorities their integrity sincerity reaffirm universality aims purposes Faith proclaim spiritual character its fundamental principles assert non-political character its Administrative institutions . . ."

There are three factors involved in this question of loyalty to government yet complete aloofness from politics: one is obedience, another is wisdom and the third is the use of approved legal channels. Too often the factor of wisdom is overlooked, and yet the Guardian made it abundantly clear that it should always be considered. In a world where the press, television and radio are hourly pouring out accusations, indictments and abuse upon the systems and policies of other nations, the Bahá'ís cannot be too wise.

In various countries he forbade the Bahá'ís to seek publicity and told them to shun all contact with certain sects and nationalities who, if they heard of the Faith or accepted it, could place the entire work of the pioneers in jeopardy. This was the essence of wisdom and every time it was ignored it led to disaster.

On the other hand, in different countries at different times, the Guardian strongly urged the Assemblies and the pioneers, wherever the way was open to do so, to protect the interests of the Faith through legal channels and through securing for it legal recognition, as well as through insuring the support of public opinion through the media of the press and radio.

In such matters of policy as these, however, which affect the international interests and well-being of the Faith, guidance and protection must come from the World Centre, which, by its very nature, is the sole authority in a position to use its judgement on such vital and delicate questions.

Another great guiding line of thought was the Guardian's exposition of what unity means in the Bahá'í teachings. Shoghi Effendi wrote that "the principle of unification which" the Cause "advocates and with which it stands identified" the enemies of the Faith "have misconceived as a shallow attempt at uniformity"; "Let there be no misgivings as to the animating purpose of the world-wide Law of Bahá'u'lláh . . . it repudiates excessive centralization on the one hand, and disclaims all attempts at uniformity on the other. Its watchword is unity in diversity . . ." The principle of the Oneness of Mankind, Shoghi Effendi stated, though it aimed at creating "a world organically unified in all the essential aspects of its life" was nevertheless to be a world "infinite in the diversity of the national characteristics of its federated units." He wrote of "the highly diversified Bahá'í society of the future" and, urging the Bahá'ís to pay special attention to winning the adherence to the Faith of different races, said, "A blending of these highly differentiated elements of the human race, harmoniously interwoven into the fabric of an all-embracing Bahá'í fraternity and assimilated through the processes of a divinely-appointed Administrative Order, and contributing each its share to the enrichment and glory of Bahá'í community life, is surely an achievement the contemplation of which must warm and thrill every Bahá'í heart." This Faith, Shoghi Effendi wrote, "does not ignore, nor does it attempt to suppress, the diversity of ethnical origins, of climate, of history, of language and tradition, of thought and habit, that differentiate the peoples and nations of the world."

In an age of proselytizing, when nations and blocks of nations, various societies and organizations are hammering away at people's minds day and night, seeking to make them over in their own image, seeking to force their political systems, their clothes, their way of living, their housing, their medical systems, their philosophy and moral and social codes on each other, it is surely of the greatest importance for Bahá'ís to ponder their own teachings and the illuminating interpretation of them given by their Guardian. The Western World today has a passion for uniformity. As far as it can it is trying to make everyone alike. The result is that while much good is undoubtedly being spread, and material benefits are reaching an ever larger number of people, many things diametrically opposed to the methods and objectives of Bahá'u'lláh are also taking place.

One of the things our western materialism is rapidly spreading—in addition to irreligion, immorality and the worship of money and possessions—is a wave of despair, unrest, and a feeling of deep inferiority among the so-called backward peoples of the world. We might well pause to contrast the impact—so deadly—that this self-importance, self-satisfaction and wealth is having upon other people with where the Guardian placed the emphasis in his relation to such peoples. Why did Shoghi Effendi keep and publish such exhaustive lists of the "races" and the "tribes" enlisted under the banner of the Faith? Did he perhaps collect them, each as a separate pearl, to weave into precious adornments for the body of Bahá'u'lláh's Cause? Why did he hang on the walls of the Mansion in Bahjí a picture of the first Pygmy Bahá'í, and the first descendant of the Inca Indians to accept the Faith? Surely it was not as curiosities or trophies but rather because the beloved Josephs of the world were come home to the tent of their Father. So well I remember when Shoghi Effendi discovered that one of his pilgrims was a descendant of the old royal family of Hawaiian kings. He seemed to radiate with a joy and delight that was almost tangible and this glow enveloped a man whose portion in life had been mostly compounded of scorn for his native blood! It must not be thought that such things were personal peculiarities of Shoghi Effendi or matters of policy. Far, far from it. It was the reflection of the very essence of the teachings that each division of the human race is endowed with gifts of its own needed to make the new Order of Bahá'u'lláh diversified, rich and perfect.

Not only did Shoghi Effendi preach this, he actively pursued it, through announcements, appeals and instructions to Bahá'í Assemblies: "First all red Indian Assembly consolidated Macy Nebraska" he cabled triumphantly in 1949. Constantly remembering 'Abdu'l-Bahá's words in the *Tablets of the Divine Plan* to *"give great importance to teaching the Indians, i.e., the aborigines of America"* Shoghi Effendi pursued this objective until the last months of his life, when he wrote, in July 1957, to the Canadian National Assembly, that the "long overdue conversion" of the American Indians, the Eskimos and other minorities, should receive such an impetus "as to astonish and stimulate the members of all Bahá'í communities throughout the length and breadth of the Western Hemisphere."

A year before, in one of Shoghi Effendi's letters to the United States National Assembly, his secretary had written: "The beloved Guardian feels that sufficient attention is not being paid to the matter of contacting minorities in the United States . . . He feels your

Assembly should appoint a special committee to survey the possibilities of this kind of work, and then instruct local Assemblies accordingly, and in the meantime encourage the Bahá'ís to be active in this field, which is one open to everybody, as the minorities are invariably lonely, and often respond to kindness much more quickly than the well-established majority of the population."

The natural outcome of this policy is the unique attitude the Bahá'í Faith has towards minorities, which was set forth so clearly by Shoghi Effendi in *The Advent of Divine Justice*: "To discriminate against any race, on the ground of its being socially backward, politically immature, and numerically in a minority, is a flagrant violation of the spirit that animates the Faith". Once a person accepts this Faith "every differentiation of class, creed, or colour must automatically be obliterated, and never be allowed, under any pretext, and however great the pressure of events or public opinion, to reassert itself." Shoghi Effendi then goes on to state a principle so at variance with the political thinking of the entire world that it deserves far more consideration than we usually give it: "If any discrimination is at all to be tolerated, it should be a discrimination not against, but rather in favour of the minority, be it racial or otherwise. Unlike the nations and peoples of the earth, be they of the East or of the West, democratic or authoritarian, communist or capitalist, whether belonging to the Old World or the New, who either ignore, trample upon, or extirpate, the racial, religious or political minorities within the sphere of their jurisdiction, every organized community, enlisted under the banner of Bahá'u'lláh should feel it to be its first and inescapable obligation to nurture, encourage, and safeguard every minority belonging to any faith, race, class, or nation within it. So great and vital is this principle that in such circumstances, as when an equal number of ballots has been cast in an election, or where the qualifications for any office are balanced as between the various races, faiths or nationalities within the community, priority should unhesitatingly be accorded the party representing the minority, and this for no other reason except to stimulate and encourage it, and afford it an opportunity to further the interests of the community." Shoghi Effendi once expressed the workings of this principle so succinctly and brilliantly that I wrote it down in his own words: "the minority of a majority is more important than the majority of a minority." In other words it is not the numerical strength or weakness in the nation that is the index of a minority, but its numerical strength or weakness inside the Bahá'í community holding the election—so great is the protection of any minority. The Guardian used to say that when the day came that a Bahá'í state existed the rights of non-Bahá'í religious minorities would be rigorously protected by the Bahá'ís.

The Bahá'í Faith not only safeguards society as a whole and protects the rights of minorities, it upholds the rights of the individual, internationally the individual nation, and within the community, the individual human being. "The unity of the human race, as envisaged by Bahá'u'lláh," Shoghi Effendi wrote, "implies the establishment of a world commonwealth . . . in which the autonomy of its state members and the personal freedom and initiative of the individuals that compose them are definitely and completely safeguarded."

Staunchly as the Guardian upheld the authority of the Assemblies, he was also a stout defender of the individual believer and had a deep bond of love with the "rank and file" of the followers of Bahá'u'lláh. Scarcely an appeal was made to the Bahá'í world or to National communities that did not address the individual Bahá'í and not only encourage his initiative, but point out that without it all plans must fail.

The humble have ever been singled out for unique blessings. In 1925 Shoghi Effendi wrote: "Not infrequently, nay oftentimes, the most lowly, untutored and inexperienced among the friends will, by sheer inspiring force of selfless and ardent devotion, contribute a distinct and memorable share to a highly involved discussion in any given Assembly." The Guardian was a passionate admirer of the meek and pure in heart and disliked aggressive and, particularly, ambitious individuals. His appeals for pioneers made his attitude quite plain: "all must participate, however humble their origin, however limited their experience, however restricted their means, however deficient their education, however pressing their cares and preoccupations, however unfavourable the environment in which they live . . . How often . . . have the lowliest adherents of the Faith, unschooled and utterly inexperienced, and with no standing whatever, and in some cases devoid of intelligence, been capable of winning victories for their Cause, before which the most brilliant achievements of the learned, the wise and the experienced have paled."

Little minds instinctively seek to circumscribe the things around them, to pull in the walls to the size of their own small existence, to get everything squared off to their own scale so they can feel safe and snug. This process invariably means that a lot of the material used in their walls is from the last house they lived in, is very much what they were accustomed to before they moved, so to speak. Big minds, on the contrary, push the horizons farther away, create new frontiers, leave room for growth. It is not difficult, when one reads over the letters to and from the Guardian, to see how he kept a perfect balance between what was wise and essential for the present stage of the Faith, and what would unduly circumscribe its unfoldment and crystallize its living teachings into a premature form, too small, too national or provincial, too sectarian or racial, to expand into a World Order, with its attendant world government and world society.

From the earliest days of his ministry Shoghi Effendi set about creating order in what was then a very small Bahá'í world, barely existing in some of the thirty-five countries which had received at least a ray of illumination from the Light of Bahá'u'lláh. The great, guiding lines were clear in his mind and as he grew older, and the community of believers grew and increased in experience, these lines became clearer and details were added. So often, as I listened to and observed Shoghi Effendi, I felt he was the only real Bahá'í in the world. Everyone else, claiming to be a Bahá'í, had a portion of the Faith, an angle on it, a concept, however large, tinctured by his own limitations, but the Guardian saw it as a whole, in all its greatness and perfect balance. He had not only the capacity to see but to analyse and express with brilliant clarity what he saw.

For instance take this epitome of what he felt the Bahá'í Faith is in the scheme of things: ". . . it should be stated that the Revelation identified with Bahá'u'lláh abrogates unconditionally all the Dispensations gone before it, upholds uncompromisingly the eternal verities they enshrine, recognizes firmly and absolutely the Divine origin of their Authors, preserves inviolate the sanctity of their authentic Scriptures, disclaims any intention of lowering the status of their Founders or of abating the spiritual ideals they inculcate, clarifies and correlates their functions, reaffirms their common, their unchangeable and fundamental purpose, reconciles their seemingly divergent claims and doctrines, readily and gratefully recognizes their respective contributions to the gradual unfoldment of one Divine Revelation, unhesitatingly acknowledges itself to be but one link in the chain of continually progressive Revelations, supplements their teachings with such laws and ordinances as conform to the imperative needs, and are dictated by the growing receptivity, of a fast evolving and constantly changing society, and proclaims its readiness and ability to fuse and incorporate the contending sects and factions into which they have fallen into a universal Fellowship, functioning within the framework, and in accordance with the precepts, of a divinely conceived, a world-unifying, a world-redeeming Order." Immediately one sees where this "greatest religious Dispensation in the spiritual history of mankind" fits into the panorama of history.

This Faith, "at once the essence, the promise, the reconciler, and the unifier of all religions", had, as its "primary mission", the establishment of a Divine Civilization. I remember in the course of a conversation Shoghi Effendi had with a former teacher of his at the American University in Beirut, how beautifully he answered this man's question as to what was the purpose of life to a Bahá'í. The Guardian answered that the object of life to a Bahá'í was to promote the oneness of mankind. He then went on to point out that Bahá'u'lláh had appeared at a time when His Message could and should be directed to the whole world and not merely to individuals; that salvation today was through world salvation, world change, world reform of society and that the world civilization resulting from this would in turn reflect upon the individuals composing it and lead to their redemption and reformation. Over and over Shoghi Effendi made it clear in his writings and talks that the two processes must go on together—reform of society, reform of personal character. There was never any doubt that individual regeneration, as he wrote to a non-Bahá'í in 1926, was the "sure and enduring foundation on which a reconstructed society" would develop and prosper. But how could one create a pattern for future society, even a tiny embryo of the future World Commonwealth of Bahá'u'lláh, if all around its fringes it was still interwoven with the fabric of that society which was dying out, must die out, to make way for the new?

Shoghi Effendi took up his scalpel—the interpretation of the writings of the Faith—and began to cut. Although the reading aright of our doctrines showed that there was only one religion, that of God Almighty, all down the ages, and the Prophets were its exponents at various times in history, the fact remained, Shoghi Effendi made us understand, that the duty of man in each new Dispensation was to adhere to it in all its forms and cut one's self away from the outer forms and secondary laws of the previous religion.

How could any honest Christian remain in the church and pray for the coming of the Father and His Kingdom while in his heart he very well knew Bahá'u'lláh was the Father and the Kingdom was beginning to emerge through the establishment of His laws and system as reflected and embodied in the Administrative Order? The Bahá'ís—East and West—had vaguely understood this to a greater or lesser degree in different places, but now, through the communications of the Guardian, they began to see a sharp line where shadow and light met, with no comfortable twilight zone of compromise with family feelings, community opinion, personal convenience left. You were expected to either get in or get out. This had a purifying and stiffening effect on the entire body of believers the world over and made them, as never before, conscious of the fact that they were a world body of people, the people of the new Day, of the new Dispensation.

It is in the light of this process that we must see how the emphasis shifted, over the years, in relation to the acceptance of new Bahá'ís. During the first decade-and-a-half of Shoghi Effendi's ministry Bahá'í bodies, in the West in particular, were encouraged to be sure that those who became Bahá'ís were well aware of the greatness of the step they took. A clear break with the past was required of them. "Otherwise", Shoghi Effendi wrote in 1927, "those whose faith is still unripe may thereby remain indefinitely along the circumference and continue in their attitude of half-hearted allegiance to the teachings of the Cause in their entirety." During those years the Faith rose in fame and stature, won in many western lands recognition as an independent religion with laws and a system of its own, was greatly helped in this process by the ruling of a Muslim court in Egypt which stated we were not part of Islám but as distinct from it as Christianity or Judaism, and became increasingly acknowledged as a Faith in its own right. Shoghi Effendi, however, constantly vigilant and unnaturally sensitive to whatever affected the life of the Cause, detected a trend amongst the administrative institutions to carry his original instruction in such matters (given in 1933) that the Assemblies should be "slow to accept" new believers, too far. A new rigidity was in danger of frustrating the main animating purpose of all Bahá'í institutions—to convert mankind to the Faith of Bahá'u'lláh. The Bahá'ís, in their eagerness to obey Shoghi Effendi's instructions, had gone to extremes and were so interested in screening applicants that it was getting difficult to become a Bahá'í at all. In 1938 Shoghi Effendi, therefore, found it necessary to instruct the American Assemblies "to desist from insisting too rigidly on the minor observations and beliefs, which might prove a stumbling block in the way of any sincere applicant" and pointed out the duty of Bahá'í communities was to nurse the new believers, subsequent to their acceptance of the Faith, into Bahá'í maturity.

As the Faith grew in inner cohesion and strength, as National Assembly after National Assembly was formed in East and West and began to function strongly and systematically, as the people of the world became increasingly aware of the existence of this new religion as an independent Revelation with a system of its own, the instructions of Shoghi Effendi changed. Particularly during the great Ten Year Plan of Teaching and Consolidation the whole emphasis in relation to the enrollment of new Bahá'ís was modified; now we were strong, now our foundations had been unassailably laid, now we could deal, at last, at last, with the masses of mankind in all the countries of the world. Fling open the doors and bring them into the ark of Bahá'u'lláh's salvation! The time had come to obey 'Abdu'l-Bahá's injunction: *"Summon the people in these countries, capitals, islands, assemblies and churches to enter the Abhá Kingdom."* In other words having achieved his end Shoghi Effendi changed his tactic. He informed the American National Assembly that the fundamental and primary requisites a candidate should have were acceptance of the stations of the Báb, the Forerunner; Bahá'u'lláh, the Author; and 'Abdu'l-Bahá, the Exemplar of the Faith; submission to whatever They had revealed; loyal and steadfast adherence to the provisions of the Will of the Master; and close association with the spirit and form of the world-wide Bahá'í Administration. These were the "principal factors" and any attempt to analyse and elucidate further, he said, would only lead to barren discussion and controversy and be detrimental to the growth of the Cause. He ended up his exposition on this delicate subject by urging the friends, unless some particular circumstance made it absolutely necessary, to "refrain from drawing rigidly the line of demarcation".

The Báb, Bahá'u'lláh, 'Abdu'l-Bahá and Shoghi Effendi were the Great Teachers. Their ministries—each so different in character—were primarily devoted to the sublime aim of bringing all mankind under the tent of this healing, peace-giving, soul-regenerating Faith. Over and over again, insistently, for thirty-six years Shoghi Effendi rallied us to "the preeminent task of teaching the Faith to

TWO VIEWS OF MT. CARMEL
Above: the Shrine of the Báb as it appeared after the passing of 'Abdu'l-Bahá. Below: the superstructure completed by Shoghi Effendi in 1953 according to the general instructions of the Master Himself

THE SHRINE ON MT. CARMEL

Part of the gardens and terraces surrounding the superstructure of the

THE SHRINE OF THE BÁB ON MT. CARMEL

THE DEVELOPMENT OF MT. CARMEL BY SHOGHI EFFENDI

The Shrine of the Báb set in its terraces and gardens, top left; the elongated Archives Building, with the arc in front of it, and the remarkable arabesque pattern of the gardens above it

the multitudes . . . a task", he assured us in his last Riḍván Message to the Bahá'í world, ". . . at once so sacred, so fundamental, and so urgent; primarily involving and challenging every single individual; the bed-rock on which the solidity and the stability of the multiplying institutions of a rising Order must rest".

If one compiled what the Guardian has written on the subject of teaching it would be a good-sized book. But one sees throughout that the objective was clear, the duty fixed, the methods adaptable and fluid. Shoghi Effendi used so many words in connection with new Bahá'ís and their acceptance of Bahá'u'lláh: he called them "converts", "candidates", "avowed adherents", "new believers", "unreserved" supporters of the Faith and many other descriptive and satisfying names; he said they were "enrolled", "converted", "declared their faith", "embraced the Faith", "enlisted" under Bahá'u'lláh's banner, "espoused His Cause", "joined the ranks" of the faithful and so on. In an age of banal, stereotyped clichés we might do well to remember this.

XIII

THE SPIRITUAL CONQUEST OF THE GLOBE

In making any attempt to give a coherent picture of what Shoghi Effendi called the first epoch in the evolution of 'Abdu'l-Bahá's Divine Plan—an epoch which he stated began in 1937 and would end in 1963, and comprised "three successive" crusades—one must go back and study his writings chronologically, for in them the clear reflection of his mind and the emergence of the scheduled pattern of his plans can be discerned. Ever since the passing of his beloved Master the whole object of the Guardian's existence was to fulfill His wishes and complete His works. The Divine Plan, conceived by Him, in one of the darkest periods in human history was, Shoghi Effendi stated, "'Abdu'l-Bahá's unique and grand design," embodied in His Tablets to those Bahá'ís of the United States and Canada, with which the destinies of the followers of Bahá'u'lláh in the North American continent would "for generations to come remain inextricably interwoven"; for twenty years it had been held in abeyance while the agencies of a slowly emerging Administrative Order were being created and perfected for "its efficient, systematic prosecution". How much importance the Guardian attached to this fundamental concept, often stressed by him, we are prone to forget, so let us turn to his actual words. During the opening years of the first Seven Year Plan, in 1939, he wrote to the American Community: "Through all the resources at their disposal, they are promoting the growth and consolidation of that pioneer movement for which the entire machinery of their Administrative Order has been primarily designed and erected." Eighteen years later Shoghi Effendi's view on this subject was the same, for he wrote to one of the European National Assemblies in 1957, shortly before his passing: "Less substantial, however, has been the progress achieved in the all-important teaching field, and far inferior the acceleration in the vital process of individual conversion for which the entire machinery of the Administrative Order has been primarily and so laboriously erected."

If we view aright what happened in 1937 at the beginning of the first Seven Year Plan, we see that Shoghi Effendi, now in his fortieth year, stepped out as the general leading an army—the North American Bahá'ís—and marched off to the spiritual conquest of the Western Hemisphere. While other generals, famous in the eyes of the world, were leading vast armies to destruction all over the planet, fighting battles of unprecedented horror in Europe, Asia and Africa, this unknown general, unrecognized and unsung, was devising and prosecuting a campaign more vital and far-reaching than anything they could ever do. Their battles were inspired by national hates and ambitions, his by love and self-sacrifice. They fought for the preservation of dying concepts and values, for the past order of things, he fought for the future, with its radiant age of peace and unity, a world society and the Kingdom of God on earth. Their names and battles are slowly being forgotten, but Shoghi Effendi's name and fame is rising steadily, and his victories rise in greatness with him, never to be forgotten.

In reviewing the overwhelming volume of material on the subject of the Guardian's Plans we must never forget that although the first organized implementation of 'Abdu'l-Bahá's Spiritual Mandate to the American believers (and let us note that this term does not refer to the Bahá'ís of the United States alone but to the believers of North America) took place with the initiation of the first Seven Year Plan, a body of devoted American followers of the Faith, the majority of whom Shoghi Effendi pointed out were "women pioneers", had already arisen, in immediate response to the *Tablets of the Divine Plan* presented to the Eleventh Annual Bahá'í Convention in New York in 1919, and had proceeded to Australia, the northernmost capitals of Europe, most of its Central States, the Balkan Peninsula, the fringes of Africa and Latin America, some countries in Asia and the islands of Tahiti in the Pacific Ocean. During thirty-six years Shoghi Effendi never forgot the services of these souls or ceased to name them. He made it clear, however, that such overseas teaching enterprises of the American Bahá'ís had been "tentative" and "intermittent". With the inauguration of the first Seven Year Plan a new epoch had begun.

When the Divine Plan will come to an end we do not know. Its significance has been elaborated by the Guardian in innumerable passages. It was, he wrote, "the weightiest spiritual enterprise launched in recorded history"; "the most potent agency for the development of the World Administrative System"; "a primary factor in the birth and efflorescence of the World Order itself in both the East and West."

With Shoghi Effendi everything was clear: there was The Plan, and then there were plans and plans! There were, after the inauguration of the first Seven Year Plan, in the course of many years, and in various parts of the world, a Nineteen Month, Two Year, Three Year, Forty-five Month, Four-and-a-Half Year, Five Year, Six Year, and other plans; but whether given by him or spontaneously initiated by the Bahá'ís themselves, he knew where to place them in the scheme of things. There was a God-given Mission, enshrined in a God-given Mandate, entrusted to the American believers; this Mission was their birthright, but they could only fulfill it by obeying the instructions given them in the Master's *Tablets of the Divine Plan* and winning every crusade they undertook; the other plans, Shoghi Effendi wrote in 1949, "are but supplements to the vast enterprise whose features have been delineated in those same Tablets and are to be regarded, by their very nature, as regional in scope, in contrast with the world-embracing character of the Mission entrusted to the community of the champion builders of the World Order of Bahá'u'lláh, and the torch-bearers of the civilization which that Order must eventually establish."

If Shoghi Effendi was the general, undoubtedly his chief of staff was the American Assembly; it got its orders direct from him and the rapport was intimate and complete. But he never forgot that the glory of an army is its soldiers, the "rank and file", as he forthrightly called them. He never ceased to appeal to them, to inspire them, to love them and to inform them that every North American believer shared a direct responsibility for the success of the Plan. Knowing how prone human nature is to be diverted from any purpose, he constantly reiterated the tasks undertaken, the responsibility assumed, the immediate need. When the different crusades approached their end and the success of various aspects of the work seemed to hang in the balance, his appeals rose in a veritable crescendo and swept the Bahá'ís to victory.

The first Seven Year Plan had a "triple task": one, to complete the exterior ornamentation of the first Mashriqu'l-Adhkár in the Western World; two, to establish one local Spiritual Assembly in every state of the United States and every province of Canada; three, to create one centre in each Latin American Republic "for whose entry into the fellowship of Bahá'u'lláh", Shoghi Effendi wrote, "the Plan was primarily formulated." Every nation in the Western Hemisphere was to be "woven into the fabric of Bahá'u'lláh's triumphant Order" and he pointed out to us that there were twenty independent Latin American Republics "constituting approximately one-third of the entire number of the world's sovereign states" and that the Plan was no less than an "arduous twofold campaign undertaken simultaneously in the homeland and in Latin America."

A little over two years after the initiation of this historic teaching drive Europe went to war; another two years passed and the United States—and practically the whole planet—was at war. Its seven-year activity took place in the face of the greatest suffering and darkest threat the New World had ever experienced. The degree to which Shoghi Effendi watched over, encouraged and guided this first great Plan of the Divine Plan is unbelievable. Messages streamed from him to the National Spiritual Assembly of the Bahá'ís of the United States and Canada. He told them the "deepening gloom" of the Old World invested their labours with a "significance and urgency" that could not be over-estimated. The Latin American campaign was "one of the most glorious chapters in the international history of the Faith." It was the "opening scene of the First Act of that superb Drama whose theme is no less than the spiritual conquest of both the Eastern and Western Hemispheres."

After two years of the Plan had run their course, when the exterior ornamentation of the Temple was satisfactorily progressing, and a series of ardent appeals from him had ensured that all the preliminary steps had been taken on the homefront, Shoghi Effendi waved his arm and directed the march of his forces down the coasts and over the islands of Central America, following, as he cabled, in a "methodical advance along line traced pen 'Abdu'l-Bahá". In spite of his own ever-growing burdens and anxieties he informed the friends he wished to keep personally in contact with pioneers in North, Central and South America. What those letters of his meant to the pioneers "holding", as he said, "their lonely posts in widely scattered areas throughout the Americas", only those who received them can truly judge, but I myself wonder if this, or later crusades would ever have been won without this communion he had with the believers. His love, encouragement and understanding kept them anchored to their posts. Not a few are still where they are because of letters signed "Your true brother, Shoghi".

In looking back on those glorious and terrible years of the last war the success of the first Seven Year Plan seems truly miraculous. While humanity was being decimated in Europe and Asia, while the World Centre of the Faith was being threatened with unprecedented danger on four sides, while the United States and Canada were engaged in a world conflict, with its attendant anxieties, restrictions and furor, a handful of people lacking in resources but rich in faith, lacking in prestige but rich in determination, succeeded in not only doubling the number of Bahá'í Assemblies in North America and ensuring the existence of at least one in every state of the Union and every province of Canada, but in completing the extremely costly exterior ornamentation of their Mother Temple sixteen months ahead of the scheduled time, and establishing not only a strong Bahá'í group in each of the twenty Latin Republics, but in addition fifteen Spiritual Assemblies throughout the entire area. In the last months of the Plan Shoghi Effendi fairly stormed the remaining unfinished tasks, with his valiant little army, too excited to feel the exhaustion of seven years' constant struggle, hard at his heels. When the sun of the second Bahá'í Century rose, it rose on triumph. To his cohorts Shoghi Effendi said that he and the entire Bahá'í world owed them a debt of gratitude no one could "measure or describe".

For twenty years, under the guidance of Shoghi Effendi, to a design he provided, the Bahá'ís wove the tapestry of the three great Crusades of his ministry. Amidst the busy, multi-coloured scenes, depicting so much work in so many places, could be discerned three sumptuous golden wheels—the three great Centenaries, historic landmarks into which he drew the threads of his plans and out of which they emerged to form still more beautiful and powerful patterns. The first of these Centenaries took place on May 23, 1944. Providentially the vast majority of Bahá'í communities throughout the world had not been cut off from communication with the Guardian at the World Centre, nor, in spite of the dangers of an encroaching theatre of war, been swallowed up in its battles. Persia, 'Iráq, Egypt, India, Great Britain, Australia, New Zealand and the Western Hemisphere had been miraculously spared. These communities, each to the degree possible under the circumstances prevailing in its own land, proceeded to celebrate the glorious occasion of the one hundredth anniversary of the Declaration of the Báb, which was at once the inception of the Bahá'í cycle as well as the birthday of 'Abdu'l-Bahá.

In spite of the fact that the Persian believers were not free to hold befitting nation-wide celebrations on the occasion of the first Centenary of the Faith which had dawned in their native land, this does not mean that worthy homage was not paid to the memory of the blessed Báb. The Guardian himself, full of tenderness for a community so perpetually afflicted, instructed its national body in detail regarding the manner in which this glorious event was to be commemorated.

For the North American Bahá'í Community a second anniversary occurred at the same time, as it was fifty years since the establishment of the Faith in the Western World. Shoghi Effendi, with his usual foresight and method, made quite clear to the American Bahá'ís in a series of messages during 1943 how he expected them to appropriately commemorate such an occasion and why he wanted them to do it on such a scale: in "its scope and magnificence" it was to "fully compensate for the disabilities which hinder so many communities in Europe and elsewhere, and even in Bahá'u'lláh's native land, from paying a befitting tribute to their beloved Faith at so glorious an hour in its history."

The celebrations the Americans would hold, he said, would not only crown their own labours but those of the entire body of their fellow-workers in both the East and the West.

Similar, though less ostentatious gatherings were being held in other countries. The close of these international festivities, Shoghi Effendi said, would mark the end of the first epoch of the Formative Age of the Faith which had lasted from 1921 to 1944.

The close of one century and the opening of another is a propitious moment to take stock of the Bahá'í world. Such a torrent of material presents itself to anyone trying to evaluate the labours of the Guardian that it is difficult indeed to know how to deal with his various achievements. He was not only a great creator of facts but an able and interested statistician and there was very little that he could not dramatize. But is not that the very essence of living—to derive interest from what superficially seems perfunctory, obligatory and therefore boring?

In 1944 Shoghi Effendi published, in Haifa, a small pamphlet, twenty-six pages long, which bore the title *The Bahá'í Faith, 1844–1944*, and under this, modestly, "Information Statistical and Comparative"; in 1950, with much more exhaustive material provided by him, the Bahá'í Publishing Committee in the United States published a similar, larger pamphlet, thirty-five pages long, with a map;

on it they put: "Compiled by Shoghi Effendi Guardian of the Bahá'í Faith". In 1952, again with material provided by him and at his instigation, both the British and American National Assemblies published the same pamphlet, with the same heading only this time twice as long and covering the period 1844–1952. Shoghi Effendi had now added a new sub-title "Ten Year International Teaching and Consolidation Plan".

It is impossible to go into details on a subject as vast as this one. On the other hand to ignore it completely would be unjust to a field of work that absorbed, for over thirteen years, a great deal of Shoghi Effendi's attention and time. One cannot argue with facts; one can disagree with ideas, pooh-pooh claims, belittle historic happenings, but when one is shown in cold print that such and such a thing is worth five-and-a-half-million dollars, or that seven National Bahá'í Assemblies have been incorporated, or that the Bahá'í Marriage Ceremony is entirely legal in fifteen states, or one reads the names of the African tribes who are represented in the Faith, the languages in which its teachings have been translated, one is forced to accept that this Faith exists in a very concrete way. Facts were part of Shoghi Effendi's ammunition with which he could defend the Faith against its enemies and through which he could not only encourage the Bahá'ís but stimulate them to greater effort.

One of his most cherished lists, the first and foremost, was that which reflected the spread of this glorious Cause entrusted to his care by 'Abdu'l-Bahá in 1921. Under "Countries opened to the Faith of Bahá'u'lláh" he had placed for the period of the Báb's Ministry: 2; Bahá'u'lláh's Ministry: 13; 'Abdu'l-Bahá's Ministry: 20. From 1921–1932, 5 were added in 11 years; 1932–1944, 38 were added in 12 years; 1944–1950, 22 were added in 6 years; 1950–1951, 6 were added in one year; 1951–1952, 22 were added in one year; 1952–1953, no increase in number; 1953–1954, 100 were added in one year; 1954–1957, 26 more were added. When Shoghi Effendi became Guardian there were 35 countries, but when he passed away he had raised this number to 254—219 added by his vision, drive and determination working through and with a dedicated, spiritually inflamed world-wide group of believers.

The Guardian devoted particular attention, in addition to creating the structural basis of the Administrative Order and assuring the rapid spread of the Faith, to ensuring that Bahá'í literature be made available, in different languages, to the people of the world.

In 1944 there were Bahá'í publications available in 41 languages; by 1957 there were 237.

He was not only eager to welcome as many different ethnic groups into the Faith as possible but constantly urged the Bahá'ís to reach people of different races so that within the communities that cardinal principle of unity in diversity might be exemplified. This was reflected in two of his statistics, the second one significantly emphasizing the great importance he attached to this aspect of our teachings; the headings of these statistics speak for themselves: "Races Represented in the Bahá'i World Community", which were listed by name. In 1944 there were 31 races; in 1955 there were about 40 races. "Minority Groups and Races with which contact has been established by Bahá'ís", likewise listed by name: in 1944 there were 9, but in 1952 they had risen to 15—12 of which were American Eskimo and Indian tribes. In 1952 a new caption was added, in spite of the insignificance of the figures involved: "African Tribes Represented in the Bahá'í Faith"; the names of 12 tribes were given—proudly. Periodically he continued to announce the increase in these figures: 1955, 90; 1956, 140; 1957, 197—an addition of 185 in 5 years.

The growth of the institutions and endowments of the Faith, a strong wall to protect its maturing Administrative Order, was another of the things to which Shoghi Effendi devoted particular attention. It is not a dream Bahá'u'lláh has come to the world to help us dream, but a reality He has given us the design to build. Incorporated bodies can hold property legally. It was and is essential that a growing Faith should own its own Temples, national and local headquarters, institutions, lands, schools, and so on. The figures in this regard speak eloquently of the progress made throughout the Guardian's ministry: in 1944 there were 5 incorporated National Assemblies and 63 locally incorporated ones in various countries; by 1957 there were over 200 incorporations of local Bahá'í Assemblies—137 being added in 13 years. Whereas in 1944, at the beginning of the second Bahá'í Century, the legal right to perform a Bahá'í marriage existed in a very few places, by 1957 this right was enjoyed by Bahá'ís in over 30 places and Bahá'í Holy Days were acknowledged as grounds for the suspension of work or school attendance in 45 places, the definition of a place being either a country, a state, or a district. In 1952, the Bahá'ís owned only 8 national headquarters, but in 1957 they owned 48. National endowments had likewise multiplied to an unprecedented degree and that same year there were 50 of them in various capital cities of the world.

With each release of statistical data the tally of National Spiritual Assemblies grew. To bring these "Pillars" of the future Universal House of Justice into existence was a task Shoghi Effendi conceived as one of his primary duties. The oldest National Assembly in the Bahá'í world, that of the United States and Canada, had existed at the time of 'Abdu'l-Bahá's passing under the name "Bahá'í Temple Unity". When the Guardian took the helm in 1921 he immediately set out to create uniformity in fundamental principles and from then on these future "Secondary Houses of Justice" were styled "National Spiritual Assemblies". By 1923 National Assemblies for the British, the German, the Indian and Burmese believers were already functioning and those of the Bahá'ís of Egypt and the Súdán, Persia, 'Iráq and Australia and New Zealand soon followed. Much as the Guardian longed to see new "Pillars" erected he had to be sure a sufficiently strong community—and especially a sufficiently strong base of local Assemblies—existed before he could permit a national body to be elected. In 1948 he launched Canada on her independent administrative destiny, followed in 1951 by two other National Assemblies, one for Central and one for South America. There was in Shoghi Effendi's mind a very clear reason for this grouping of two or more countries under a single National Assembly, which he explained to an Indian Bahá'í pilgrim in 1929, who wrote down his words at the time: "He is against separation of Burma and India for he says we have very few workers and separation will dissipate our forces and energy while what we most need at the present time is consolidation of all our resources and forces . . ."

With the formation of these two giant Central and South American bodies, whose title was National Assembly but whose composition and function was regional in nature, a new phase in the administrative development of the Faith began. Shoghi Effendi was never intimidated by the magnitude or difficulty of a task, nor was he any respecter of current views or methods. For nine years he was to constitute nothing but these vast National "Regional" Assemblies—except in the case of the National Assembly of the Bahá'ís of Italy and Switzerland, elected in 1953—which were truly immense in scope. The two Latin American ones comprised 20 countries and the four African ones, formed in 1956, represented 57 territories. This meant that nine people, often residing in countries over a thousand miles apart, had to consult and administer the affairs of scattered, mostly young and inexperienced Assemblies and communities, spread over hundreds of thousands of square miles.

There was now a choice corps of experienced Bahá'í pioneers, administrators, and teachers, in Latin America and in Africa, but they were not sufficient in number for the work of 20 independent administrative bodies in Central and South America and far, far from sufficient to provide experienced Bahá'ís for 57 territories in Africa. The answer was these interim National Assemblies which were to be broken down into ever smaller units pending the day when each nation had a sufficiently strong network of local Assemblies, of more mature believers, deepened in the teachings they had so recently embraced, who could assume responsibility for the administration and advancement of the Cause in their own territories. The remarkable feats achieved by these Regional Assemblies, constantly urged on and encouraged by Shoghi Effendi in the discharge of their historic tasks, fully justified his method.

In his selection of the countries he associated under one national body the Guardian amply demonstrated the fact that the Bahá'ís are far more than international, they are supra-national—above nation—in their beliefs and policy. No consideration of national prejudices, political animosities, or religious differences influenced his choice of those who were to work together under one Assembly. For him such worldly considerations were not allowed to weigh, albeit he was a keen student of current affairs and never blind to facts. It was those Divine forces within the Faith that he utilized—a Faith which, as he so beautifully expressed it, "feeds itself upon . . . hidden springs of celestial strength" and "propagates itself by ways mysterious and utterly at variance with the standards accepted by the generality of mankind."

It was not until 1957 that he resumed the formation of purely National Assemblies; in April of that year Alaska, Pákistán and New Zealand elected their own permanent Bahá'í bodies. It was an historic occasion in the evolution of the Administrative Order for no less than eleven new National Assemblies came into existence that year at one time, the others being Regional Assemblies for North East Asia, South East Asia, the Benelux Countries, Arabia, the Iberian Peninsula, Scandinavia and Finland, the Antilles, and the northern countries of South America which formed a new body. What had hitherto been one National Assembly for South America and one for Central America now became two smaller Regional ones in South America while Central America was partially pared away and its island republics joined in electing an Assembly of their own. Ere Shoghi Effendi's last great Crusade drew to a close every republic of Latin America had its own independent national body, as he himself had planned when, in his statistical pamphlet published on the eve of the Centenary of 1953, he had included within the "Ten Year International Bahá'í Teaching and Consolidation Plan" as one of its most thrilling and challenging provisions the task of more than quadrupling the existing National Assemblies through raising their number to over fifty.

The example set through the achievements of the first Seven Year Plan inspired other communities to dare greatly. The increasing awareness of the glorious possibilities of service opening before the Bahá'í world in the second century of its own era was constantly fanned into flame by the Guardian's messages to various National Assemblies. He frequently quoted Bahá'u'lláh's admonition: *"Vie ye with each other in the service of God and of His Cause"*, and openly encouraged a competitive spirit in its noblest form. His use of statistics was one example of the way he did this, his own words another: "Spiritual competition", he cabled America in 1941, "galvanizing organized followers Bahá'u'lláh East West waxes keener as first Bahá'í Century speeds to its close."

The news of the victories being won during the first Seven Year Plan, passed on by the Guardian in a steady flow of inspiring messages to the believers of Persia, was, Shoghi Effendi cabled in 1943, "thrilling Eastern communities Bahá'í world with delight admiration and wonder . . . Ninety-five Persian families emulating example American trail-blazers Faith" had left their homes and were on their way to hoist its banner in Afghánistán, Balúchistán, Sulaymáníyyih, Ḥijáz and Baḥrayn. India and Egypt were stirring, and the 'Iráqí Bahá'ís were hastening their own plans to crown the end of the first century with local victories. The Bahá'ís of both the East and the West were writing the last glorious pages in their own chapters of the first century of their Faith.

Three months after the May 1944 celebrations were ended, the Guardian informed the North American Community: "A memorable chapter in the history of the Faith of Bahá'u'lláh in the West has been closed. A new chapter is now opening, a chapter which, ere its termination, must eclipse the most shining victories won so heroically by those who have so fearlessly launched the first stage of the Great Plan conceived by 'Abdu'l-Bahá for the American believers."

When a "war-ravaged, disillusioned and bankrupt society" paused in its bloody battles after six years and began, with the cessation of European hostilities in the summer of 1945, to lick its wounds, Shoghi Effendi told the American Bahá'ís that the prosecutors of the Divine Plan must "gird up their loins, muster their resources" and prepare themselves for the next step in their destiny. The appeals he made, during the months that preceded the launching of the second Seven Year Plan, to the minds and the feelings of the American believers were profound. He told these "ambassadors of the Faith of Bahá'u'lláh" that the "sorrow-stricken, war-lacerated, sorely bewildered nations and peoples" of Europe were waiting in their turn for the healing influence of the Faith to be extended to them as it had been extended to the peoples throughout the Americas. News he received of the plight of the believers in Germany and Burma—two old and tried communities—greatly touched him and was so distressing that he hastened to appeal to "their fellow workers in lands which have providentially been spared the horrors of invasion and all the evils and miseries attendant upon it" to take immediate and collective action to mitigate their plight. He appealed particularly to the American community, which "of all its sister communities in East and West, enjoyed the greatest immunity" during the war and had in addition been privileged to successfully prosecute so great a Plan, to do all in its power to help financially and by any other means at its disposal.

The official inception of the second Seven Year Plan, the "second collective enterprise undertaken in American Bahá'í history," took place at the 1946 Convention. It would seem as if all the work so successfully undertaken since 1921 had been designed to create in the Western Hemisphere a vast homefront from which the New World could launch a well-organized attack on the Old World—on Europe, its parent continent. The child of one hemisphere, now a fully-grown young giant, was ready to return, vital and fresh, destined, as Shoghi Effendi wrote "through successive decades to achieve the spiritual conquest of the continent unconquered by Islám, rightly regarded as the mother of Christendom, the fountain head of American culture, the mainspring of Western civilization . . ."

Again we see the design in Shoghi Effendi's great tapestry drawn into another blazing wheel of glory—this time the second great Centenary of the Faith in 1953 which would, he informed us, commemorate the Year Nine marking the mystic birth of Bahá'u'lláh's prophetic mission as He lay in the Síyáh-<u>Ch</u>ál of Ṭihrán.

The objectives of this new Plan, of which Europe was the "preeminent" goal, and which came to be known as the European Campaign, were as follows: consolidation of work throughout the Americas; completion of the interior ornamentation of the Mother Temple of the West in time for the celebration of its fiftieth anniversary in 1953; erection of three pillars of the future Universal House of Justice through the election of the Canadian, the Central and the South American National Assemblies; a systematic teaching campaign in Europe aimed at the establishment of Spiritual Assemblies in the Iberian Peninsula (Spain and Portugal), the Low Countries (Holland and Belgium), the Scandinavian states (Norway, Sweden and Denmark), and Italy. He ended his message by saying that he himself was pledging ten thousand dollars as his initial contribution for the "manifold purposes glorious Crusade surpassing every enterprise undertaken by followers Faith Bahá'u'lláh course first Bahá'í Century."

Six weeks later a cable from Shoghi Effendi informed the American National Assembly that "nine competent pioneers" should be promptly dispatched to Europe to as many countries as feasible, that the Duchy of Luxembourg should be added to the Low Countries and Switzerland also included. With these two, and the previous eight, the "Ten Goal Countries" came into existence in our Bahá'í vocabulary. Some time later, in view of the marked progress being made in the north of Europe, Finland was also added to the scope of the Plan. Although, in addition to Britain and Germany there were still Bahá'ís living in France, Switzerland, Norway, Sweden, Denmark, Yugoslavia, Czechoslovakia, Bulgaria and perhaps other places, they were for the most part too isolated or too suppressed to undertake large-scale teaching activities. The opening of this systematic well-organized Plan in "war-torn, spiritually famished" Europe meant that the American Community now found itself "launched in both hemispheres on a second, incomparably more glorious stage, of the systematic Crusade designed to culminate, in the fullness of time, in the spiritual conquest of the entire planet." It meant that the American Community was to be engaged in strenuous work in thirty countries, in addition to ensuring that proper foundations were laid for the election in 1948, of the National Spiritual Assembly of Canada, whose essential local Assemblies in various provinces were in most cases new and weak.

The continent of Europe was "turbulent, politically convulsed, economically disrupted and spiritually depleted." But it was the arena where the American Community must now carry out the "first stage of its transatlantic missionary enterprises", "amidst a people so disillusioned, so varied in race, language, and outlook, so impoverished spiritually, so paralyzed with fear, so confused in thought, so abased in their moral standards, so rent by internal schisms . . ."

When these "trail blazers" of the second Seven Year Plan began their mission there were only two European Bahá'í communities worthy of the name, those of the British Isles and Germany, both long-standing and both of which had had active National Assemblies before the war; the first had never ceased to function; the second, dissolved by the Nazi authorities in 1937 when all Bahá'í activity was officially suspended, was now reconstituted and heroically gathering its war-torn flock about it. With these the European Teaching Committee of the American National Assembly and the ever swelling group of pioneers in the Ten Goal Countries closely co-operated. This great European undertaking truly fired the imagination of the Bahá'ís all over the world, including the new communities of Latin America—who were even able to send some of their own pioneers to assist in this new Crusade.

During these difficult years the numerically much smaller Canadian Community—co-partner with the American Community in the execution of the Divine Plan—was so preoccupied with the Five Year Plan the Guardian had instructed it to initiate when the independent stage of its development was reached in 1948, that it was in no position to offer much assistance to the main body of believers in the United States, and the formation in 1951 of two more National Assemblies, one in Central and one in South America, made further demands on their tenacity, resources and courage. Yet with all their burdens their triumphs during the last years of the second Seven Year Plan continued to multiply.

The winning of so many victories by the Bahá'ís of the United States as well as Canada—to which had been added in the closing years of this Crusade services in the African continent never contemplated in the original Plan—far exceeding in substance the misty prizes which had loomed, beckoning but vague, in the fog surrounding the world at the end of the war, now encouraged the Guardian to add another offering on the altar of Bahá'u'lláh, one he termed the "fairest fruit" of the mighty European project. In 1952 he cabled that "ere termination American Community's sec-

THE TRANSFORMATION OF MT. CARMEL

Looking down on the golden dome of the Báb's Shrine (left) and the International Bahá'í Archives, built in the Greek style (right)

BUILDINGS ERECTED BY SHOGHI EFFENDI

Left: International Archives building. Right: Shrine of the Báb. The curved path is part of the arc around which other international buildings will be constructed.

THAT SACRED SPOT

Left to right: the monuments marking the resting-places of the brother, mother, wife and sister of 'Abdu'l-Bahá above which, facing an arc-shaped path, will cluster the International Administrative Institutions of the Faith

THE RESTING-PLACE OF THE GREATEST HOLY LEAF

Brethren and fellow-mourners in the Faith of Bahá'u'lláh

A sorrow, inexpressible in its poignancy, the overwhelming grief caused by 'Abdu'l-Bahá's sudden removal from our midst has stirred the Bahá'í world to its foundations. The Greatest Holy Leaf, the well-beloved and treasured Remnant of Bahá'u'lláh entrusted to our stern and unworthy hands by our departed Master, has passed to the Great Beyond, leaving a legacy that time can never dim.

The Community of the Most Great Name, in its entirety and to its very core, feels the sting of this cruel loss. Invariable though this calamitous event appeared to us all, however acute our apprehensions of its steady approach, the fear, connected with the final consummation of this invisible hour, leaves us, whose souls have been invigorated by the energizing influence of her love, prostrated and disconsolate.

How can my feeble pen, so utterly inadequate to glorify so august a station, so impotent to portray the experiences of so sublime a life, so dejected to recount the blessings she showered upon

a heavenly Father," for we no less than the ardent lovers of her winsome beauty and ardent admirers of the Cause of her glorious brother have known under her loving guardianship, the solace, the joy, the inspiration of tender motherly love. Her acts of kindness, of charity, of loving care for her kindred, her friends, and even for strangers are but shining examples of her imperishable love, and should constitute for those whom she left behind, real lively, real inspiring examples of true self-sacrificing consecration to the invisible person of the Great Beloved.

Whatever betide us, however distressing the vicissitudes which the nascent Faith of God may yet experience, we pledge ourselves, before the mighty task of His previous Father, to hand on, unimpaired and undivided, to generations yet unborn, the glory of that tradition of which she was herself its most brilliant exemplar.

In the innermost recesses of our hearts, O Blessed Leaf of the Abhá Paradise, we have raised for thee a shining mansion that the hand of time can never undermine, a shrine which shall eternally, the march of eternity, resound with the passionate whisper, the fire of thy consuming love, the voice of thy communing love shall burn for ever.

Shoghi

The servants of the Lord and His handmaids of the merciful throughout the West.

July 17, 1932.

THE HANDWRITING OF SHOGHI EFFENDI

Facsimile of the first and last pages of his letter in English concerning the passing of the Greatest Holy Leaf

AERIAL VIEW OF BAHJÍ

Looking northward: the large building is the Mansion of Bahá'u'lláh, the pointed roof on the left His Shrine. The extensive gardens created by Shoghi Effendi are shown to the southwest and north. Note at end of winding path the small white room from the roof of which he surveyed the work

ond Seven Year Plan" the National Spiritual Assembly of the Bahá'ís of Italy and Switzerland should be formed, and added: "Advise European Teaching Committee upon consummation glorious enterprise issue formal invitation their spiritual offspring newly emerged National Spiritual Assembly participate together with sister National Assemblies United States, British Isles, Germany Intercontinental Conference August same year capital city Sweden". He explained he was planning to entrust this youngest Assembly of the Bahá'í world with a specific plan of its own as part of the Global Crusade to be embarked upon between the second and third Century celebrations. It had become an established procedure of the Guardian for these new National Bahá'í babies to be born with a plan in their mouths!

It may well be imagined how excited, how heartened, all the followers of Bahá'u'lláh were by news so thrilling as this. They saw what seemed to them little short of miracles taking place, and their loving "true brother", in his humility, his praises and kindness, led them to believe such miracles were all theirs. That Italy should have, from a vacuum, succeeded in one decade in building up a foundation of local Assemblies strong enough, with its Swiss companion, to bear the weight of an independent National Assembly was a feat far beyond anyone's fairest dreams.

In order to grasp, in however dim a way, why the third Seven Year Plan—which the Guardian had repeatedly referred to since the end of the first Bahá'í Century—became a Ten Year Plan instead, we must understand a fundamental teaching of our Faith. A just and loving God does not require of any soul what He will not give it the strength to accomplish. Privileges involve responsibilities, for peoples, nations, individuals. To the degree to which they arise to meet their responsibilities they are blessed and sustained; to the degree they fail they are automatically deprived and punished. Shoghi Effendi had written at the beginning of the first Seven Year Plan that "failure to exploit these golden opportunities would . . . signify the loss of the rarest privilege conferred by Providence upon the American Bahá'í Community." "*The Kingdom of God*", 'Abdu'l-Bahá had said, "*is possessed of limitless potency. Audacious must be the army of life if the confirming aid of that Kingdom is to be repeatedly vouchsafed to it . . .*" It was in pursuance of the operation of this great law that the followers of Bahá'u'lláh who had been entrusted with the Divine Plan, rising to meet their challenge, pulling down from on high through their services an ever-greater measure of celestial aid, discharging their sacred responsibility in so noble a fashion, found destiny hastening to meet them, a step in advance. A victorious army, having swept all barriers before it, is often so exhilarated by its exploits it needs no respite. It is ready to march on, fired by its victories. This was the mood of the Bahá'í world as 1953 approached and it was about to enter the Holy Year. Their Commander-in-Chief was a general who needed very little encouragement to induce him to go on and who never rested. So it was inevitable that given the hour, the mood and the man the Bahá'ís should find themselves with no "three year respite" but rather twelve completely evolved plans—one for each National Assembly—ready to be put into operation the moment the trumpet sounded the reveille in Riḍván 1953.

Wonderful as had been the celebration of the hundredth anniversary of the Bahá'í Faith, in 1944, by Bahá'í communities living in the shadow of the worst war the world had ever known, it was dwarfed by the events associated with the hundredth anniversary of the revelation Bahá'u'lláh received in the Síyáh-Chál of Ṭihrán. Poignantly, in the months preceding the commemoration of that event, the Guardian recalled to the Bahá'í world the tidal wave of persecution and martyrdom which had swept so many disciples of the Báb, so many heroes, so many innocent women and even children, from the scene a century before and had culminated in casting the Supreme Manifestation of God into a loathsome subterranean dungeon immediately following the abortive attempt on the life of Náṣiri'd-Dín Sháh on August 15, 1852. The Guardian chose as the commencement of the Holy Year—the celebration of the Anniversary of the "Year Nine"—the middle of October 1952. A veritable fever of anticipation swept over the believers East and West, now free in every part of the globe to give their hearts to unreserved rejoicing. Perhaps for the first time in their history the Bahá'ís had a throbbing sense of their true oneness as a world community. What had always been a matter of doctrine, taught and firmly believed in, was now sensed by every individual as a great and glorious reality. The plans for the future, set in motion by a series of dynamic messages from Shoghi Effendi, served to inflame this new awareness.

At the end of November 1951, in a cable addressing all National Assemblies of the Bahá'í world, Shoghi Effendi informed us that the long anticipated intercontinental stage was now at hand. We had, he pointed out, passed through the phases of local, regional, national and international activity and were emerging, at such an auspicious moment, into a new kind of Bahá'í world, one in which we began to think in terms of the entire planet with its continents in relation to our teaching strategy. Shoghi Effendi took the Centenary—this great golden wheel in his tapestry—and fashioned it in such a way that two entirely different things were made to react on each other and at the same time blend into each other in one great creative centre of force. One was the past, the commemoration of such soul-shaking events as the martyrdoms, the imprisonment of Bahá'u'lláh, His mystic experience of His own station in the Síyáh-Chál, His exile and all that these events signified for the progress of man in his journey towards his Creator; the other was the marshalling, this time of all the organized Bahá'í communities of the planet, in a vast Plan, the next step in the unfoldment of 'Abdu'l-Bahá's Divine Plan.

It was beginning to take shape in his mind long before its detailed provisions were released through the publication in 1952 of his pamphlet, *The Bahá'í Faith 1844–1952*, with its supplement "Ten Year International Teaching and Consolidation Plan", which was made public at the inception of the Holy Year. Previously he had requested different National Assemblies to provide him with the names of the territories and major islands of the five continents where Bahá'í activity was in progress, thus supplementing his own exhaustive list, which included the countries mentioned by 'Abdu'l-Bahá Himself in the *Tablets of the Divine Plan*, and which he had carefully compiled with the aid of atlases and works of reference.

The highlights of the Holy Year were four great Intercontinental Teaching Conferences which were announced in that same November 1951 cable and were to be held in four continents: the first in Africa, in Kampala, Uganda in the spring of 1953; the second in Chicago, in the United States during Riḍván; the third in Stockholm, Sweden during the summer and the fourth in New Delhi, India in autumn. The pattern of these great Conferences—which were announced a year before the new Plan itself was disclosed— became clear as the hour approached for them to take place. All Hands of the Cause were invited to attend as many of them as possible; to each one the Guardian would send as his own special representative one of the Hands "honoured direct association newly-initiated enterprises World Centre". In chronological order, these were Leroy Ioas, Amatu'l-Bahá Rúḥíyyih Khánum, Ugo Giachery and Mason Remey; these emissaries would fulfil a four-fold mission: they would bear a reproduction of a miniature portrait of the Báb to show to the friends gathered on such an historic occasion; they would deliver the Guardian's own message to the assembled attendants; they would elucidate the character and purposes of the Spiritual World Crusade; they would rally the participants to an energetic, sustained, enthusiastic prosecution of the colossal tasks that lay ahead.

Before going into more detail it would be well to recall that although, in his November 1951 message announcing these Conferences to be held during the Holy Year, Shoghi Effendi had given a faint hint of things to come when he stated they would initiate a new stage of intercontinental activity and would reflect a degree of Bahá'í solidarity of unprecedented scope and intensity, still, as far as the Bahá'í world knew, they were designed as great jubilee gatherings to commemorate the Year Nine, to celebrate the end of the victorious second Seven Year Plan, and many regional ones as well. Indeed, only a week before the cable announcing those Conferences reached the Bahá'í world the Guardian had, in another message, still been referring to a "third Seven Year Plan" so that there was in 1951 no association in the minds of the Bahá'ís of the commencement of a new crusade with these festival gatherings. The extraordinary success the Bahá'ís were meeting with all over the world, the enthusiasm of National Assemblies such as America and Britain, who had been winning remarkable victories in Europe and in Africa respectively, swung the compass on a new course, a course that in reality started three years before the inauguration of the Ten Year Plan. So vast is the range covered by the provisions of this Plan, so numerous the communications from Shoghi Effendi on this subject—his lists, his announcements and his statistics, beginning in 1952 and carried on until his death in November 1957— that to give more than a brief outline of them here is impossible. On the other hand this Crusade crowned his ministry and his life's work, was a source of deep happiness to him, and its unfolding victories a comfort to his often sad and over-burdened heart. Therefore it must be dealt with, however inadequately.

No words can better sum up the very essence of this supreme Plan conceived of and organized by him than his own definition of it: "Let there be no mistake. The avowed, the primary aim of this Spiritual Crusade is none other than the conquest of the citadels of men's hearts. The theatre of its operations is the entire planet. Its duration a whole decade. Its commencement synchronizes with the

Centenary of the birth of Bahá'u'lláh's Mission. Its culmination will coincide with the Centenary of the Declaration of that same mission."

Although all believers were welcome to be present at the four great Conferences of the Holy Year, a special category was singled out and invited to attend by Shoghi Effendi, namely, representatives of those National Assemblies and communities who were intimately concerned with the work which was to go forward in each of the four continents. If we begin with the first Conference held in February, in Africa, and analyse what the most crucial phase of the entire Crusade involved there—the opening of new territories and the consolidation of the work in those already opened—we will get an idea of the shattering impact these historic gatherings had on Bahá'í history: 57 territories were to be the subject of concentrated teaching activities for which six national bodies would be responsible, namely, the National Spiritual Assemblies of the British, the American, the Persian, the Egyptian and Súdánese, the 'Iráqí and the Indian, Pákistání and Burmese believers, who were to open 33 new territories and consolidate the work already begun in 24. The tasks allotted the whole Western Hemisphere community, through its four National Assemblies, those of the United States, Canada, Central America and South America, were equally staggering: 56 territories, 27 to be opened and 29 to be consolidated, involving such widely separated and difficult goals as the Yukon and Keewatin in the north and the Falkland Islands in the south. The Asian goals were even more formidable: 84 territories in all, 41 to be opened and 43 to be consolidated, ranging from countries in the Himalayas to dots in the Pacific Ocean; these were divided between the nine National Assemblies of Persia; India, Pákistán and Burma; 'Iráq; Australia and New Zealand; the United States; Canada; Central America; South America and the British Isles. At the European Conference five National Assemblies received 52 territories as their share of the Plan, 30 to be opened and 22 to be consolidated. Seated amongst its elders, the National Assemblies of the United States, Canada, the British Isles, Germany and Austria, was the baby national body of the Bahá'í world—that of Italy and Switzerland, scarcely three months old—which was given by the Guardian territories all its own, 7 in number.

At these historic gatherings, more than 3,400 believers were present, representing, Shoghi Effendi announced, not only all the principal races of mankind, but more than 80 countries. Each of the

Conferences had some special distinction of its own: the first, the African one, attended by no less than ten Hands of the Cause, friends from 19 countries and representatives of over 30 tribes and races, being particularly blessed by having over 100 of the new African believers present as the personal guests of the Guardian himself, a mark of consideration on his part that clearly showed his deep attachment to the new African Bahá'ís. Indeed, in his highly significant message to the first Conference of the Holy Year he was at pains to quote the words of Bahá'u'lláh Who had compared the coloured people to the *"black pupil of the eye"* through which *"the light of the spirit shineth forth."* Shoghi Effendi not only praised the African race, he praised the African continent, a continent that had "remained uncontaminated by the evils of a gross, a rampant and cancerous materialism undermining the fabric of human society alike in the East and the West, eating into the vitals of the conflicting peoples and races inhabiting the American, the European, and the Asiatic continents, and, alas, threatening to engulf in one common catastrophic convulsion the generality of mankind." Should such a warning, given at such an historic juncture in the fortunes of Africa, not be remembered more insistently by the band of Bahá'u'lláh's followers labouring there to establish a spiritually based World Order?

The second, "without doubt," Shoghi Effendi wrote, "the most distinguished of the four Intercontinental Teaching Conferences commemorating the Centenary of the inception of the Mission of Bahá'u'lláh" and marking the launching of that "epochal, global, spiritual decade-long Crusade", took place in the middle of the Holy Year and constituted the central feature of that year's celebrations and the highest point of its festivities. This great all-America Conference was held in the heart of North America, in Chicago, the very city where sixty years before Bahá'u'lláh's name had first been publicly mentioned in the Western World during a session of the World Parliament of Religions held in connection with the World's Columbian Exposition which opened on May 1, 1893. Its sessions were preceded by the consummation of a fifty-year-old enterprise—the dedication to public worship, on May 2nd, of the Mother Temple of the West, which was, Shoghi Effendi assured us, not only "the holiest House of Worship ever to be reared to the glory of the Most Great Name" but that no House of Worship would "ever possess the immeasurable potentialities with which it has been endowed" and that the "role it is destined to play in hastening the emergence of the World Order of Bahá'u'lláh" could not as yet be fathomed.

The unveiling of the model of the future Bahá'í Temple to be erected on Mt. Carmel at the World Centre of the Faith was another event which Shoghi Effendi himself had planned to take place in conjunction with that Conference—a Conference which he said will "go down in history as the most momentous gathering held since the close of the Heroic Age of the Faith, and will be regarded as the most potent agency in paving the way for the launching of one of the most brilliant phases of the grandest crusade ever undertaken by the followers of Bahá'u'lláh since the inception of His Faith . . ."

The lion's share of this new Crusade in prosecution of 'Abdu'l-Bahá's Divine Plan had been given by Shoghi Effendi to those he so lovingly said were not only "ever ready to bear the brunt of responsibility" but were, indeed, that Plan's "appointed" and "chief trustees". They had performed in the past "unflagging and herculean labours", now, through their two national bodies, that of the United States and of Canada, in competition with ten other National Assemblies, each of which had received a goodly portion of goals, this Community would indeed have to struggle hard to maintain its lead and win the new victories expected of it. There were 131 virgin territories throughout the world to be opened to the Faith of Bahá'u'lláh in ten years and 118 territories already opened but still requiring a great deal of consolidation. Of these 249 places, most of them large, independent nations, the United States and Canada received 69, or 28 percent of the total; 48 new National Assemblies were to be formed before 1963, 36 of them by the United States alone. The first dependency ever to be erected in the vicinity of a Bahá'í Temple was likewise to be undertaken by this Community; in addition, it was to purchase two sites for future Houses of Worship, one in Toronto, Canada, and one in Panama City, Panama; translate and publish Bahá'í literature in 10 Western Hemisphere Indian languages, and achieve many other goals besides.

In the presence of the twelve Hands of the Cause attending this Conference—to which Bahá'ís from over 33 countries had come—well over 100 believers arose and offered themselves as pioneers to set in motion the accomplishment of the great tasks the Guardian had just made so dazzlingly clear in his message.

The opening of the doors of the Mother Temple to public worship, the public meetings addressed by prominent Bahá'ís and non-

Bahá'ís alike during the jubilee celebrations attracted thousands of people and received enthusiastic nation-wide publicity in the press, on television and over the radio. During the Holy Year the light of the Faith truly shone most brightly in the Great Republic of the West, the chosen cradle of its Administrative Order.

The third Intercontinental Bahá'í Teaching Conference, which convened in Stockholm during July, was honoured by having the largest attendance of Hands of the Cause of any of the others, fourteen being present, the five Persian Hands and one African Hand having just come from extensive travels in the Western Hemisphere, undertaken at the instruction of the Guardian, immediately following the launching of the Crusade in Chicago. It would not be inaccurate to characterize this third gathering as the "executive conference". Though numerically much smaller than the American one, circumstances permitted a hard core of the most dedicated and active National Assembly members, teachers, administrators and pioneers to be present from all over Europe, including 110 believers from the Ten Goal Countries. The attendants, from thirty countries, devoted themselves during six days not only to the solemn yet joyous recapitulation of those events which had transpired a century before and which the Holy Year commemorated, but to a studious analysis of the work their beloved Guardian had entrusted to the three European National Assemblies and that of the United States, the only other national body involved in the European work being that of Canada, which had been given Iceland as a consolidation goal.

In his message on this historic occasion Shoghi Effendi recalled not only the history of the Bahá'í Faith in relation to Europe—"a continent which, in the course of the last two thousand years, has exercised on the destiny of the human race a pervasive influence unequalled by that of any other continent of the globe"—but the effect both Christianity and Islám had had upon the unfoldment of its fortunes. In recapitulating the advances made and victories won since the end of the last World War the Guardian pointed out that these had been largely due to "the dynamic impact of a series of national Plans preparatory to the launching of a World Spiritual Crusade". Those Plans had been the second Seven Year Plan, conducted by the North American believers, a Six Year Plan and a Two Year Plan launched by the British Bahá'ís, and a Five Year Plan prosecuted by the German and Austrian Bahá'í Communities. The result of these well-organized labours had been the establishment of local Assemblies in Eire, Northern Ireland, Scotland and Wales and in each of the capitals of the Ten Goal Countries, a large increase in the number of Assemblies, centres and believers throughout Europe, the election of yet another independent national body, and the acquisition of a national Bahá'í headquarters in Frankfurt. The hour was now ripe, Shoghi Effendi wrote, for them "to initiate befittingly and prosecute energetically the European campaign of a Global Crusade" which would not only broaden the foundations of the Faith in Europe but would "diffuse its light over the neighbouring islands" and would "God willing, carry its radiance to the Eastern territories of that continent, and beyond them as far as the heart of Asia".

Words such as these fired the attendants to take immediate action and there were not only 63 offers from among those present to pioneer to European goals, but, what was much more unusual, various national bodies and committees, whose members were present in numbers, immediately took up these offers and before the Conference ended pioneers had been allocated to every goal given the European believers with the exception of those territories within the Soviet orbit. The thrilling objective of the erection of one of the two Bahá'í Temples called for in the original outline of the "Ten Year Teaching and Consolidation Plan"—the Mother Temple of Europe to be built in Germany—received substantial financial pledges, as did three other European projects involving large sums of money, namely, the purchase of the National Ḥaẓíratu'l-Quds of the British Bahá'ís and the sites for two future Bahá'í Temples, one in Stockholm and one in Rome. The convocation of such a Conference met with wide and favourable publicity and the public meeting held in conjunction with it attracted one of the largest audiences gathered under Bahá'í auspices that had yet been seen on the continent.

Twelve months after the beginning of the Holy Year, ushered in during mid-October 1952, the great Asian Intercontinental Teaching Conference took place in New Delhi, India. Though the logical place for such a gathering would have been Persia, or failing this, 'Iráq, the temperature of the fanatical populations of these countries and the constant and unchanging animosity of the Muslim clergy made the choice of either place impossible. It was therefore highly befitting that the great sister country to the east—opened in the earliest days of Bahá'u'lláh's Ministry—should receive this honour. To it flocked hundreds of His followers from all over the world from places as far apart as Europe, Africa, Australia, New Zealand, Japan, many countries in the Western Hemisphere, and particularly Persia, as well as all five Asiatic Hands, who had already attended, at the request of the Guardian, the African, American and European Conferences. There were also present six other Hands of the Cause from the Holy Land, Europe, America, Africa and Australia. In his message to this last of the great Teaching Conferences Shoghi Effendi, after greeting its attendants "with high hopes and a joyful heart", pointed out the unique circumstances and significance of the work in Asia: in this "world girdling crusade" the "triple Campaign, embracing the Asiatic mainland, the Australian Continent and the islands of the Pacific Ocean" might "well be regarded as the most extensive, the most arduous and the most momentous of all the Campaigns". Its scope was "unparalleled in the history of the Faith in the Eastern Hemisphere"; it was to take place in a continent on whose soil "more than a century ago, so much sacred blood was shed", a continent enjoying an unrivalled position in the Bahá'í world, a continent where the overwhelming majority of Bahá'u'lláh's followers resided, a continent that was "the cradle of the principal religions of mankind; the home of so many of the oldest and mightiest civilizations which have flourished on this planet; the crossways of so many kindreds and races; the battleground of so many peoples and nations;" above whose horizon in modern times the suns of two independent Revelations had successively risen; and within whose boundaries such holy places as the Qiblih of our Faith (Bahjí), the "Mother of the World" (Ṭihrán) and the "Cynosure of an adoring world" (Baghdád) are embosomed. The Guardian ended his message with an expression of assurance as well as a sad foreboding of what might lie ahead: "May this Crusade, launched simultaneously on the Asiatic mainland, its neighbouring islands and the Antipodes . . . provide, as it unfolds, an effective antidote to the baneful forces of atheism, nationalism, secularism and materialism that are tearing at the vitals of this turbulent continent, and may it re-enact those scenes of spiritual heroism which more than any of the secular revolutions which have agitated its face, have left their everlasting imprint on the fortunes of the peoples and nations dwelling within its borders."

No less enthusiasm for the tasks ahead—the most staggering of which was work in 84 territories, half of them virgin areas—filled the hearts of the Bahá'ís gathered in New Delhi than had characterized the reaction of their brothers and sisters attending the three previous Conferences. This enthusiasm was further heightened when a cable was received from the Guardian giving the glad-tidings that his own personal hope—expressed before the festivities of the Holy Year began—had been attained through the completion of the superstructure of the Báb's Holy Sepulchre. The Bahá'ís rallied strongly to meet their given goals: offers to pioneer were received from over 70 people, 25 of whom proceeded to their posts shortly after the Conference ended; funds were lavishly contributed towards the purchase of the three sites for future Bahá'í Temples—Baghdád, Sydney and Delhi, 9 acres of land for the latter being acquired before the Conference rose; substantial donations were received for that most precious and longed-for Temple to be erected in Bahá'u'lláh's native city, the capital of Persia, which was one of the two Temples originally scheduled to be built during the World Crusade; public meetings and a reception for over a thousand guests were held at which many important figures were present; India's President, Dr. Rajendra Prasad, as well as her famous Prime Minister, Jawaharlal Nehru, received delegations from the Conference and the publicity was wide and friendly. At the end of the Conference Shoghi Effendi instructed the Hands attending it to disperse on trips lasting some months, himself providing both assistance and directions as to their itineraries.

In addition to what might be called his routine work, already consuming daily an alarming amount of his time, for over two years Shoghi Effendi not only worked on and fully elaborated the details of this global Crusade but made the exhaustive plans necessary for these great jubilee celebrations and constantly directed the Hands of the Cause and the National Assemblies who were to implement their programmes. One might have thought that a lull in his creative output would ensue, but such was not the case. Cables and letters streamed from him at the end of each of the Conferences like missiles towards targets. For four years he never let the white hot heat he had engendered wane. A typical example of this is the tone in which, immediately after the American Conference ended, when the bemused Bahá'í world had scarcely begun to recover from the first glorious revelation of the new Plan, he cabled the Persian National Assembly: "Announce friends no less 128 believers offered pioneer services during celebrations Wilmette including offer pioneer leper colony. Appeal friends not allow themselves surpassed western brethren. Hundreds must arise. Enumerated goals at home abroad must promptly be fulfilled. Upon response progress protection victory entire community depends. Eagerly awaiting evidence action." Such oft-repeated appeals had such an effect on a community which had lived its entire existence in a wretched cage of prejudice and persecution that the Persian believers, seeing, unbelievably, a door open before them, began to pour forth to the four corners of the world in ever-swelling numbers; without their assistance, their strong financial support and their constant readiness to sacrifice, the Crusade could never have been won on the scale that marked its triumphal conclusion in 1963.

But let us return to the newly inaugurated "fate-laden, soul-stirring, decade-long, world-embracing Spiritual Crusade . . ." with its four objectives: Development of the institutions at the World Centre of the Faith; consolidation of the homefronts of the twelve territories serving as the administrative bases of the twelve Plans which were component parts of The Plan; consolidation of all the territories already opened to the Faith; opening of the remaining chief virgin territories of the planet. Although the administration of the Crusade had been entrusted to the twelve National Assemblies, nevertheless every single believer, irrespective of his race, nation, class, colour, age or sex, was to lend his particular assistance to the accomplishment of this "gigantic enterprise". In a colourful passage of scintillating prose Shoghi Effendi lifted the curtain on the arena of the new Plan: Where? Why, everywhere—in the Arctic Circle, in the deserts, the jungles, the isles of the cold North Sea and the torrid climes of the Indian and Pacific Oceans. To whom? Why, to all peoples—to the tribes of Africa, the Eskimos of Canada and Greenland, the Lapps of the far north, the Polynesians, the Australian Aborigines, the red Indians of the Americas. Under what circumstances? Not only in the wilderness, but in the cities, "immersed in crass materialism", where people breathed the fetid air of "aggressive racialism" bound by the chains of "haughty intellectualism", surrounded by "blind and militant nationalism", immersed in "narrow and intolerant ecclesiasticism". What strongholds must Bahá'u'lláh's soldiers storm? The strongholds of Hinduism, the monasteries of Buddhism, the jungles of the Amazon, the mountains of Tibet, the steppes of Russia, the wastes of Siberia, the interior of China, Mongolia, Japan, with their teeming multitudes—nor should they forget to sit with the leper and consort with the outcast in their colonies. "I direct my impassioned appeal," he wrote, "to obey, as befits His warriors, the summons of the Lord of Hosts and prepare for that Day of Days, when His victorious battalions will, to the accompaniment of hosannas from the invisible angels in the Abhá Kingdom, celebrate the hour of final victory."

It is clear that the Guardian envisaged this Ten Year undertaking as no more and no less than a battle, the battle of the "world-wide, loyal, unbreachable army" of "Bahá'u'lláh's warriors", His "army of light", against the entrenched battalions of darkness holding the globe. Its "Supreme Commander" was 'Abdu'l-Bahá; behind Him stood His Father, the "King of Kings", His aid pledged "to every crusader battling for His Cause". "Invisible battalions" were mustered "rank upon rank, ready to pour forth reinforcements from on high". And so the little band of God's heroes assembled, ready to go forth and "emblazon on their shields the emblems of new victories", ready to implant the "earthly symbols of Bahá'u'lláh's unearthly sovereignty" in every country of the world, ready to lay the unassailable administrative foundation of His Christ-promised Kingdom of God upon earth.

Nine months after the opening of the Crusade the Guardian could announce that almost ninety territories had been opened, three-quarters of the total number, exclusive of those within the Soviet orbit, and in his Riḍván Message of 1954 he was able to give the glad-tidings that they had reached 100. Having seized these 100 new prizes the army of Bahá'u'lláh was now engaged in depth. Shoghi Effendi, his mind more or less at rest about the progress of the front lines, immediately set about digging in. The second phase of the Plan, now opening, was primarily concerned with consolidation. In that same Message the Guardian listed 13 points which were to be concentrated upon during the coming two years: prosecution of the all-important teaching work; preservation of all prizes won; maintenance of all local assemblies; multiplication of groups and centres—all to hasten the emergence of the 48 National Assemblies scheduled to be formed during the Crusade; purchase of Temple sites; initiation of special funds for purchase of the specified National Ḥaẓíratu'l-Quds; speedy fulfilment of various language tasks; acquisition of historic Bahá'í sites in Persia; measures for the erection of the Ṭihrán and Frankfurt Temples; establishment of the Wilmette Temple dependency; inauguration of national endowments; incorporation of local Assemblies; establishment of the new Publishing Trusts. He directed his "fervent plea" to accomplish such monumental labours as these to the

108 people constituting the 12 National Assemblies of the Bahá'í world, out of the teeming millions of human beings on the planet!

The miracle was that such an appeal, to what in the eyes of the sophisticated could not but appear to be pitifully weak instruments, should have had such an effect. All over the Bahá'í world the leaders and the rank and file redoubled their efforts and sweeping victories were won. In 1955 Shoghi Effendi informed the believers in his annual Riḍván Message, which was his main instrument for conveying news of the progress of the Faith, that the Plan was "forging ahead, gaining momentum with every passing day, tearing down barriers in all climes and amidst divers peoples and races, widening irresistibly the scope of its beneficent operations, and revealing ever more compelling signs of its inherent strength as it marches towards the spiritual conquest of the entire planet."

It was during this second phase of the World Crusade that the Bahá'ís accomplished such feats as purchasing 10 of the 11 Temple sites enumerated as goals of their Ten Year Plan, at a cost of over $100,000, of acquiring 30 out of the 51 national endowments at an estimated $100,000, and of buying 43 of the 49 national Bahá'í headquarters, for over half-a-million dollars in various continents of the globe—the latter being a feat which Shoghi Effendi cryptically and significantly stated was "amply compensating for the seizure and occupation of the National Administrative Headquarters of the Faith and the demolition of its dome by the military authorities in the Persian capital."

There were many brilliant victories during these early years of the Crusade: the Síyáh-Chál, scene of the first intimation of Bahá'u'lláh's Prophetic Mission, was purchased; His banner was planted in Islám's very heart through the establishment of a Spiritual Assembly in Mecca; the particularly welcome news reached the Guardian that there were Bahá'ís—remnants of the former communities in the Caucasus and Turkistán—in some of the Soviet states listed at the inception of the Crusade as unopened, but which might now be regarded as open, however faint and feeble the solitary candles burning there; 98 islands throughout the world now had Bahá'ís; work on the erection of the International Archives Building at the World Centre was begun.

It was in a period of victories such as these that Shoghi Effendi took the momentous decision to erect not two but three Houses of Worship during the Ten Year Plan. The significance given in the Writings of Bahá'u'lláh and 'Abdu'l-Bahá to these Mashriqu'l-

Adhkárs (dawning places of the mention of God) is very great: they are erected, Shoghi Effendi said, for "the worship of the one true God, and to the glory of His Manifestation for this Day." They are strongly linked to both the spiritual life of the individual and the communal life of the believers.

At the inception of the Crusade the Guardian turned his attention to the problem of erecting the first Bahá'í Temple in Bahá'u'lláh's native land. He decided on a conservative concept, worked out with his personal approval in Haifa, and which he said, "incorporates a dome reminiscent of that of the Báb's Holy Sepulchre". Already the enthusiastic Persian believers had started a five year plan to raise twelve million tumans for its construction and the Guardian himself had had its design unveiled at the meeting in Bahjí on the first day of Riḍván, 1953. It was a project to which Shoghi Effendi attached the greatest importance and the outlawing of all Bahá'í activity in Persia in 1955 came as a severe blow to him for he realized that the situation there, far from having improved in the quarter of a century of his ministry, had again deteriorated to such a point that there was little hope of such a building being erected before the end of the Ten Year Plan. In spite of the fact that the first Mashriqu'l-Adhkár of Europe—the second Temple of the Plan—could still be built, he immediately struck back at the enemies of the Faith through a cable sent in November 1955: "Historic decision arrived at raise Mother Temple Africa in City Kampala situated its heart and constituting supreme consolation masses oppressed valiant brethren cradle Faith. Every continent globe except Australasia will thereby pride itself on derive direct spiritual benefit its own Mashriqu'l-Adhkár. Befitting recognition will moreover have been accorded marvelous expansion Faith amazing multiplication its administrative institutions throughout continent . . ." Thus the African believers received what he characterized as "the stupendous, the momentous and unique project of the construction of Africa's Mother Temple."

Whereas Ṭihrán was to have the third great Temple of the Bahá'í world and Germany the fourth, in reality the European one became third in priority and Africa the fourth. The design for the African Temple was made under Shoghi Effendi's supervision in Haifa and met with his full approval. The situation as regards the German one was different: he himself had chosen a design and sent it to the National Assembly of the Bahá'ís of Germany and Austria, but there was already so much strong church-aroused opposition to the erection of a Bahá'í House of Worship that the National Assembly had informed him they felt the conservative nature of the design he had chosen would, in a land favouring at the moment extremely modern-style buildings, complicate its erection, as a building permit might be refused on this pretext. Shoghi Effendi therefore permitted them to hold a competition and of the designs sent him he favoured the one which was later built. Frankfurt was in the heart of Germany, Germany was in the heart of Europe. It was the logical place for the European Temple.

Still thoroughly aroused by the persecution of the main body of the faithful who resided in Bahá'u'lláh's native land, Shoghi Effendi quietly set a new plan in motion. He had chosen a third Temple design and instructed the National Assembly of the Bahá'ís of Australia and New Zealand to make enquiries, confidentially, as to how much such a building would cost if erected in Sydney. When he received an estimate which he felt would not add too heavily to the financial burden the Crusade was already carrying, he made his thrilling announcement, in his Riḍván Message of 1957, of the launching of an "ambitious three-fold enterprise, designed to compensate for the disabilities suffered by the sorely-tried Community of the followers of His Faith in the land of His birth, aiming at the erection in localities as far apart as Frankfurt, Sydney and Kampala, of the Mother Temples of the European, the Australian and the African continents, at a cost of approximately one million dollars, complementing the Temples already constructed in the Asiatic and American continents." This announcement meant that the loss to the Persian believers of their first Mashriqu'l-Adhkár would be compensated for by the erection in the Pacific of what the Guardian called "The Mother Temple of the Antipodes, and indeed of the whole Pacific area" and the construction in the heart of the African continent of another House of Worship which he said was "destined to enormously influence the onward march of the Cause of God the world over, to consolidate to a marked degree the rising institutions of a divinely appointed Order and noise abroad its fame in every continent of the globe." The Guardian also announced in this Riḍván Message that the designs for all three of these "monumental edifices, each designed to serve as a house for the indwelling Spirit of God and a tabernacle for the glorification of His appointed Messenger in this day" would be shown to "the assembled delegates at the thirteen historic Bahá'í National Conventions being held for the first time during this year's Riḍván Festival."

It was during this second phase of the World Crusade that the American National Assembly purchased the land for its first Temple dependency. The Guardian had advised that Assembly that he did not consider a library—the first proposal—sufficiently demonstrative of the purpose and significance of the institution of the Ma<u>sh</u>riqu'l-A<u>dh</u>kár in Bahá'í society and it was therefore decided to build a Home for the Aged. One of his last letters was to urge that Assembly to commence work on the Home, as it would impress on the public that one of the chief functions of our Faith is to serve humanity, regardless of creed, race or denomination, and be sure to attract attention and publicity.

XIV

A UNIQUE MINISTRY

The Guardian had fused in the alembic of his creative mind all the elements of the Faith of Bahá'u'lláh into one great indivisible whole; he had created an organized community of His followers which was the receptacle of His teachings, His laws, and His Administrative Order; the teachings of the Twin Manifestations of God and the Perfect Exemplar had been woven into a shining cloak that would clothe and protect man for a thousand years, a cloak on which the fingers of Shoghi Effendi had picked out the patterns, knitted the seams, fashioned the brilliant protective clasps of his interpretations of the Sacred Texts, never to be sundered, never to be torn away until that day when a new Law-giver comes to the world and once again wraps His creature man in yet another divine garment.

The Master's grandson had been sublimed by the forces released in His Testament into the Guardian of the Faith; belonging to the sovereign caste of his divine Forefathers, he was himself a sovereign. To the primacy conferred by ties of consanguinity had been added the powers of infallible guidance with which the operation of God's Covenant had invested him. Shoghi Effendi's divine and indefeasible right to assume the helm of the Cause of God had been fully vindicated through thirty-six years of unremitting, heartbreaking toil. It would be hard indeed to find a comparable figure in history who, in a little over a third of a century, set so many different operations in motion, who found the time to devote his attention to minute details on one hand and on the other to cover the range of an entire planet with his plans, his instructions, his guidance and his leadership. He had laid the foundations of that future society Bahá'u'lláh had fathered upon the mind of the Master, and which He in turn had gestated to a point of perfection, passing it upon His death into the safe hands of His successor.

Patiently, as a master jeweller works at his designs, picking out from his stock of gems some kingly stone, setting it amidst smaller but equally precious ones, so would Shoghi Effendi choose a theme from the Teachings, pluck it out, study it, polish its facets, and set it amidst his brilliant commentaries, where it would flash and catch our eye as never before when it had laid buried beneath a heap of other jewels. It would be no exaggeration to say that we Bahá'ís now live in a room entirely surrounded by these glorious, blazing motifs Shoghi Effendi created. It is as if he had caught the sunlight of this Revelation in a prism and enabled us to appreciate the number of colours and rays that make up the blinding light of Bahá'u'lláh's words.

Things we knew all our lives suddenly, startlingly, took on a new and added significance. We were challenged, rebuked, stimulated. We found ourselves arising to serve, to pioneer, to sacrifice. We grew under his aegis and the Faith grew with us into something vastly different from what had existed before. Let us take a few of these master jewels, these themes Shoghi Effendi set before us in such a brilliant manner. One day Bahá'u'lláh rested on Mt. Carmel. He pointed out a spot to 'Abdu'l-Bahá and said buy this land and bring the body of the Báb and inter Him here. The Master brought the Precious Trust and placed it in the heart of the mountain and covered it with the building he erected with so many tears. The Guardian completed the sacred Edifice, and now the glorious Shrine of the Forerunner of the Faith rests in queenly splendour on Mt. Carmel, the cynosure of all eyes.

The Master sent a handful of precious Tablets, written during dark and dangerous days, to America after the First World War and a pleasant ceremony was held called the "unveiling of the Divine Plan" at which pairs of children and young people (myself included) pulled strings and one of the Tablets duly appeared on the draped background of the platform. 'Abdu'l-Bahá had sent a king's ransom to the North American believers, who rejoiced but did not understand. Shoghi Effendi, never losing sight of this gleaming hoard that had been deposited on the other side of the world, set about working his way to it. It took him almost two decades, but at last, having painfully and feverishly erected the machinery of the Administrative Order, he was in a position to take up those jewels and set them. The North was conquered, the South was conquered, the East and the West alike began to glow and blaze in all their parts with the light of new Bahá'í centres and

Assemblies, more than 4,200 throughout the world. Into the various territories of the globe—251 in number—which Shoghi Effendi had ensured should either be awakened or reanimated by the breezes of the Divine Plan, he had spilled the river of the translations of the literature of the Faith in 230 languages. For twenty years, since he first set in motion the power 'Abdu'l-Bahá had concealed in those Tablets, Shoghi Effendi had never ceased to wave forward an army of pioneers, battalion after battalion marching forth to conquer at his bidding the whole planet and implant, wherever it conquered, the Banner of Bahá'u'lláh.

Grasping the hidden import of Bahá'u'lláh's Tablet of Carmel the Guardian entombed the Greatest Holy Leaf near the Shrine of the Báb, brought her mother and brother to rest beside her, designated this spot as the heart of a world-wide administration, drew an arc above it on the mountainside which he associated with Bahá'u'lláh's words *"the seat of God's Throne"*, built the first of the great edifices that will rise about that arc, and in innumerable passages pointed out the nature of the progress that must pour out from this great spiritual hub to all the peoples and nations of the world, a progress based on the teachings of a Faith that is "essentially supernatural, supranational, entirely non-political, non-partisan, and diametrically opposed to any policy or school of thought that seeks to exalt any particular race, class or nation"; a Faith whose "followers view mankind as one entity, and profoundly attached to its vital interests, will not hesitate to subordinate every particular interest, be it personal, regional or national, to the over-riding interests of the generality of mankind, knowing full well that in a world of interdependent peoples and nations the advantage of the part is best to be reached by the advantage of the whole"; a Faith the embryo of which, Shoghi Effendi explained, had developed during the Heroic Age, whose child, the social Order contained in the teachings of Bahá'u'lláh would grow during the Formative Age, whose adolescence would witness the establishment of the World Order, and whose maturity in the distant reaches of the Golden Age would flower in a world civilization, a global civilization without precedent, which would mark "the furthermost limits in the organization of human society", which would never decline, in which mankind would continue to progress indefinitely and ascend to ever greater heights of spiritual power.

He divided the events that had taken place, and were taking place in the Cause of God, into sections, relating each to the whole evolution of the Faith, creating a map in relief that enabled us to see at a glance where our present labours fitted in, how much the achievement of an immediate objective would pave the way for the next inevitable step we must take in our service to Bahá'u'lláh's Cause. The definitions and divisions he employed were not arbitrary, but implicit in the teachings and in the course of events transpiring within the Faith. The Prophetic Cycle—which began with Adam and culminated with Muḥammad—in the school of whose Prophets man had been educated and prepared for the age of his maturity, had given way to the Cycle of Fulfilment, inaugurated by Bahá'u'lláh. The unity of the planet, which science had made possible, would enable, nay, oblige man to create a new society in which a world at peace could devote itself exclusively to the material and spiritual unfoldment of man. Because of the very greatness of this transformation Bahá'u'lláh's shadow would be cast over the planet for five thousand centuries, the first ten of which would be governed by the laws, ordinances, teachings and principles He had laid down.

This thousand-year-long Dispensation Shoghi Effendi divided into great Ages. The first, commencing with the declaration of the Báb and ending with the ascension of the Master, lasted seventy-seven years and was styled by the Guardian the Apostolic or Heroic Age of the Faith because of the nature of the events that transpired within it and the blood-bath that had characterized its inception and swept away 20,000 souls, including the Báb Himself. This Age was divided into three epochs by the Guardian, associated with the Ministry of the Báb, Bahá'u'lláh and 'Abdu'l-Bahá, respectively. The second Age, which Shoghi Effendi called the Formative Age, the Age of Transition, the Iron Age of the Faith, was that period during which its Administrative Order—the very hall-mark of this Age—must evolve, reach perfection and effloresce into the World Order of Bahá'u'lláh. The first epoch of this Age spanned the period from the ascension of 'Abdu'l-Bahá in 1921 until the centenary of the inception of the Faith in 1944 and the events immediately following upon it, and the second epoch was consummated by the termination of the World Crusade in 1963, coinciding with the hundredth anniversary of the Declaration of Bahá'u'lláh. Although the Guardian never stated exactly how many epochs would characterize this Formative Age, he implied that others, equally vital, equally thrilling would take place as the Faith steadily advanced towards what he called its Golden Age, which on more than one occasion, he intimated would probably arise in the later centuries of the Dispensation of Bahá'u'lláh.

Shoghi Effendi said the Cause of God would pass from obscurity and persecution into the light of recognition as a world religion; it would achieve full emancipation from the shackles of the past, become a state religion and eventually the Bahá'í state itself would emerge, a new and unique creation in the world's religious history. When the Formative Age passed and man entered the Golden Age, he would have entered that Age foretold in the Bible in Habakkuk, 2:14: "For the earth shall be filled with the knowledge of the glory of the Lord, as the waters cover the sea."

The historic implementation of 'Abdu'l-Bahá Divine Plan by Shoghi Effendi was likewise divided into epochs by him and these in turn subdivided into specific phases, a device that enabled the Bahá'ís to follow closely the course of their own activities and to concentrate on specific goals. The first epoch of the Divine Plan passed through three phases, the first Seven Year Plan, the second Seven Year Plan and the Ten Year Teaching and Consolidation Plan which we came to term the World Crusade. This Crusade itself Shoghi Effendi divided into a series of phases: the first of these lasted one year, 1953–1954; during it, Shoghi Effendi said, the vital objective of the Plan had been virtually attained through the addition of no less than 100 new countries enlisted under the Banner of Bahá'u'lláh; the second phase, from 1954–1956, was marked by a unique measure of consolidation as well as expansion, which not only paved the way for the election of the forty-eight new national bodies which was scheduled to take place before the Plan was consummated, but was characterized by unprecedented expenditures through the purchase of National Ḥaẓíratu'l-Quds and Temple sites as well as the formation of Bahá'í Publishing Trusts; "the third and what promises to be the most brilliant phase of a world spiritual Crusade" he wrote, would take place between 1956–1958, and was to be distinguished by an unparalleled multiplication of Bahá'í centres throughout the entire world as well as the formation of sixteen new National Assemblies. Before he passed away the Guardian indicated that the fourth phase of his mighty Plan, which would stretch from 1958 to 1963, must be distinguished not only by an unprecedented increase in the number of believers and centres all over the world but by progress in the erection of the three Temples which now formed part of the goals of the Ten Year Plan.

But for us, the end of this great leadership, that had given us such concepts as these, that had fulfilled in so brilliant a manner the work begun by 'Abdu'l-Bahá, that had so worthily implemented not only His own instructions but the supreme guidance of the Manifestation of God Himself, was at hand. No one could know, no one could bear to know, that when the Bahá'í world received the message dated October 1957, it would be the last message of Shoghi Effendi. It was a happy and victorious message, full of hope, full of new plans, a last priceless gift from the man who as he wrote it was in reality laying down his pen and turning his face from the world and its sorrows for all time. Soon, Shoghi Effendi informed us, the Global Spiritual Crusade would reach its midway point. That point was to be marked by the convocation of a series of five Intercontinental Conferences to be held in January, March, May, July and September of 1958, in Africa, the Antipodes, America, Europe and Asia, respectively. Following a pattern similar to the one he employed at the time of the convocation of the first four Intercontinental Conferences held during the Holy Year at the inception of the Crusade, Shoghi Effendi specified the five bodies under whose auspices these great gatherings would be held and whose chairmen were to act as their convenors. The Central and East African Regional Assembly was made responsible for the first Conference (surely it is not by chance that Africa, twice in a period of five years, led the way in the series by holding the first Conference?); the National Assembly of Australia for the second; the National Assembly of the United States for the third; the National Assembly of the Bahá'ís of Germany and Austria for the fourth; and the Regional Assembly of South-East Asia the final one. "They are to be convened", Shoghi Effendi wrote, ". . . for the five-fold purpose of offering humble thanksgiving to the Divine Author of our Faith, Who has graciously enabled His followers, during a period of deepening anxiety and amidst the confusion and uncertainties of a critical phase in the fortunes of mankind, to prosecute uninterruptedly the Ten Year Plan formulated for the execution of the Grand Design conceived by 'Abdu'l-Bahá; of reviewing and celebrating the series of signal victories won so rapidly in the course of each of the campaigns of this world-encircling Crusade; of deliberating on ways and means that will ensure its triumphant consummation; and of lending simultaneously a powerful impetus, the world over, to the vital process of individual conversion—the pre-eminent purpose underlying the Plan in all its ramifications—and to the construction and completion of the three Mother Temples to be built in the European, the African, and Australian continents."

BAHÁ'U'LLÁH'S TOMB IN BAHJÍ

Above: Appearance of the entrance to the Shrine about 1921;
below, the majestic beautification of the entrance to His Tomb, 1957

THE MOST HOLY TOMB
Above: the Shrine of Bahá'u'lláh at Bahjí; below: some of the 96 lamp posts illuminating the Shrine gardens at night

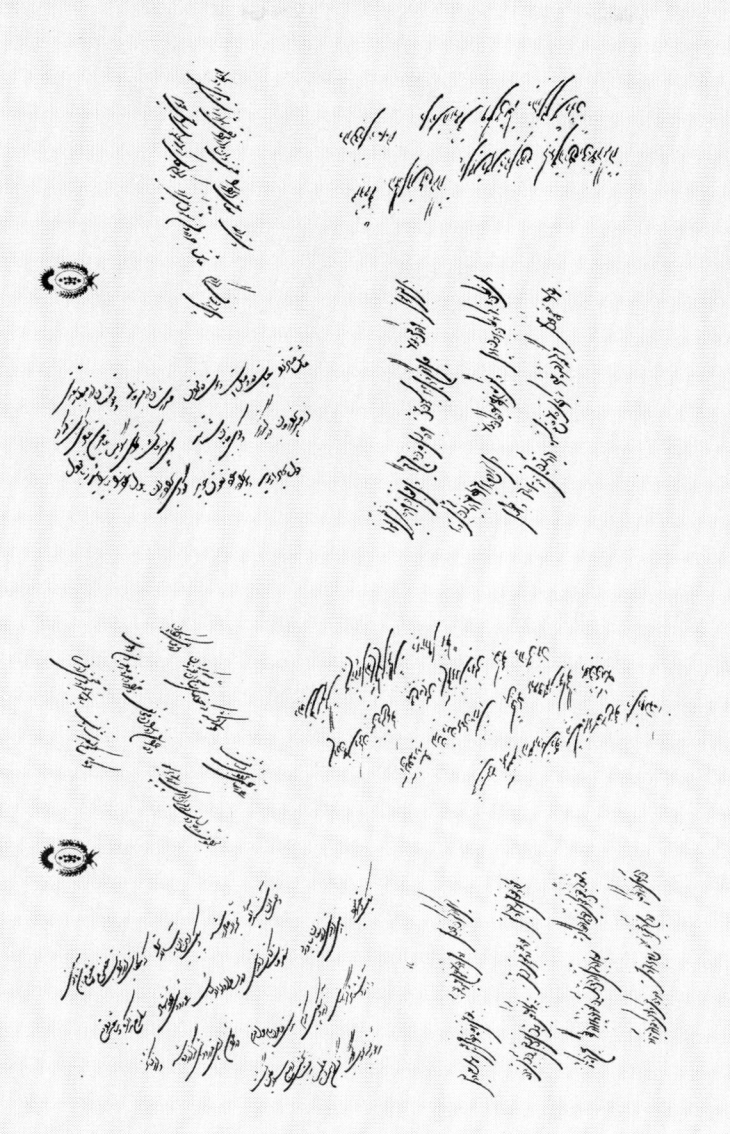

FACSIMILE OF SHOGHI EFFENDI'S HANDWRITING

On the left is an excerpt from a letter to the Baháʼís of the East dated November 1927, concerning the services of Miss Martha Root; on the right, a few of the "Hidden Words"

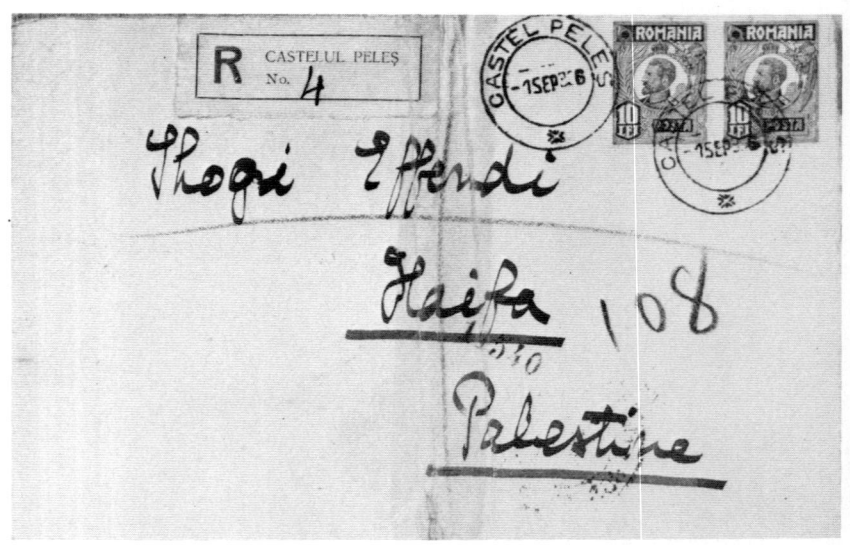

FACSIMILES OF QUEEN MARIE'S HANDWRITING

Above: envelope addressed to Shoghi Effendi by the Queen of Rumania, which contained her first letter to him written on 27 August 1926, from Bran, her favourite residence. Facing page: One of Her Majesty's written testimonials to the significance of the Bahá'í teachings

The Bahai teaching brings peace and understanding.

It is like a wide embrace gathering together all those who have long searched for words of hope.

It accepts all great prophets gone before, it destroys no other creeds and leaves all doors open.

Saddened by the continual strife amongst believers of many confessions and wearied of their intolerance towards eachother, I discovered in the Bahai teaching the real spirit of Christ so often denied and misunderstood:

Unity instead of strife, Hope instead of condemnation, Love instead of hate, and a great reassurance for all men.

Marie.

THE GUARDIAN
The last photograph of Shoghi Effendi taken a few months before he passed away. Enlarged from a very small snapshot it conveys something of the gentle, noble, humble nature of the Guardian. The majesty and power that so strongly radiated from him are lacking in this picture

THE FUNERAL OF SHOGHI EFFENDI IN LONDON
Grief-stricken farewells take place as the Bahá'ís file past the coffin of their Guardian at the foot of his open grave, November 9, 1957

THE GRAVE OF THE GUARDIAN
White Carrara marble, a Corinthian column, a globe showing the map of Africa, and his own Japanese eagle on top, symbol of victory

Shoghi Effendi informed us that, "The phenomenal advances made since the inception of this globe-girdling Crusade, in the brief space of less than five years, eclipse . . . in both the number and quality of the feats achieved by its prosecutors, any previous collective enterprise undertaken . . . since the close of . . . the Heroic Age . . ." With evident joy, he recapitulated these feats and enumerated the victories won, characterizing them as "so marvellous a progress, embracing so vast a field, achieved in so short a time, by so small a band of heroic souls".

It was in this message that the Guardian appointed his last contingent of Hands of the Cause of God—eight more individuals to join this "august institution"—thus raising the total number of "high-ranking officers of a fast evolving World Administrative Order" to twenty-seven, an act which, in view of their recent assumption "of their sacred responsibility as protectors of the Faith", called for the formation of another Auxiliary Board, equal to the previous one in number, which would be "charged with the specific duty of watching over the security of the Faith". The five Hands who had been chosen by Shoghi Effendi to work at the World Centre were to attend these five Intercontinental Conferences as his special representatives. Two of them would place in the foundations of the Mother Temples being built in Kampala and Sydney "a portion of the blessed earth from the inmost Shrine of Bahá'u'lláh"; another portion of that sacred soil would be delivered in Frankfurt to the National Spiritual Assembly of Germany and Austria, pending the time when it could be placed in the foundations of the first European Mashriqu'l-Adhkár. A reproduction of the portrait of Bahá'u'lláh and a lock of His precious hair would not only be shown to the attendants at the European, Australian and African Conferences, but deposited with the national bodies in whose areas these great Houses of Worship were being erected, as a permanent and loving gift of their Guardian. The Guardian would send with the Hand who was to attend the Conference in Asia another reproduction of the portrait of Bahá'u'lláh for the assembled believers to view, but this was to be brought back for safe keeping to the Holy Land. At the Conference to be convened in Chicago, Shoghi Effendi's representative would exhibit to the believers the portraits of Bahá'u'lláh and the Báb which he had previously entrusted to the care of the American National Assembly. These were the final gestures of love Shoghi Effendi was able to shower on the believers, that host of the faithful over whom he had watched, who had followed him so unfailingly, for so many history-making years.

When thousands of Bahá'ís from innumerable lands gathered during 1958, in fulfilment of Shoghi Effendi's plan and wish, at these five great Intercontinental Conferences, it was not only with awe that they gazed on the sacred portrait of the Founder of their Faith, but with grief-filled hearts and tear-filled eyes. Why had He, before Whose glory they bowed themselves, Whose teachings they had espoused, into the depths of Whose deep and all-knowing eyes they were now gazing, seen fit to remove His scion from their midst? They not only cried out for their Guardian, they asked where was the Guardianship itself? It was the supreme test of faith: God had given, and God had taken back, and "He doth what He pleaseth. He chooseth; and none may question His choice." When the Báb was martyred Bahá'u'lláh had remained; when Bahá'u'lláh ascended 'Abdu'l-Bahá had remained; when 'Abdu'l-Bahá passed away Shoghi Effendi remained. But now it was as if a procession of Kings—albeit each different, vastly different in station from the other—had gone into a room of their own and closed the door. We Bahá'ís looked at the door and kept asking, like children whose parents have been killed in an earthquake and disappeared, why had it been closed?

Perhaps at no point in its history will the deepness of the root of belief that binds the Bahá'ís to their religion be again laid as bare as it was in the year after the passing of Shoghi Effendi. They bowed their heads in the agony of the grief that swept them, but they held. Had not the Guardian provided these five great rallying points at which the believers could come together in such large numbers, console each other and receive guidance from the Hands of the Cause who had arisen to complete the Guardian's Plan and ensure the election of the divinely-guided Universal House of Justice, it is hard to imagine how greatly affected the body of the Faith might have been by the sudden and totally unexpected death of its beloved Head. The fact that the friends were actively engaged in a Plan, the fact that the attention of the Bahá'í world was now focussed on its midway point, the fact that at these Conferences five specific themes were to be given special attention, and the fact that they repeatedly received messages of love, faith and encouragement from the Hands of the Cause—all exerted a binding and unifying influence upon the Bahá'ís of the world. The very calamity itself brought to their hearts, cleansed by the rushing freshets of their grief, a new fortitude and called forth a deeper love. They were not going to fail Shoghi Effendi. He had told them to consider ways and means of ensuring the triumphal conclusion of the Plan—very well, they would do so, they would see it crowned befittingly in 1963 with a success that would have thrilled his heart and brought from his pen one of those rushes of praise and gratitude so dearly prized by them.

No testimony to the truth and strength of the Cause could have been greater than the triumphal conclusion of the Guardian's World Crusade which the believers achieved. It had been a hard, an overwhelming task to begin with. That the Bahá'ís achieved it, that for over five years they worked and sacrificed to a greater degree than ever before in their history without his leadership, without those appeals, those reports, those marvellous word-pictures he painted for them in his messages, without the knowledge that he was there at the helm, their so dearly-loved captain steering them to victory and safety, is little short of a miracle and testifies not only to how well he builded, but to those words of the Master: *"there is a mysterious power in this Cause, far far above the ken of men and angels."*

Life and death are so closely allied that they are the two halves of one heartbeat and yet death never seems very real to us in the normal course of events—who therefore awaited Shoghi Effendi's death! He had been in very good health that last summer, better than for a long time, a fact that he not only mentioned himself but which his doctor commented upon at the time he examined him some weeks prior to his passing. No one dreamed that the time clock inside that heart was reaching the end of its allotted span. Many times people have asked me if I did not notice indications that the end was near. My answer is a hesitant no. If a terrible storm comes suddenly into the midst of a perfect day one can later imagine one saw straws floating by on the wind and pretend they had been portents. I do remember a very few things that might have been significant, but certainly they meant nothing to me at the time. I could never have survived the slightest foreknowledge of the Guardian's death, and only survived it in the end because I could not abandon him and his precious work, which had killed him long before any one believed his life would end.

One of the goals of the Ten Year Plan associated with the World Centre, a goal the Guardian had allotted himself, was what he termed the "codification of the laws and ordinances of the *Kitáb-i-Aqdas*, the Mother Book of the Bahá'í Revelation." Any work involving a book of this magnitude, which Shoghi Effendi had stated was, together with the *Will and Testament* of 'Abdu'l-Bahá, "the chief depository wherein are enshrined those priceless elements of that Divine Civilization, the establishment of which is the primary mission of the Bahá'í Faith", would certainly be unsuitable for any one but the Head of the Faith to undertake. Shoghi Effendi worked on this for about three weeks or so in the spring of 1957 prior to his departure from Haifa. As I often sat in the room with him while he worked, reading out loud and making notes, I realized from what he told me that he was not planning at that time a legal codification of the provisions in the Aqdas but rather a compilation, placing subject with subject, which would enable the Bahá'ís to comprehend the nature of the laws and ordinances given by Bahá'u'lláh to His followers. It was at this time that Shoghi Effendi remarked more than once that he did not feel he could ever finish this task he had undertaken. I attached no particular importance to this, as he sometimes fretted under the terrible load of his ever-increasing work, and attributed it to his great fatigue at the end of the long, exhausting, unbroken stretch of labour he had passed through during his months at home. After his death I remembered and wondered.

That last summer he went back to visit many of his favourite scenes in the mountains and I wondered about this too, when the blow fell, but at the time I was only happy to see him happy, forgetting, for a few fleeting moments, the burdens and sorrows of his life.

In 1958 his grave was built of the same dazzling white Carrara marble he had himself chosen for the monuments of his illustrious relatives in Haifa, a simple grave as he would have wished it to be. A single marble column, crowned by a Corinthian capital is surmounted by a globe, the map of Africa facing forward—for had not the victories won in Africa brought him the greatest joy during that last year of his life?—and on this globe is a large gilded bronze eagle, a reproduction of a beautiful Japanese sculpture of an eagle which he greatly admired and which he had placed in his own room. No better emblem than this symbol of victory could have been found for the resting-place of him who had won so many victories as he led the hosts of Bahá'u'lláh's followers on their ceaseless conquests through the five continents of the world.

Having, with adamantine fortitude in the face of every trial, accomplished "the toilsome task of fixing the pattern, of laying the foundations, of erecting the machinery, and of setting in operation the Administrative Order" to use the Guardian's own words; having effected the world-wide spread and establishment of the Cause of God through the implementation of 'Abdu'l-Bahá's Divine Plan; having, through that rare spirit of his so admirably compounded of audacity and sobriety, guided the Faith of Bahá'u'lláh to heights it had never before reached; having carried the work his Lord had entrusted to him as far forward as his failing strength would permit; bearing the scars of innumerable personal attacks made upon him during the course of his ministry, Shoghi Effendi departed from the scene of his labours. The man had been "called by sorrow and a strange desolation of hopes into quietness."

> *Well is it with him that seeketh the shelter of his shade that shadoweth all mankind.*
> 'ABDU'L-BAHÁ

INDEX

The transliteration for Persian and Arabic words in this book is according to a system established at one of the International Oriental Congresses.

Aba Khoushy (Mayor of Haifa) 143
'Abdu'l-Bahá (The Master, Centre of the Covenant, Sir 'Abbás Effendi) 1-27, 60, 61, 62, 66, 79, 95, 100, 124, 141, 142, 149, 153, 157, 164, 165, 169, 195, 223, 229, 236
  alludes to His successor 1
  ascension, and its effects, 13-27, 59, 66, 232
  departs for Egypt 7
  first letter to Shoghi Effendi 4
  health improved with good news 9
  knighthood from British Government 10
  lays Báb's remains to rest on Mount Carmel 84
  love for Shoghi Effendi 3, 7
  moves to Haifa 5
  prophecies of, fulfilled 109
  release from bondage 2
  record of His voice 184
  relics of 117
  Shoghi Effendi and 1-15, 65, 71
  Will and Testament of 1, 2, 14, 15, 16, 23, 26, 86, 99, 106, 108, 112, 114, 115, 145, 163, 194, 229, 238
  Writings translated by Shoghi Effendi 86, 87, 97
'Abdu'l-Hamíd (Sultan of Turkey) 1, 2, 76
Adana (in Turkey), local Bahá'ís imprisoned 158-9
Administrative Order of the Bahá'í Faith 67, 111, 115, 153, 165, 174, 187, 194, 197, 199, 201-4, 229, 230, 232, 235, 239
  cradle of (North America) 93, 163, 170, 218
  development and evolution of 108-19, 145-9, 206
  divine in origin 153, 162-3, 167
  purpose of administrative bodies 163-4
  rigidity in essentials, fluidity in non-essentials 162, 165
  structure and principles of 147, 162
Advent of Divine Justice, The 58, 71, 93-4, 189
Afghánistán, pioneers to 207
Afnáns, the 2, 99, 111, 117
Afnán, Nayyir 15
Africa 111, 114, 171, 180, 197, 210, 214, 222, 238
  Bahá'ís of 204, 206, 216, 220
  Intercontinental Teaching Conferences in 213, 215, 216, 220, 234, 235
  Mother Temple of Continent 225, 226, 234
  pioneers to 198
  Regional Assemblies, purpose of 162-3
  Shoghi Effendi's praise for race and continent 216
  North 171
  South 111
  West 111
  (*See also* Spiritual Assemblies)
Ages (of the Baháí Dispensation),
  Apostolic, Heroic 100, 150, 169, 217, 231, 232, 235
  Formative, Iron, of Transition 41, 87-8, 100, 114, 118, 145, 202, 231, 232
  Close of First Epoch (1944) 232
  Golden 145, 169, 183, 231
'Akká (Acre) 1, 2, 5, 99, 116, 134, 135, 137, 141
  Governor of 18
  Muftí of 18
'Alá'í, Shu'á'u'lláh (Hand of the Cause) 111
Alexander, Agnes (Hand of the Cause) 112
Alexander, Grand Duke of Russia 123
Alexandria (Egypt) 7, 48, 53, 73
Allenby, Sir (later Lord) Edmund (Commander in Chief, Armed Forces in Palestine W.W.I.) 10
Amazon jungles 222
America (the Americas) 7, 78, 110, 114,

INDEX

169, 182, 208, 216, 220
Bahá'ís of 15, 16, 20, 42, 61, 65, 69, 73, 74, 76, 78, 106, 123, 150, 163, 171, 179, 184, 208, 209
culture 208, 218
Intercontinental Teaching Conferences in 213, 216-8, 220, 221, 234
Central 113, Pioneers in 200
Latin (Central and South America) Bahá'ís of 73, 206, Bahá'í communities send pioneers to Europe 210, Pioneers in 198-201, 206, Republics, importance of in Divine Plan 199-200
North (United States and Canada) 'Abdu'l-Bahá's visit to 7, 180. Bahá'ís of 93, 169-7, 197-202, 207, 230. Bahá'í Conventions 20, 170, 198, 208. Cradle of Administrative Order (World Order of Bahá'u'lláh) 93, 163, 170, 218
Excessively materialistic 178.
Guardian's early relationship with 170. Guardian's marriage reinforced ties with North America 70.
Newspapers 43. Pioneers in 200.
Queen Marie of Rumania visits 43.
Spiritual primacy of 169. Station of 169-70.
World mission of 169, 199
South 113. Pioneers in 200.
United States 21, 111. 'Abdu'l-Bahá's visit to 39. Bahá'ís of 33, 198. Cradle of Administrative Order 218. Foremost protagonist of godless materialism 179-80. Guardian's predictions of future tribulations for 79, 177-81. President of 153, Qualities of which it must be rid 179. Role in establishing Lesser Peace 79
(*See also* Spiritual Assemblies)
American Bahá'i Publishing Committee 48
Angora (in Turkey) 158
Antilles, the (*see* Spiritual Assemblies)
Antipodes 220
Intercontinental Teaching Conference in 234, 235
Mother Temple of the Antipodes (and indeed of the whole Pacific area) 226
Apocalyptic upheavals 76-81, 176-81, 216
Arabian Peninsula 111 (*see also* Spiritual Assemblies)
Arctic Circle 222
Art 181, 182
Asia 11, 110, 113, 114, 180, 197, 216, 219, 220

Intercontinental Teaching Conferences in 213, 216-8, 220, 221, 234, 235.
Pioneers to 198
Significance of 220
(*See also* Spiritual Assemblies)
Atom bomb 77
Australia 33, 111, 113, 114, 198, 201, 220
Bahá'ís of 20, 24, 171, 220
Intercontinental Teaching Conference in 234, 235
Mother Temple of Continent 226, 234
(*See also* Spiritual Assemblies)
Austria, Bahá'ís of 34 (*see also* Spiritual Assemblies)
Auxiliary Boards (of the Hands of the Cause of God) 113-5, 235

Báb, the 84, 95, 149, 194, 236
portrait of 184, 214, 235
relics of 117
safe-keeping of His remains 101
interment Mt. Carmel 103
Writings translated by Shoghi Effendi 86, 97
(*See also* Holy Places)
Badí'u'lláh (younger brother of Muhammad-'Alí) 18
Baghdád 220
High Commissioner in 34
(*See also* Holy Places *and* Temples)
Baghdádi, Dr. Zia 4, 5
Bahá'í Community, world-wide 109, 114, 173
at different stages of development 163-4
oneness of 212-3
Bahá'í Declaration of Human Rights and Obligations, A (submitted to United Nations) 148
Bahá'í Esperanto Magazine 107
Bahá'í Faith, acknowledgement of its independence 133-9, 159-61
aim of 134
"Cause of God, the" 21, 24, 169, 231, 233, 239
chief function of 227
description of by Guardian 134, 231
enemies of (within and without) 23, 73, 114, 149-50
evolution of 169, 232
for all, irrespective of social standing 60
fundamental truths of 169-98
greatest exploits will coincide with lowest ebb of mankind's fortunes 78
growth and progress 203

INDEX

outlawed in Germany 149. In Persia 149-54, In Russia 149, 154-7
pattern of its history 149
protection of 114
recognition of 26, 148-9, 153-4, 193-4
regenerates mankind 25
should reflect racial diversity 61
West, extraordinary brilliancy in 169
Bahá'í Faith, The, 1844-1944 202
Bahá'í Faith, The, 1844-1952 203, 213
Bahá'í International Community (at the United Nations) 153
Bahá'í laws 159-62, 164-5
regarding matters of personal status (a compilation) 161
Bahá'í marriage, considered invalid in Muslim countries 161, 203-4
Legal in many places 203
recognised in Palestine 101, 130
Bahá'í News 7
Bahá'í News of India 173
Bahá'í Temple Unity 205
Bahá'í World, The 46, 48, 88-91, 123, 133
Bahá'ís 17, 25-6, 53-4, 73, 134, 160-1, 172, 185. at different stages of development 165. duties and privileges 164, 211. Primary duty 25. immaturity of 171-2. Need wisdom 186. nature of their work 157 new 163-4, 194-5. Enrolment of 163, 194
purpose of life for 192
Bahá'u'lláh, ascension of 1, 2, 84-5, 94-5, 108, 114, 149, 165, 167, 181, 184, 189, 191, 192, 194, 195, 220, 223, 229, 230, 236
prophecies of, fulfilled 109
relics 117. Sent to five Intercontinental Teaching Conferences 235-6
Writings translated by Shoghi Effendi 86, 91, 93-4, 97
Bahá'u'lláh and the New Era 42
Bahrayn, pioneers to 207
Baker, Dorothy (Hand of the Cause) 110, 111
Balkan Peninsula, pioneers to 198
Balúchistán, pioneers to 207
Balyuzi, Ḥasan (Hand of the Cause) 111
Banání, Músá (Hand of the Cause) 111, 116
Bayán, The 87
Beba (Egypt), Appelate religious courts 159-61, 193
Bedekian, Victoria ("Auntie Victoria") 54
Beirut 6, 53
American University (formerly Syrian Protestant College) 6, 9, 92, 192
Bahá'í students at 8

Belgium (*see also* Spiritual Assemblies)
Ben-Gurion, David (first Prime Minister of Israel) 136, 137
Bentwich, Prof. Norman 126
Ben-Zvi, Itzhak (President of Israel) 139-40
Ben-Zvi, Mrs, 140
Bible, King James version 12, 233
Blomfield, Lady Sara 13
Boris, King of Bulgaria 46
Bottomley, Gordon (playwright) 92
Bran (Rumania) 43
Britain (British Isles) 21, 111, 201
Bahá'ís of 34, 73, 171, 209, 210, 218
Government of 35
honour conferred on British peoples through Guardian's marriage 70
National Ḥaẓíratu'l-Quds purchased 219
(*See also* Spiritual Assemblies)
Buddhism 222
Bulgaria, Bahá'ís in 209
Burma 8, 21
Bahá'ís of 8, 21, 73, 171. Pilgrims from 20, 33. Plight at end of W.W.II 208
(*See also* Spiritual Assemblies)

Cairo (Egypt) 49
Rumanian Minister in 49
Cambridge (England) 11
Canada 20, 53, 111, 199
Bahá'ís of 34, 61, 65, 171. Pilgrim from 59
Eskimos of 222 (*See also* Minorities)
Newspapers 43
Queen Marie of Rumania visits 39
(*See also* Spiritual Assemblies)
Capitalism 180
Carlyle, Thomas 12
Carrara (in Italy), marble columns for Shrine of Báb acquired 106
Caucasus, the, Bahá'ís of 20, 33, 154, 171, 222
Bahá'í Faith banned in 155
(*See also* Spiritual Assemblies)
Centenaries and Anniversaries, of the birth of the Bahá'í Faith, Declaration of the Báb, birth of 'Abdu'l-Bahá 96, 106, 207, 211, 212, 232
of the Year Nine (Holy Year, Oct. 1952—Oct. 1953) 113, 207, 208-9, 211, 212, 215, 234
50th anniversary of establishment of Bahá'í Faith in Western World 202.
Centralization 187
Chancellor, Sir John (High Commissioner of Palestine) 130

"Charters, three mighty" 112
Chase, Thornton (first American believer) 6
Chicago (*see* Conferences, Intercontinental Teaching)
China 222
  Bahá'ís in 33, 48
Ciffrin, Dr. (submits design to 'Abdu'l-Bahá for Báb's Monumental Stairway) 141
Cities, negative characteristics of 222
Civilization 71, 93-4
Clayton, Sir Gilbert (Chief Secretary to Palestine Administration) 23
Collins, Amelia (Hand of the Cause) 110, 115
  Vice-President, International Bahá'í Council 109, 110.
Communications 172-3
Communism 180
Compensation, principle of 56, 154, 202, 224
Conferences, Fourth European Teaching (1951) 78, 108.
  Indian Asian Women's (1930) 126
  Intercontinental Teaching 213-21, 234-6 (1953). "Shattering impact on Bahá'í history" 215. Africa (Kampala, Uganda) 213, 215, 216, 220. America (Chicago, U.S.A.) 213, 216-8, 220, 221. Asia (New Delhi, India) 213, 219-21. Europe (Stockholm, Sweden) 211, 213, 215, 218-9, 221.
  (1958) "five-fold purpose" 234 Africa (Kampala, Uganda) 234, 235. America (Chicago, U.S.A.) 234. Antipodes, the (Sydney, Australia) 234, 235. Europe (Frankfurt, W. Germany) 234, 235.
  World Congress of Faiths (1926) 125
  World's Parliament of Religions (1893) 216
  World's Columbian Exposition (1893) 216
Constantinople (*see* Spiritual Assemblies)
Covenant-breakers ("Nakeseens") 16, 22, 137, 138.
Crete 73
Cycles (of religious history) 230-33
  Prophetic 232
Cyprus, Queen Marie of Rumania visits 48
Czechoslovakia, Bahá'ís of 209

Danzig (Gdansk, Poland) 124
Dawn, The 173

Dawn-Breakers, The - Nabil's Narrative 87, 91-3, 97, 132
Decline and Fall of the Roman Empire, The 12
Deepening 172
Demagogy 174
Democracy 174
Denmark Bahá'ís of (*see also* Spiritual Assemblies)
Despotism 174
Ḍíyá'íyyih Khánum ("Ziaiyyih", mother of Shoghi Effendi, eldest daughter of 'Abdu'l-Bahá) 2, 69
Dispensation of Bahá'u'lláh, The 27
Diversity 61, 187, 216
  (*See also* Minorities)
Divine Assistance 211-2, 223
Dodge, Prof. Bayard 92
Dreyfus-Barney, Hippolyte 20
Dumit (Domets) 123, 131, 132
Dunn, Clara (Hand of the Cause) 111

Ecclesiasticism 222
Egypt 20, 53, 161, 193
  'Abdu'l-Bahá's visit to 7
  Bahá'ís of 171, 201, 207. Persecuted 149, 159-61. Pilgrims from 20
  Queen Marie of Rumania visits 43
  (*See also* Spiritual Assemblies)
Eire (*see* Spiritual Assemblies)
England, Bahá'ís of 21.
  Pilgrims from 20
  Shoghi Effendi in 12
Epistle to the Son of the Wolf 95
Equality, meaning of 61
Esperantists 124
  (*See also* languages)
Esslemont, Dr. John (Hand of the Cause) 35, 42
Ethical Cultural Society 92
Europe 7, 19, 20, 71, 111, 113, 114, 197, 214, 216, 218
  'Abdu'l-Bahá's visit to 7, 180
  Bahá'ís of 73, 163, 171, 220
  Cradle lamentably defective civilization 179-80
  Mother Temple of Continent 225-6, 234
  pioneers to 219
  Shoghi Effendi in 19-21
  World War II and its aftermath 208, 210-1
  Central States 198
  Northernmost capitals 198
  (*See also* conferences, Intercontinental Teaching *and* Spiritual Assemblies)

INDEX

Eynath, Mr. S. (Legal Adviser to Israeli Government) 139
Eytan, Walter (Director-General of Ministry for Foreign Affairs, Israeli Government) 139

Faith, meaning of 71
Faizí, Abú'l-Qásim (Hand of the Cause) 111
Falkland Islands 215
Far East 8, 72
Featherstone, Collis (Hand of the Cause) 111
Feisal, King of 'Iráq 33
Ferraby, John (Hand of the Cause) 111
Finland 209
  (*See also* Spiritual Assemblies)
France, Bahá'ís of 20, 34, 48, 171, 209.
  Pilgrims from 20
Frankfurt (West Germany), acquisition of a national Bahá'í headquarters in 219
  (*See also* Conferences, Intercontinental Teaching *and* Temples)
Fujita 69
Funds 114, 165-7
Furútan, 'Alí-Akbar (Hand of the Cause) 110
Future, dark 76-7

Germany, Bahá'ís of 20, 34, 171, 209, 210.
  Persecuted by authorities 149. Plight at end of W. W. I. 208
  Shoghi Effendi in 20
  (*See also* conferences, Intercontinental Teaching, Spiritual Assemblies *and* Temples)
Giachery, Dr. Ugo (Hand of the Cause) 110, 111
  Italian connection construction of Shrine of the Báb 106, 110
  member-at-large, International Bahá'í Council 110, 138
  represents Shoghi Effendi at Stockholm Intercontinental Teaching Conference, 213
Gibbon, (historian), 12, 85
Gleanings from the Writings of Bahá'u'lláh 93, 133
God Passes By 75, 83, 91, 95-6, 97, 136, 161
Goldman, Julia 124
Governments, obedience to 156, 162, 185
  exception recantation Faith 162
Grand, Miss 13
Greatest Holy Leaf (Bahíyyih Khánum,

'Abdu'l-Bahá's sister) 7, 16, 19, 85, 116, 126
  announces provisions of 'Abdu'l-Bahá's Will to Bahá'í world 14
  description of 66
  Guardian eulogises her life 66
  passing of 65-8
  qualities of 14
  station of 66
  support for Shoghi Effendi 15-16, 19-20, 65-7
Greenland, Eskimos of 222
Gregory, Louis (Hand of the Cause) 7
Grossmann, Hermann (Hand of the Cause) 111
Guardianship 69-70, 113, 115, 235
  Seat of 118

Haifa 2, 6, 7, 16, 19, 20, 21, 53, 58, 69, 72, 85, 88, 99, 109, 127-30, 134, 136, 141-3, 238
Haifa Relief Fund 11
Ḥakím, Dr. Luṭfu'lláh (Eastern Assistant Secretary, International Bahá'í Council) 109, 110
Hamburg (Germany) 107
Haney, Paul (Hand of the Cause) 111
Hands of the Cause, appointments 110-12, 115, 152, 235, 236. Guardian's Method of appointing 111-2, 115-6
  Auxiliary Boards formed 113, 115, 235.
  Distribution and functions 113-4, 235.
  functions 113
  Members of International Bahá'í Council 110.
  participation in conferences 213-4, 216-8, 220-1
  represent Guardian at Intercontinental Teaching Conferences, 1953 and 1958 113, 213-4, 235. At National Conventions, 1957 114.
  Seat of 118
  station of 113
  travels 113, 218, 221
  (*See entries under individual names*)
Hawaii 188
Hebrew Technical College 143
Hebrew University 125
Ḥijáz pioneers to 207
Hinduism 222
Hitler, Adolf 76
Holley, Horace (Hand of the Cause) 88, 90, 110
Holy Days 151, 173, 204
Holy Land 8, 21, 22, 72, 74-5, 110, 112, 114,

129, 220, 235
  Bahá'í holdings in 55, 75-6, 121, 133-5
  "Heart and nerve centre" of the Faith 121-44
Holy Places associated with the Báb.
  House in <u>Sh</u>íráz 152
  Shrine of, on Mt. Carmel 30, 58, 62, 63, 75, 83, 99, 101, 112, 131, 134, 141, 143-4, 183, 225, 230. Building of 96, 101-6, 109, 116, 117, 121, 122, 120
Holy Places associated with Bahá'ulláh.
  Ba<u>gh</u>dád House of ("Most Holy House") 23, 33-4, 36, 128
  Bahjí, Mansion of (His Tomb and Shrine, Qiblih of the Bahá'í world) 5, 18, 23, 30-2, 45, 56, 62, 63, 68-9, 88, 99, 100, 101, 121, 122, 128, 134, 137, 138, 188, 220, 235
  Garden of Riḍván ('Akká) 5
  House of 'Abbúd in 'Akká 63, 99, 144
  Mazra'ih, Mansion of 57, 63, 137
  Síyáh-<u>Ch</u>ál (dungeon in Ṭihrán) 209, 212, 213, 224
  Turkish military barracks in 'Akká 2, 143
Holy Places, other. At the World Centre 99, 101. Exempted from tax 122, 132. House of 'Abdu'lláh-Pá<u>sh</u>á in 'Akká 2. Protected by Israeli Government 76. On Mt. Carmel, arc 58, 117-9. Monument Gardens 133, 231. Monument to Greatest Holy Leaf 32, 63, 67, 116-7, 118, 121, 231, Muníríh <u>Kh</u>ánum (wife of 'Abdu'l-Bahá) 116-7, Navváb 116-7, 118, 121, 231, Purest Branch 116-7, 118, 121, 131
Honolulu (Hawaii) 41
Hoover, Herbert (President of U.S.A.) 41
Human Rights 190
Ḥusayn (son of 'Abdu'l-Bahá) 3

Iceland 218
Ileana, Princess (daughter of Queen Marie) 47, 48, 49 visits Egypt 48
India 201, 209
  Bahá'ís of 8, 21, 26, 33, 73, 161, 171, 201, 207. Pilgrims from 20, 107, 205
  (*See also* Spiritual Assemblies)
Indian Ocean 222
Individual 192
  Bahá'í 190, 192, 199-200
  Initiative 190-1
Intellectualism, haughty 222
International Bahá'í Bureau (in Geneva) 107

International Bahá'í Council 109-11
  appointment and membership 109
  enlargement of 110
  functions 109
Ioas, Leroy (Hand of the Cause) 110, 140
  Secretary-General, International Bahá'í Council 110, 138
  represents <u>Sh</u>oghi Effendi at Kampala Intercontinental Teaching Conference, 213
Ioas, Sylvia (member, International Bahá'í Council) 110
Írán (*see* Persia)
'Iráq 219
  Abortive revolution 72
  Bahá'ís of 33, 73, 201, 207
  British High Commissioner in 34
  (*See also* Holy Places *and* Spiritual Assemblies)
Ireland, Northern (*see* Spiritual Assemblies)
Irreligion 177-179, 188-9
'I<u>sh</u>qábád 173
  Bahá'ís of 154. Persecuted by authorities 155-7
  (*See also* Temples)
'Ismat Pá<u>sh</u>á 158
Israel 136-8
  Government of 136, 138, 142. Department for Bahá'í Faith in Ministry for Religious Affairs 137-8, 160-1
Italy, Bahá'ís of 21, 171. Pilgrims from 20 Supplies materials and craftsmen for International Archives Building 118; Monuments of the Greatest Holy Leaf, the mother, brother and wife of 'Abdu'l-Bahá 67, 116; Shrine of the Báb 106, resting-place of <u>Sh</u>oghi Effendi
  (*See also* Spiritual Assemblies)

Jack, Marion ("General Jack") 53
Jahrom (Jahrum, in Írán), Bahá'ís martyred 36, 45
Jamal Pá<u>sh</u>á 76
Japan 20, 222
  Bahá'ís of 17, 33, 73, 170, 220
  Emperor of 41
Jerusalem 18, 22, 138, 140, 142
  Grand Muftí of (enemy of both the Faith and the Guardian) 73
Jesuits 6
Justice 146, 176

INDEX

Kadria, Princess of Egypt 124
Kampala (Uganda) (*see* Conferences, Intercontinental Teaching *and* Temples)
Ka<u>sh</u>án (Írán), Bahá'í Schools closed 151
Keewatin 215
Keith-Roach, Edward O.B.E. (District Commissioner for Haifa) 127-8, 130
<u>Kh</u>ádem, <u>Dh</u>ikru'lláh (Hand of the Cause) 111
<u>Kh</u>ázeh, Jalál (Hand of the Cause) 111
<u>Kh</u>or<u>sh</u>id-i-<u>Kh</u>ávar (publication) 173
Kingdom of God 97, 146, 211, 223, 231
Kirmán<u>sh</u>áh (Írán), Bahá'ís persecuted by authorities 151
Kitáb-i-Aqdas (The Most Holy Book) 99, 108, 165, 237-8
Kitáb-i-Íqán (The Book of Certitude) 91
Kitalya Prison (in Uganda), Bahá'ís of 60

Lamington, Lord 124
Languages 217, 231
  Arabic 83, 86, 96, 147, 182
  English 83, 86, 87, 91-2, 96, 147, 182
  Esperanto 124
  French 107, 147
  German 107, 147
  Persian 83, 86, 91, 96, 129, 147, 182
League of Nations 35
  Permanent Mandates Commission 35
Lebanon 73
Levy, Shabatay (Mayor of Haifa) 136
Libya 73
Literature 181, 182, 217, 231
Locke, Prof. Alaine 30
London 10, 30, 47
  Shoghi Effendi receives news of 'Abdu'l-Bahá's passing 13
  University of 92
Luxembourg, Duchy of (*see* Spiritual Assemblies)

Macaulay, Thomas Babbington (quoted) 83
McNeill, Mrs. 51
Macy, Nebraska (U.S.A.) (*see* Spiritual Assemblies)
Malta 51
Man, God respites 176
  heedlessness of 94, 176
Marie, Queen of Rumania 39-52, 93, 124, 157
  cables Shoghi Effendi 46-7
  childhood friend lived in Mazra'ih 51
  disapproved of by her "own caste" 43, 46
  first Bahá'í Queen 52
  interview with Martha Root 45.
  Relationship with her 45-46
  Guardian's gifts to 46, 49
  Guardian's tribute to 52
  Guardian writes to 40, 43, 47, 50-1
  receives copy of *Gleanings* 51, 93
  responds to Guardian's first communication 43-4
  sends Guardian signed portrait 47
  station explained by Guardian 52
  statements on the Bahá'í religion 43, 157
  visits America 39, 43
  visits Cyprus 47
  visits Egypt 48
  writings of 44-5
Marina, Princess of Greece (later Duchess of Kent) 124
Martin, Dr. Alfred W. 93
Martyrs, twenty thousand 162
Materialism 78, 180, 188, 216, 222
  definition 177-78
Ma<u>sh</u>riqu'l-A<u>dh</u>kárs (*see* Temples)
Maxwell, May 68, 69, 103
Maxwell, Mary (*see* Rúḥíyyih <u>Kh</u>ánum)
Maxwell, Sutherland (Hand of the Cause) 70, 103-6, 110, 111
  architect of the Shrine of the Báb 104-6
  relationship with Shoghi Effendi 103
Mecca (*see* Spiritual Assemblies)
Medicine 181
Mihdí, Mírzá (The Purest Branch, brother of 'Abdu'l-Bahá) 67, 116, 231
Minorities 61, 188-190, 204, 205, 216
  discrimination in favour of 190
  protection of 190
  African tribes 189, 222
  Australian Aborigines 222
  Eskimos 189, 222
  Lapps 222
  Polynesians 222
  Pygmies 188
  Red Indians 60-1, 188-9, 222
Moderation 54
Mongolia 222
Montreal (Canada) 105
Morality 185
Moscow (U.S.S.R.) Bahá'ís of 33
  (*See also* Spiritual Assemblies)
Muhájir, Dr. Raḥmatu'lláh (Hand of the Cause) 111
Mühlschlegel, Adelbert (Hand of the Cause) 111

Muḥammad-'Alí, Mírzá (Arch-Covenant-breaker, half-brother of 'Abdu'l-Bahá) 18, 33, 99, 100, 101
Music 181

Náṣiri'-d-Dín Sháh 212
Nationalism 178, 222
Navváb (wife of Bahá'u'lláh, mother of 'Abdu'l-Bahá and the Greatest Holy Leaf) 67, 116
Nazis 73, 210
Nehru, Jawaharlal (first Prime Minister of India) 221
New Delhi (India) (*see* Conferences, International Teaching, *and* Temples)
New History Society 136
New York (*see* Spiritual Assemblies)
New Zealand 201, 205
   Bahá'ís of 24, 34, 53, 201, 220
   (*See also* Spiritual Assemblies)
Nicolas A.L.M. 87
North Sea, isles of 222
Norway, Bahá'ís of 209

"Old World" 180-1, 208
   Standards 180
Oligarchy 174
Olinga, Enoch (Hand of the Cause) 111
Orient 1
Oxford (England), Shoghi Effendi at University 11-12

Pacific Islands 21, 24, 111, 215, 220, 222
   Bahá'ís of 34, 41, 171
   Mother Temple of whole Pacific area 226
Pákistán (*see* Spiritual Assemblies)
Palestine, Bahá'ís of 21, 72, 129-30, 133-5, 171
   High Commissioner for 22, 101, 123, 124
   relation of Shoghi Effendi with authorities 126-44
Panama City (*see* Temples)
Peace, Lesser 77, 80
   Most Great 81
Persecution of Bahá'ís 149
   of Bábís 212
   principal agent in propelling growth of the Faith 149
   in Egypt 149, 159-61
   in Germany 149, 159
   in Persia 149-54. "Aid the Persecuted" fund 154
   in Russia 149, 154-7. Distinction between hardships of Russian and Persian Bahá'ís 155
   in Turkey 149, 159
Persecution, racial and religious 178
Persia 41, 84, 111, 132, 161, 175, 201-2, 219, 223
   Bahá'ís of 16, 21, 26, 33, 53, 69, 73, 106, 151, 169, 171, 220, 225. Martyred 36, 150-200. Persecuted 149-54, 225.
   Pilgrims from 8, 11, 20
   Sháh of 150, 153. Pahlavi Dynasty 150
   (*See also* Persecution *and* Spiritual Assemblies)
Philadephia Evening Bulletin 44
Pilgrims 10, 53, 57, 58
   American negro 59-60
   early western 2, 59-60
Pioneering 26, 190, 193, 200, 221
Plans 57, 207-8
   Divine Plan 26, 169, 213, 217, 233, 239. "Second stage" 74
   Seven Year Plan (first, American) 41, 75, 106, 197, 199, 207, 233
   Seven Year Plan (second, "European Campaign") 76, 77, 208-11, 218, 233
   "Ten Goal Countries" 56, 209, 210, 218-9
   Ten Year Crusade 112, 113-4, 115, 117, 149, 194, 207, 232, 233-4. Achievements of 234-5
   Defined by Guardian 233. Goals of 201, 209-15
   Objectives of 222. Phases of 223, 233. Started as "Third Seven Year Plan" 56, 211. Thirteen points of 223.
Pole, Major Tudor 13, 22, 23
Politics 172, 179, 181
Port Said (Egypt) 7
Portugal (*see* Spiritual Assemblies)
Prasad, Dr. Rajendra (President of India) 221
Prayers and Meditations by Bahá'u'lláh 93
Progressive revelation 192
Promised Day Is Come, The 58, 72, 73, 75, 91, 94, 176
Psychology 182

Qazvín (Írán) 151

Races 204, 216
   Eskimo 59, 204, 222
   Inca 188
   Mongolian 61
   Red Indian 60-1, 188-9, 204, 222
   (*See also* Minorities)

INDEX

Racialism 222
Ramleh (Egypt) 7
Rashíd-'Alí (War-time Head of Government of 'Iráq) 72
Remey, Mason (Hand of the Cause) 110
  President, International Bahá'í Council 109, 110, 138
  represents Shoghi Effendi at New Delhi Intercontinental Teaching Conference 213
Revell, Ethel (Western Assistant Secretary, International Bahá'í Council) 108, 110
Revell, Jessie (Treasurer, International Bahá'í Council) 108, 110
Reverence 61
Reward and punishment 182
Robarts, John (Hand of the Cause) 111
Roman Empire, fall of 178
Rome (see Temples)
Rommel, General 72
Root, Martha (Hand of the Cause) 39-42,

Revell, Jessie (Treasurer, International Bahá'í Council) 108, 110
Reverence 61
Reward and punishment 182
Robarts, John (Hand of the Cause) 111
Roman Empire, fall of 178
Rome (see Temples)
Rommel, General 72
Root, Martha (Hand of the Cause) 39-42, 44, 45, 47, 49, 71, 93, 103, 124
  first interview with Queen Marie of Rumania 42
  Guardian's tributes to 40, 41-2, 54, 115
  Guardian's relations with 41-2
  passes away in Honolulu 41
Ross, Sir E. Denison 92
Roumie, Syed Mustafa 8
Rubaiyyat of Omar Khayyam (Fitzgerald's translation) 92
Rúhíyyih Khánum, Amatu'l-Bahá (Mary Maxwell, Hand of the Cause) 111, 116, 140
  Liaison between Guardian and International Bahá'í Council 110
  marriage with Shoghi Effendi 67, 68-9
  represents Shoghi Effendi at 1953 Inter-Continental Conference, Chicago, launching Ten Year Plan 213
Rumania, royal family of 47
Russia 41, 185, 222
  (See also Persecution of Bahá'ís, Spiritual Assemblies and Temples)

Sacrifice 54
Salvation 192
Samandarí, Tarázu'lláh (Hand of the Cause) 110
Samuel, Sir Herbert (High Commissioner for Palestine, later Lord Samuel) 17, 126, 128
  Writes to Shoghi Effendi 129
Samuel, Lady 126
Sandstrom, Justice Emil (Chairman of U.N. Special Committee on Palestine) 133
Scandinavia 41
  (See also Spiritual Assemblies)
Schopflocher, Fred (Hand of the Cause) 111, 116
Scotland (see Spiritual Assemblies)
Sears, William (Hand of the Cause) 111
Serbia, Queen of 46
  royal family of 47
Service 54
Sharett, Moshe 126
Shíráz (see Holy Places)
Shírází, Mírzá Hádí, father of Shoghi Effendi 2
Shoghi Effendi
  birth and parentage 2
  named by 'Abdu'l-Bahá 2
  appearance and character as a child 3-4
  to school at Jesuit Collège des Frères 6. Unhappy there 6
  attends Protestant Syrian College (American College) in Beirut 6
  purpose of his studies 6, 12
  Bahá'í activities as a student 8
  receives B.A. Degree 9
  appearance and character as a youth 6, 10, 29
  relationship with 'Abdu'l-Bahá 1-15, 71
  becomes 'Abdu'l-Bahá's secretary 9
  introduced to readers of Star of the West 9
  accompanies 'Abdu'l-Bahá to official functions 10
  to Balliol College, Oxford 11
  receives news of 'Abdu'l-Bahá's ascension, and his reaction 13-27
  returns to Haifa 13-14
  appointed 'Abdu'l-Bahá's successor in His Will and Testament 15
  support from Greatest Holy Leaf 14, 15, 19, 47, 116, 126-7
  received with love and loyalty by Bahá'ís 16, 24
  authority attacked by Covenant-breakers

18-19, 136
appoints tentative Assembly in Haifa, withdraws to Switzerland 19-20
letters to Bahá'í world on resuming duties 21-2
whole object was to fulfill master's wishes and complete His works 197
refused to imitate 'Abdu'l-Bahá 100
marriage 67, 68-9, 130
foresees Second World War 71-2
his life in wartime Haifa 72-4
exhausted by strain of war years 75
personal characteristics:
Catholicity of spirit 123. Compassion 103, 135. Courage 23, 58. Courtesy 123. Determination 55-6, 74. Devotion 10. Dignity 16, 30. Disliked being photographed 30. Economy 57. Energy 10, 30, 220-222. Enthusiasm 10, 30, 74. Frankness 57. Generosity 57-8, 167. Honesty 57. Humility 20, 26-7. Humour 30, 55. Ingenuity 56, 63. Kindness 53, 58. Logic 30. Mastery of detail and orderliness 31-2, 54. Modesty 91. Neatness 63. Nobility 30. Openness 57, 59. Patience 182. Power to rise again after sustaining blows 14, 35-6. Quickness 31-2. Radiance 20. Reverence 61-2. Sensitivity 6, 7-8. Shrewdness 56. Strength 16, 30. Sympathy for downtrodden and outcast 60. Tidiness 63. Will-power 3. Wisdom 16, 162, 188
aesthetic and intellectual characteristics:
Able statistician 202. "Architect's eye" 62. Artistic sense 62. Love of light 32; mountains 20; music 184; ornamental beauty 183; symmetry 182-3. "Painter's eye" 62. Sense of proportion 32, 62. Style of the Holy Places created by him 63. Politically observant 71. Taste in architecture 118; art 182; literature 24, 83-97, 182. His Writings 181-2; evolution of his style; joy in words 9, 24; maintained highest standard of English 12, 83, 182.
Siberia 222
Social science 181
Society, divisions in 77
reformation of 193
Sofia (Bulgaria) 54
Sohrab, Ahmad 137
Spain (*see* Spiritual Assemblies)
Spiritual Assemblies, local 67, 108, 156, 171-2, 223, 230

in Canada 199, 201
in Eire 219
in the Iberian Peninsula 209
in Italy 209
in the Low Countries 209
in North America 24
in Northern Ireland 219
in Russia 149
in the Scandinavian States 209,
in Scotland 219
in the U.S.A. 153, 177, 194, 199, 201,
in Wales 219
Constantinople 157
Haifa 173
'Ishqábád 154-7
Macy, Nebraska (U.S.A.), first all-Red Indian Assembly 188
Mecca 224
Moscow 154, 155
New York 170. By-Laws serve as pattern for every local community throughout Bahá'í world 147
Spiritual Assemblies, National 57, 61, 67, 73, 107, 109, 113, 114, 115, 145-66, 186, 205, 212, 223, 233
Europe 197, 218
Palestine Branches of 99-100, 121-2, 123, 132, 135
Alaska 122, 206
Australia 122, 234
Australia and New Zealand 205, 215, 226
British Isles 122, 203, 210, 211, 214, 216
Canada 122, 188, 205, 209, 215, 217, 218
Caucasus 154
Egypt and the Súdán 161, 205, 215
Germany and Austria 205, 210, 211, 215, 225, 234, 235
India and Burma 107, 122, 205
India, Pákistán and Burma 215
'Iráq 205, 215
Italy and Switzerland 59, 205, 211, 215
New Zealand 122, 206
Pákistán 122, 206
Persia 36, 122, 150-1, 158, 205, 215, 221
Turkistán 154
United States and Canada 42, 69-70, 87, 89, 121, 122-3, 132, 135, 146
United States of America 153, 203, 211, 214, 215, 217, 218, 227, 235
Spiritual Assemblies, Regional 205
African 205-6
Antilles 206
Arabia 206
Benelux Countries 206

Central America 205-6, 207, 209, 210, 215
  Island Republics of 207
  Central and East Africa 234
  Iberian Peninsula 206
  Latin America 205, 209, 210, 215 Independent National Assemblies in every republic 206
  North East Asia 206
  Scandinavia and Finland 206
  South America 205, 209, 210, 215.
    Northern countries of 206
  South East Asia 206, 234.
Stannard, Mrs. (International Bahá'í Bureau, Geneva) 107
Star of the West 9-10, 172, 173
Stockholm (Sweden) (see Conferences, Intercontinental Teaching and Temples)
Storrs, Sir Ronald (Governor of Cyprus), 47, 126
Súdán 127
  (See also Spiritual Assemblies)
Sulaymáníyyih, pioneers to 207
Sun of Truth 173
Sweden, Bahá'ís of 21, 171
  (See also Conferences, Intercontinental Teaching and Spiritual Assemblies)
Switzerland, Bahá'ís of 21, 58, 171, 173, 210
  Shoghi Effendi in 59-60
  (See also Spiritual Assemblies and Temples)
Symes, Col. Sir G. Stewart, Governor of Phoenicia, later Governor of Haifa) 23, 126-7, 128, 130, 141
Symes, Mrs. 128, 141
Syria, Bahá'ís of 21, 171

Tablet of Carmel, The 112, 231
Tablets of the Divine Plan 39, 112, 188, 197, 213, 230-1
Tahiti, pioneers to 198
Tarbiyat School (Írán)
Tasmania, Bahá'ís of 24
Teaching 17, 24, 163-4, 170-5, 183-192, 193-195, 197-202, 222-3. deputization 167
Temples, significance of 183, 225
  Frankfurt 219, 223, 225-6, 234, 235
  'Ishqábád 149, 154-7, 185-6
  Kampala 56, 154, 183, 225, 226, 234, 235
  Mount Carmel 121, 183, 217
  Sydney 56, 183, 226, 234, 235
  Ṭihrán 183, 221, 223, 225
  Wilmette 52, 65, 167, 199-201, 209, 216-8, 226. Bahíyyih Khánum Fund for 68.

  First dependency 217, 223, 227
  Sites acquired, Baghdád 221. Delhi 221. Panama City 217. Rome 219. Stockholm 219. Switzerland 59. Sydney 221. Toronto 217.
Tibet 222
Ṭihrán 36, 150, 209, 220
  Ḥaẓíratu'l-Quds destroyed 152, 224
  (See also Temples)
Times, The 42
Toronto Daily Star 39, 44
Townshend, George (Hand of the Cause) 110, 112, 113
True, Corrine (Hand of the Cause) 111
Turkey 41
  Bahá'ís of 149-71. Persecuted 157-9
Turkistán, Bahá'ís of 21, 53, 154, 171, 224
  (See also Spiritual Assemblies)

Uganda 60
United Nations 76, 133, 148-9, 153
  Bahá'í U.N. Committee 148
  Secretary-General 149
  Special Committee on Palestine 133-5, 175
Unity 123, 146, 190, 192, 230-1.
  meaning of 187
Universal House of Justice 15, 67, 106, 108, 112, 113, 114, 174, 205, 209, 236
  conference on establishment of 106-7
  formation anticipated 106-7, 110
  functions of 108
  powers of 108
  seat of 118
Universal participation 194

Varqá, 'Alí-Muḥammad (Hand of the Cause) 111
  Trustee of Huqúqu'lláh 111
Varqá, Valíyu'lláh (Hand of the Cause) 110, 111
  Trustee of Huqúqú'lláh 111
Victoria, Queen 49
Voting rights 164

War 76-7, 200-1, 208, 212, 218, 230
  World War One 8, 17, 230
  World War Two 71-4, 78, 106, 184, 200, 212, 218. Communications during 73. Guardian anticipates 71-2.
    Guardian during 72-4. Real cause of 72-4. Reason for 94. Significance for Bahá'ís 73
  Possible future wars 77

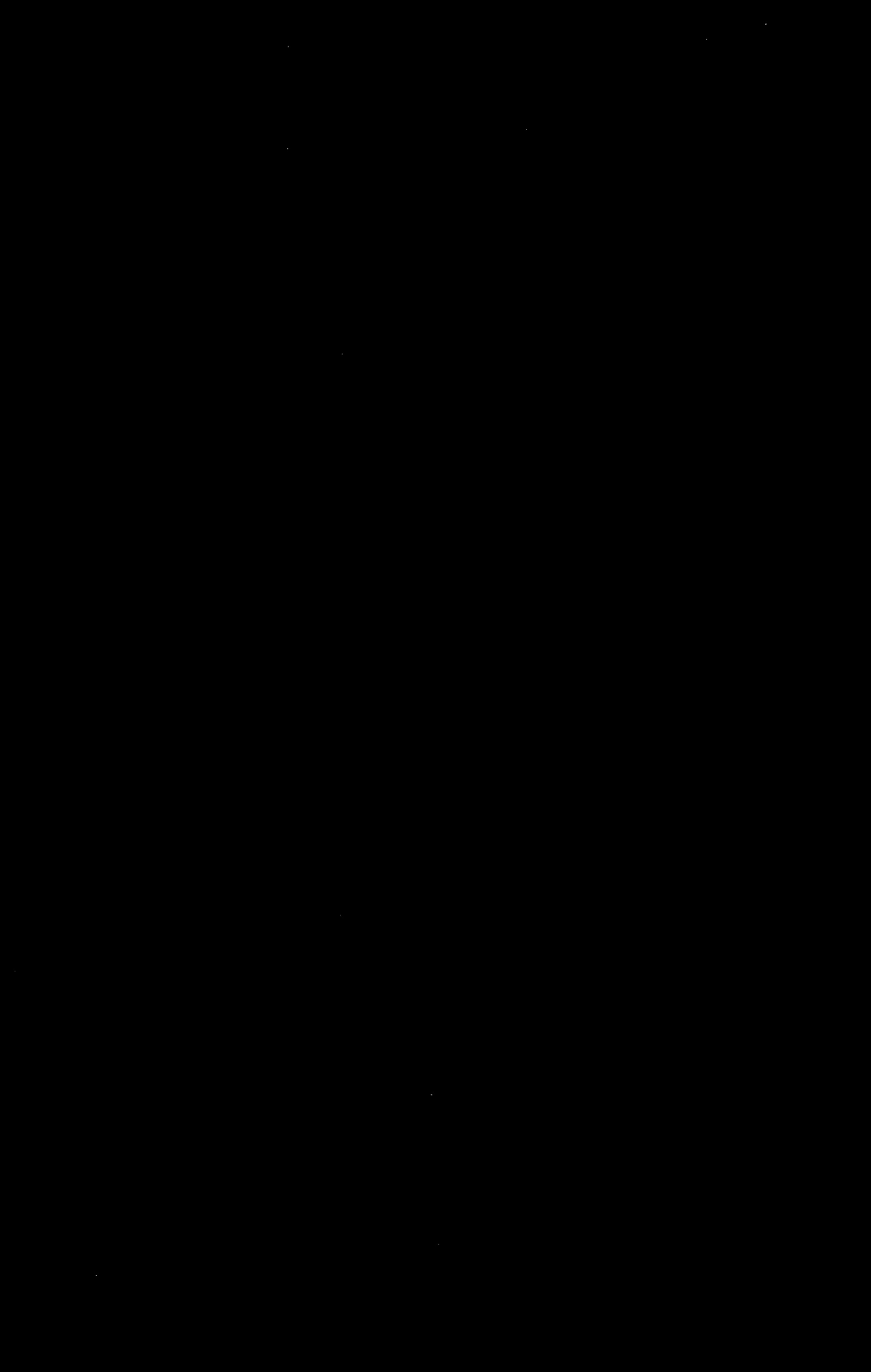